**Conversations with
Orhan Pamuk**

Literary Conversations Series
Monika Gehlawat
General Editor

Conversations with Orhan Pamuk

Edited by Erdağ Göknar and Pelin Kıvrak

University Press of Mississippi / Jackson

The University Press of Mississippi is the scholarly publishing agency of the Mississippi Institutions of Higher Learning: Alcorn State University, Delta State University, Jackson State University, Mississippi State University, Mississippi University for Women, Mississippi Valley State University, University of Mississippi, and University of Southern Mississippi.

www.upress.state.ms.us

The University Press of Mississippi is a member of the Association of University Presses.

Copyright © 2024 by University Press of Mississippi
All rights reserved
Manufactured in the United States of America
∞

Library of Congress Cataloging Number 2023036852

Hardback ISBN 978-1-4968-4941-0
Paperback ISBN 978-1-4968-4942-7
Epub single ISBN 978-1-4968-4943-4
Epub institutional ISBN 978-1-4968-4944-1
PDF single ISBN 978-1-4968-4945-8
PDF institutional ISBN 978-1-4968-4946-5

British Library Cataloging-in-Publication Data available

Books by Orhan Pamuk

English translations of the original Turkish titles are in **bold**.

Novels

Cevdet Bey ve Oğulları ("Cevdet Bey and Sons"). İstanbul: Karacan, 1982.
Sessiz Ev. Istanbul: Can, 1983.
Silent House. New York: Knopf, 2012.
Beyaz Kale. Istanbul: İletişim, 1985.
The White Castle. New York: Braziller, 1991.
Kara Kitap. Istanbul: İletişim, 1990.
The Black Book. New York: Farrar, Straus, & Giroux, 1994; Vintage, 2006.
Yeni Hayat. Istanbul: İletişim, 1994.
The New Life. New York: Farrar, Straus, & Giroux, 1997.
Benim Adım Kırmızı. Istanbul: İletişim, 1998.
My Name Is Red. New York: Knopf, 2001.
Kar. İstanbul: İletişim, 2002.
Snow. New York: Knopf, 2004.
Masumiyet Müzesi. Istanbul: İletişim, 2008.
The Museum of Innocence. New York: Knopf, 2009.
Kafamda Bir Tuhaflık. Istanbul: Yapı Kredi, 2014.
A Strangeness in My Mind. New York: Knopf, 2015.
Kırmızı Saçlı Kadın. Istanbul: Yapı Kredi, 2016.
The Red-Haired Woman. New York: Knopf, 2017.
Veba Geceleri. Istanbul: Yapı Kredi, 2021.
Nights of Plague. New York: Knopf, 2022.

Memoirs and Nonfiction

Öteki Renkler. Istanbul: İletişim, 1999.
Other Colors. New York: Knopf, 2007.
İstanbul: Hatıralar ve Şehir. Istanbul: Yapı Kredi, 2003.
Istanbul: Memories and the City. New York: Knopf, 2005.

The Naïve and Sentimental Novelist. Cambridge: Harvard, 2010.
Manzaradan Parçalar: Hayat, Sokaklar, Edebiyat ("Fragments of the View: Life, Streets, Literature"). Istanbul: İletişim, 2010.
Uzak Dağlar ve Hatıralar ("Memories of Distant Mountains"). Istanbul: Yapı Kredi, 2022.

Photography and Art Books

The Innocence of Objects. New York: Abrams, 2012.
Balkon. Göttingen: Steidl, 2018.
Orange. Göttingen: Steidl, 2020.

Screenplays

Gizli Yüz ("The Secret Face"). Istanbul: Can, 1992.
The Innocence of Memories (documentary). London: Faber & Faber, 2018.

Contents

Introduction   xi

Chronology   xxiii

"One Should Seek to Be a People's Writer Rather Than an Elite Writer"   3
  Nursel Duruel / 1982

"I Wanted to Show How Everything Eventually Sinks into the Overwhelming Banality of the Dreary Thing Called Everyday Life"   6
  Konur Ertop / 1983

Orhan Pamuk from *Cevdet Bey* to *The White Castle*—"I Started Out with Lukács"   9
  Fatih Özgüven / 1986

Orhan Pamuk: "Enigma Is Sovereign"   13
  Judy Stone / 1994

The Best Seller of Byzantium   17
  Fernanda Eberstadt / 1997

Turkish Interview Excerpts from *Öteki Renkler* (*Other Colors: Essays and a Story*)   22
  Various / 1982–1999

Sense of the City: Istanbul   39
  BBC Editorial Board / 2003

"I Was Not a Political Person"   41
  Alexander Star / 2004

The Most Hated Turk   45
   Peer Teuwsen / 2005

"One's Novels Can Be Seen as the Milestones in the Development of One's Spirit"   52
   Ángel Gurría-Quintana / 2005

Orhan Pamuk and the Turkish Paradox   66
   Der Spiegel / 2005

Nobel Foundation Telephone Interview with Orhan Pamuk   71
   Adam Smith / 2006

Nobel Prize in Literature Interview: Orhan Pamuk   75
   Horace Engdahl / 2006

"No One Drives Me into Exile"   80
   Der Spiegel / 2007

"Novels Are Encyclopedias"   84
   Carol Becker / 2007

Orhan Pamuk and Salman Rushdie on "Homeland"   92
   Deborah Triesman / 2007

A Conversation with the Nobel Prize-Winning Author of *The Museum of Innocence*   102
   Bigthink.com / 2009

Orhan Pamuk Interview: Painting and Literature   107
   Charlie Rose / 2009

Orhan Pamuk Interview: Turkish Geopolitics   110
   Charlie Rose / 2011

Orhan Pamuk: *Silent House*   112
   Diane Rehm / 2012

Orhan Pamuk: "A Book Is a Promise" 117
  Sameer Rahim / 2012

Orhan Pamuk on Taksim Square, the Effects of *Breaking Bad*, and Why the Future of the Novel Is in the East 120
  Pankaj Mishra / 2013

On Writing *A Strangeness in My Mind* 126
  Erdağ Göknar / 2015

"I Am an Accidental Politician" 131
  Bruce Robbins / 2016

"I Don't Write My Books to Explain My Country to Others" 140
  Isaac Chotiner / 2017

Politics & Prose Presents Orhan Pamuk 144
  Azar Nafisi / 2017

On the Photographs in *Balkon* 149
  Gerhard Steidl / 2019

"I Am Content with My Novel" 151
  Erkan Irmak / 2019

"*Nights of Plague*, the Novel I Am Currently Writing, Is Also Something of an East-West Novel" 159
  Ramil Ahmedov / 2021

Turkish Interview Excerpts on *Nights of Plague* 164
  Various / 2021–2022

An Interview about Interviews 174
  Pelin Kıvrak and Erdağ Göknar / 2022

Index 179

All interviews reprinted with permission of Orhan Pamuk. All translations from the Turkish rendered by the editors unless otherwise indicated.

Introduction

Nobel laureate Orhan Pamuk writes with a focus on Turkish culture, history, and politics while developing techniques of the global novel. Most of his work is set in Istanbul, Turkey, the former capital of the Ottoman Empire and the city of his birth (1952). Pamuk was raised in a family like the ones described in his novels *Cevdet Bey ve Oğulları* ("Cevdet Bey and Sons," 1982), *The Black Book* (1990), and *The Museum of Innocence* (2008), in the upscale district of Nişantaşı. As he writes in his memoir *Istanbul: Memories and the City* (2003), from his childhood until the age of twenty-two he devoted himself largely to painting. After graduating from high school at the American Robert College in Istanbul, he studied architecture at Istanbul Technical University for three years but abandoned the course when he found his passion for writing and literature. He went on to graduate in journalism from Istanbul University but never worked as a journalist. At the age of twenty-three, Pamuk decided to become a novelist and withdrew from social life. His first novel, *Cevdet Bey and Sons*, was published seven years later in 1982, when he was thirty years old.

Pamuk is a faithful practitioner of what is termed the "East-West novel" in Turkish literature, a genre that addresses fraught encounters of modernity between Ottoman or Turkish Muslim and European cultures. His prose is often complex and philosophical, and he is known for formal innovations that incorporate traditional, realist, modern, postmodern, and postcolonial forms. Pamuk's work contains autobiographical flourishes, literary innovation, and Ottoman or Turkish cultural history focused on Istanbul. *Cevdet Bey and Sons* is the award-winning story of three generations of a wealthy Istanbul family living in Nişantaşı. Pamuk's second novel *Silent House* (1983), about a declining modern Istanbul family, was the first to win an international award in French translation (the 1991 Prix de la découverte européenne). His third novel, *The White Castle* (1985), is a historical novel set in the seventeenth century about the frictions and friendship between a Venetian slave and an Ottoman scholar. Developing the theme of doubles, or the doppelgänger, the plot focuses on the tensions between two characters who represent distinct Eastern and Western worldviews. It was the first Pamuk novel translated into English, in 1990 (and subsequently many other languages), bringing the novelist to international attention. The novel marked Pamuk's early experimentation with postmodern literary techniques.

From 1985 to 1988, Pamuk lived in the United States as a visiting scholar at Columbia University in New York City. There, he wrote most of his complex urban novel *The Black Book* (1990), in which the streets, history, and culture of Istanbul are described through the story of a lawyer seeking his missing wife, Rüya (literally "dream"). *The Black Book*, with its dramatic ironies, Sufi themes, and Borgesian winks to the reader, increased Pamuk's fame both in Turkey and internationally as an author at once popular and experimental, writing intertextual fiction. That year saw the production of a Turkish film, *Gizli Yüz* ("The Secret Face," 1992), whose screenplay by Pamuk was based on a one-page story in *The Black Book*.

Mixing and melding historical, romance, detective, political, and autobiographical genres, Pamuk includes tropes in his work such as the double, identity, obsessive love, coups, Sufism, Islamic art, conspiracy, and murder mystery. He began to interweave multiple popular genres in his novel *The New Life* (1994), about young university students influenced by a mysterious book. Becoming one of the fastest selling and most widely read books in Turkish literature, the novel introduced a secular-religious Mobius strip that established an ironic, mystical, Sufi relationship between the characters and "the book."

Starting in the mid-1990s, Pamuk began to take a critical stance toward the Turkish state in articles about human rights and freedom of thought, although he had little interest in engaged politics per se. Under the title *Other Colors* (1999), he published a selection of articles on literature and culture written for newspapers and magazines in Turkey and abroad, together with a selection of writings from his notebooks. The Turkish version of this collection also includes commentary from Turkish interviews on individual novels, excerpts of which are included here in English translation for the first time (see Turkish Interview Excerpts from *Öteki Renkler*).

Focusing on Islamic book arts and notions of the sacred and the profane, the sixteenth-century historical novel *My Name Is Red* (1998) depicts Ottoman artists and their ways of seeing and portraying the non-Western world, told through a love story and family saga. Formally, the novel skillfully hones literary techniques such as multiperspectivalism, multigenre, political allegory, and intertextuality. Positive reviews, including in the *New*

Yorker and the *New York Times Book Review* (cover), underscored Pamuk's candidacy for the Nobel Prize, which he was awarded in 2006.

Pamuk describes *Snow* (2002) as his "first and last political novel." Set in the small city of Kars in northeastern Turkey, the novel tells the story of political violence and tension among Islamists, the state, secularists, and Kurdish and Turkish nationalists. In his interview with Bruce Robbins, Pamuk states, "Generations of Turkish intellectuals were destroyed by military coups." By the time Pamuk was thirty, he had lived through three military coups—in 1960, 1971, and 1980—that supported an authoritarian trajectory of secular modernity in Turkey. Additionally, in 1997 the military forced the resignation of Prime Minister Erbakan of the Islamist Welfare Party to assuage public fears of politically enfranchised Islam, an event openly decried by Pamuk. It was this "postmodern coup" that inspired *Snow*. The novel, in turn, later shed prescient light on the "failed coup" of 2016. *Snow* was selected as one of the best one hundred books of 2004 by the *New York Times*.

Pamuk's memoir, *Istanbul: Memories and the City*, is an accessible, poetic work that combines the author's early memoirs up to the age of twenty-two as well as essays about the city of Istanbul, illustrated with black-and-white photographs. Here, Pamuk explains the strong tone of loss and lament in Turkish culture, which he describes as a form of collective melancholy that he identifies as *hüzün*.

The author's first post-Nobel novel, *The Museum of Innocence* (2008), focuses on personal and historic objects in the context of a doomed Istanbul romance. The novel became the basis for a series of innovative creative projects: the Museum of Innocence (an actual museum in Cihangir, Istanbul, 2012); *The Innocence of Objects* (a glossy museum catalog, 2012); and *The Innocence of Memories* (a video documentary about the novel-cum-museum, 2015; screenplay, 2018). Engaging in a sort of social ethnography, *A Strangeness in My Mind* (2015) traces the lifeworlds of Istanbul street vendors, particularly sellers of yogurt and traditional Turkish boza, a fermented wheat drink. The novel provides a generational overview of the enfranchisement of Anatolian migrant laborers residing in Istanbul's *gecekondu* shanties, which later were developed into modern apartment buildings—thus raising their social and economic status.

The Red-Haired Woman (2018) explores iconic father-son mythologies in Eastern and Western traditions through a modern-day story that traces the position of a female protagonist navigating these relationships. Begun before the COVID-19 pandemic, Pamuk's most recent novel, *Nights of Plague*

(2021), addresses the plight of Muslim and Greek Orthodox inhabitants of an imaginary Mediterranean island overcome by plague during the late Ottoman Empire. This allegorical novel also relies on multiple genres such as murder mystery, modernization history, romance, and the political novel.

Pamuk's books, informed by intertextual allusions to the classics of Turkish and world literature, have been translated into sixty languages, including Georgian, Malayan, Czech, Danish, Japanese, and Catalan, and have sold over fifteen million copies globally. Apart from three years in New York, Orhan Pamuk has spent all his life in the same streets and district of Istanbul. While continuing to write novels, in the past decade, Pamuk has also expanded his aesthetic focus to painting and photography.

Duality, Hybridity, and Intertextuality

As the interviews collected here show, Pamuk's work makes repeated allusions to literary texts from Eastern and Western traditions in a hybrid manner. In his conversation with Fernanda Eberstadt, he describes this as a kind of "double consciousness." Among the sustained and recurring tropes in Pamuk's fiction is duality or, by extension, the confluence of two cultural currents that form the basis for literary innovation. Istanbul itself is a city of two continents, and Pamuk admonishes his readers to not be afraid of having "two souls" (see *Paris Review* interview). Pamuk's novels are also self-consciously concerned with dramatizing textual production. Generally, his plots assume a metafictional aspect that traces the creation of a book or novel, a technique of international postmodernism.

For example, based on an Ottoman ("Eastern") manuscript found in an archive, the modern-day protagonist Faruk Darvınoğlu produces a ("Western") novel, *The White Castle*. The story focuses on writing, as the two main characters sit at a table and write various kinds of texts: treatises, dream interpretations, attempts at autobiography, and so on. The hybrid text (or intertext) that emerges out of the plot is the novel we read. Pamuk, again, resolves civilizational duality through literary techniques that advocate for hybridity as a vantage of critique. Perhaps the operative Turkish term here is *terkip* (hybridity or a sort of synthesis), an idea that Pamuk adopted from the Turkish modernist author-intellectual Ahmet Hamdi Tanpınar (1901–1962). The concept dovetails with much postcolonial thought regarding mimicry, divided selves, and hybridity.

Intertextuality in Pamuk's work also refers to the mixing of genres. *The Black Book* intertwines the genre of the Western detective story with an Eastern mystical romance story that has Sufi allusions. In Pamuk's world, the popular theme of the quest is both for the beloved and for authorship of a book—a theme that persists, in different historical contexts, in *The New Life*, *My Name Is Red*, and *Snow*. In addition to its multigenre structure, *My Name Is Red* introduces intertextuality both through words and images, or experiments with ekphrasis (prose that depicts art), as miniature painting and perspectivalism intersect with storytelling in various ways. The book at the center of that novel is deemed blasphemous because it aims to represent an Islamic world through European aesthetic perspectives. The novelist tells Erkan Irmak in an interview twenty years after the publication of *My Name Is Red* that "it is perhaps [his] best novel" and he wanted it to be as much about the "genuine pleasures of painting" as tensions arising from a kaleidoscope of unique perspectives intertwining seeing, thinking, identity, guilt, death, and happiness.

The Museum of Innocence reorients Pamuk's intertextual focus away from an image/text axis to one of object/memory. Exploring the way things contain stories, in the world of this novel, objects contain memories and affect, constituting idiosyncratic museums for viewers/readers. Furthermore, the Museum of Innocence located in Istanbul is a multifaceted, genre-crossing project based on the novel. The latter tells the love story between Kemal, a young man from an upper-class family, and Füsun, a distant relative, while providing a panorama of daily life in Istanbul during the final quarter of the twentieth century. Building on these themes, the museum's collection consists of nostalgic objects and furniture, bric-a-brac, and personal effects that resemble objects found in the novel, curated in eighty-three display boxes to mirror each chapter of the book. The museum building in Istanbul, constructed in 1897, reflects the architecture of a typical late Ottoman residential building of the period. Apart from displaying intriguing still life interplays between fiction, history, and reality, the Museum of Innocence emerges as the one and only city museum depicting everyday life in Istanbul. There, the viewer is exposed to what might be termed "literary curation": the museum as a novel and the novel as a museum.

The intertextuality of the East-West genre returns in Pamuk's two most recent novels. *The Red-Haired Woman* plays on dominant myths of Oedipus (from *Oedipus Rex*) and Rostam (from the *Shahnameh*) as master plots of intersecting Eastern and Western patriarchy and patrimony. The myths become metaphors for generational change and transformation. As Azar Nafisi indicates in her interview, Pamuk explores in the novel the ways that "story" has the power to overwrite our fate. *Nights of Plague*, in a historical and allegorical vein, juxtaposes Christian and Muslim responses to state-sponsored quarantine measures during an epidemic. The difference is treated as a measure of modern progress on the peripheries of Europe during the late Ottoman Empire.

Pamuk and the Global Novel

Conversations with Orhan Pamuk reveals that Pamuk's novels are predicated on methodical research, at times archival and scholarly, investigative and journalistic, or ethnographic. One could say the Pamuk novel *is* method. His fictions are constructed through intricate clockwork. Certain elements recur. There is always an engagement with an Ottoman or Turkish historical period, usually set wholly or partially in Istanbul, the erstwhile imperial capital. The author—a curator of sorts—has a prominent role in the text as a character, creating a doubled narrative structure reminiscent of authors like Joseph Conrad. His narratives are textually focused, tracing the production of a book or revealing the central place of the library or archive in literary production (showing the influences of Jorge Luis Borges, Italo Calvino, or Umberto Eco, for example). Whereas the characters in the plots of his novels are often struggling writers, at times condemned to writer's block or failure, the Pamuk narrator perseveres through the plot as a redemptive figure of the successful global author. In Pamuk's reliance on techniques from multiple traditions, his work engages realism, modernism, postmodernism, and a variety of Turkish postcolonialism related to the Ottoman legacy.

The interview conducted with both Pamuk and Salman Rushdie, an icon of postcolonial literature, reveals their positions as global novelists. Both authors convey a cosmopolitan secular worldview—a discomfort with being treated as representatives of their Muslim homelands/nations in world literary contexts—and both lament being valued as political instead of cultural figures. Both are practitioners of international postmodernism linked to the Global South and employ techniques of mimicry, passing, and intertextuality. Whereas there is a clear colonial context for Rushdie and India, Pamuk's postcolonialism is at once more subtle and more complex because it addresses Ottoman imperialism as well as the profound European colonial influences on Turkish modernization. Pairing the two authors in a single interview indicates their representational stature in terms of Muslim culture, the secular modern, and world literature. In many respects, both authors speak back to literary traditions that have constructed, or orientalized, the regions of India and Turkey.

Today, about 85 percent of Pamuk's readers read him in languages other than Turkish. In Pamuk's reception outside of Turkey, however, geopolitics often takes precedence over literature. The interview with Charlie Rose, for example, is evidence of the non-European author's valuation as a political commentator above his value as a novelist. Rose focuses on Turkish geopolitics until Pamuk is forced to politely state, "I'm not a political commentator; I'm a, you know, novelist." The interview then finally turns to the impending opening of the Museum of Innocence. In the *Paris Review* interview, Pamuk points to a process of racialization he experiences in which his Turkishness is emphasized outside of Turkey and he is considered to be a writer *of* or *about Turkey* rather than a writer per se. The tendency for Pamuk to be treated as a political commentator instead of a literary figure runs throughout the interviews as a point of tension.

Additionally, there are some interviews in which Pamuk seems to be tasked with establishing his credentials as a Western author. The interview with the permanent secretary of the Swedish Academy in the wake of the Nobel Prize reveals interesting moments in this regard. The conversation focuses on minutiae specific to European authors such as Michel de Montaigne and Gérard de Nerval, and Pamuk is put in the position of establishing his expertise in the Western canon. The interviewer constantly refers to the parochial figure of the "Western reader," one that, ironically, Pamuk's work has effectively deconstructed. The idea of literary modernity emerging from the periphery of Europe or a non-European context is lost in the conversation. The interview makes important insights while, however, reifying specters of binary logic such as "center" and "periphery," "self" and "other," and "colonizer" and "colonized."

The Interview as an Alternative Literary History

Conversations with Orhan Pamuk not only compiles and curates Pamuk's most compelling interviews in multiple languages but also adds to the decade-long debates about the tendentious rise of the literary interview in the twenty-first century. Author Sarah Fay, in her 2012 article in *The Atlantic*, "The Precarious State of the Literary Interview," argues that the emerging precarity of the genre is attached to a declining quality in substance and style despite the abundance of literary conversations with writers that turned the 2010s into "the age of the interview." She reminds us of early eighteenth-century essayist and literary critic William Hazlitt's claim about authors being good interviewees because there is "more to be learnt from interviews than from their books." The present volume, when read from beginning to end, confirms Hazlitt's thesis, as it allows the reader to conceive of another Pamuk who is not only the writer but also an interpretive reader of his own books as well as a bold critic of political and social realities unfolding in Turkey and the world. This collection depicts the intellectual, critical, and political development of one of the greatest literary minds of the past century in "a hybrid genre between media and literary domains."[1]

We argue that the interviews in this volume, which span forty years, constitute an alternative literary history through the insights they provide into influence, method, form, and content. The interviews open windows into Pamuk's everyday life, influences, craft, and process from aspirations to be a "people's writer" to becoming a global novelist. They contain affective responses and can be humorous, pedantic, or grave. At times they situate or interpret individual works, give an overview of a series of publications, or survey his entire oeuvre to date. They address and trace the differences between national and international audiences and track the author's development and changing readership. They are indexed to specific political and historical events as well as to international prizes, revealing cultural and ideological attitudes toward the author and his literary styles.

Reading the interviews as context shows that Pamuk has always been engaged with literary theory and world literature, consciously connecting them to the Turkish novel. References in his first interviews to the influence of Marxist political thinker and literary theorist György Lukács (1885–1971) establish Pamuk's early concerns with an aesthetic of historical realism, and even class consciousness. Pamuk's first novel also reveals a historical consciousness in the late Ottoman and Turkish context that could be described as Lukácsian and open to notions of revolutionary art. Lukács opposed modernist innovation; however, Pamuk adopted it, showing the influence of authors like James Joyce, Virginia Woolf, and William Faulkner while establishing his own literary modernity, which included experimentation in form.

The interviews as a corpus also uncover Pamuk's ambitions as a novelist with a globalized literary imagination who has experimented with the genre of the encyclopedic novel since *Cevdet Bey and Sons*. From the beginning of his career, Pamuk has struck readers as a bold and confident novelist with a deep knowledge of the so-called canon of world literature, French philosophy, and regional history. In fact, in her 1997 interview for the *New York Times Magazine*, Fernanda Eberstadt quotes the famous Turkish literary critic Jale Parla's review of Pamuk's early novels: "His source of inspiration has been more literature than life." Yet, while his ambitions remain, Pamuk's inspirations have become increasingly more embedded in the details of everyday life.

An aspect of Pamuk's writing life that remains constant throughout his career, as the interviews reveal, is his structured work habits. He always has a humorous attitude toward his studiousness while admitting that he was not a good student during his school years. He shares that his writing routine (seven days a week from 9 a.m. to 8 p.m.) has not left any time for him to socialize with friends and enjoy nights of drinking raki with literary circles, especially in his youth, when the aspiring novelist was smoking and writing at his desk every night. He subverts the dismissive Turkish phrase "to work like a clerk" and says that he has always been proud of attaining whatever number of pages that he sets for himself in the morning.

In an interview by Ramil Ahmedov, when the novelist is asked the difference between Orhan Pamuk after his first novel and after his tenth, he answers without hesitation: "I've been doing the same thing for forty years. I think I can do it for another four hundred years." After he says that he has been writing the same way, even at the same desk, for forty years, he also admits that his insecurities and vulnerabilities have remained as well, and he gets discouraged from time to time by the thought that a particular scene he is working on will not turn out well. In 2005, a year before he won the Nobel Prize, he confided to Ángel Gurría-Quintana of the *Paris Review* that sometimes he feels his character should enter a room, but he still doesn't know how to make him enter. "Still," he adds in half frustration, half humor, "after thirty years!"

In this vein, the interviews might also be read as windows into the writing process and a guide for young novelists and storytellers who get discouraged when they cannot make a character enter a room. In each interview, even in the most political ones, Pamuk shares firsthand wisdom about how to "explore the inner depths of one's soul" while also aiming to write for a globalized world. When read with a notebook and a pen in hand, these interviews provide enough detail to produce several book lists of what Pamuk has read since early in his career, how he has composed scenes in which to place his characters, and the research he has conducted for every novel—in various libraries or museums around the world, through interviews, or in conversations that model the scenes in his mind's eye.

Pamuk's interviews also reveal his reception in the Turkish literary establishment, shedding significant light on the prominent place and function of the novel in Turkish society as a cultural vehicle for progress and modernity. So why has Pamuk been met with such visceral reactions? His Turkish interviewers can be suspicious and cynical, at times looking for the hidden secret to unprecedented success, especially when an author's international fame far exceeds his national renown. Is it simply dedication and hard work?

Pamuk broke new ground after the 1980 coup by distancing himself from a Cold War generation of socially engaged authors in Turkey. He was neither an ideological writer under the influence of the state nor a revolutionary vanguard; he came from the wrong class for political causes or village novels. This military coup marked a turning point in the young author's career. By subsequently embracing postmodern techniques, Pamuk was regarded by some as having relinquished the role of the writer as a beacon of the people. He was considered, broadly, to be writing difficult novels that were hard for the reading public to comprehend. But he was also something of a scholar in the field of word literature, in no small part due to access to his father's library of great books. Perhaps he had begun to outgrow his local readership. Pamuk at times struggled with being a left-leaning liberal humanist writing in and about a nationalist Sunni Muslim country. His internationalism and cosmopolitanism shone through his pages, and in that regard, he was no longer considered to be writing for the nation or its people. The unfair refrain was that he wasn't writing for Turks.

This attitude, promoted by ultranationalists in Turkey, was amplified in a Swiss interview that appears here in its entirety in English for the first time. The interview by Peer Teuwsen, titled "The Most Hated Turk," led to a media polemic and the aborted trial of Pamuk in 2005 for "insulting Turkishness" because of comments he made about the mass killing of Armenians and Kurds in the late Ottoman and Turkish republican eras, respectively. At the time, the conservative AK Party (Justice and Development Party) was in its first term of power and Turkish accession talks were slated to start with the European Union in eight months. The position of the Swiss interviewer and the Turkish author revealed tense European and Turkish relations and can even be read allegorically. The interview developed into a literary scene all its own, working through layers of nationalist and orientalist discourses. Pamuk became both a cause célèbre and a target of nationalists. The charges were later dropped, but he has continued to receive threats such that he has had to have a state-appointed bodyguard to the present day.

The Interview as a Paratext

Pamuk is probably one of the most interviewed novelists of this century. As a living Nobel Laureate, he has been invited to countless literary fairs, academic conferences, book signings, readings, and seminars, and he has given talks and lectures at various university campuses around the world. The interviews we have chosen for this volume also reveal different aspects of the author that are intertwined with his identity as a novelist or that have shaped that identity over decades. For example, in some interviews and conversations, we come across his witty side, which occasionally resurfaces even in his most dramatic and tragic novels, such as *Snow*, *The Museum of Innocence*, and *Nights of Plague*. Or we witness the hardworking novelist looking back and evaluating his previous books and learning lessons from each. Or we learn about the canon of world classics or historical documents in public libraries that the novelist has read. The interviews, furthermore, point to one of the most important aspects of Pamuk's process that makes him such a prolific and innovative novelist: Pamuk is a meticulous archivist.

A short tour of the novelist's apartment office in Cihangir, Istanbul, or of the Museum of Innocence in the same neighborhood, confirms this. Archiving is something of a novelistic method for Pamuk. In this context, the author's interviews and conversations form a bridge between the literary archive consisting of his own novels and writings and the material archives that he has curated by collecting books and objects from the places surrounding him. How else could we appreciate that while writing *A Strangeness in My Mind*, he might very well buy an object for the Museum of Innocence from a junk dealer that he discovered wandering alone through neighborhoods doing research? Or that when he puts on his historian's hat to write *Nights of Plague*, he realizes that if he were a historian, he would write through objects, and his biggest inspiration would be to follow in the footsteps of Reşat Ekrem Koçu (1905–1975), the famous Turkish writer and historian of everyday life whom Pamuk wrote about in *Istanbul*. Reading Pamuk's interviews is like seeing a collage of text and image in his mind that creates a new whole at every glance.

Conversations with Orhan Pamuk traces the dominant themes of the author's oeuvre as well as their variations. In this regard, the interview as genre functions as what French literary critic Gérard Genette calls a "paratext," that is, supplemental material to literature that frames and situates the reception of that literature. Genette explains that a paratext is "a threshold, or [. . .] a 'vestibule' that offers the world at large the possibility of either stepping inside or turning back. It is an 'undefined zone' between the inside and the outside, a zone without any hard and fast boundary."[2] Pamuk himself indicates that the literary interview is paratextual in the last selection in this volume, "An Interview about Interviews." In our reading it is, moreover, the discursive space of literary history where writing, politics, and the everyday intersect and where the politics of literature can be located.

The editors would like to thank Ezgi Üstündağ and Johanna Schuster-Craig for translations from Turkish and German, respectively; Renée Ragin Randall for editorial assistance; and Kenan Sharpe for proofreading and indexing. The Josiah Charles Trent Memorial Endowment Fund at Duke University and the National Humanities Center in Durham, North Carolina, provided support for the completion of this volume. We are grateful to the editors and staff at the University Press of Mississippi for their support in the publication of *Conversations with Orhan Pamuk*.

EG
PK

Notes

1. Anneleen Masschelein, Christophe Meurée, David Martens, and Stéphanie Vanasten, "The Literary Interview: Toward a Poetics of a Hybrid Genre," *Poetics Today* 35, nos. 1–2 (2014): 1–2.

2. Gérard Genette, *Paratexts: Thresholds of Interpretation*, trans. Jane E. Lewin (Cambridge: Cambridge University Press, 1997).

Chronology

1952 Born June 7 in the Nişantaşı neighborhood of Istanbul, Turkey. He devotes himself to painting in his youth.
1972 Enrolls in Istanbul Technical University to study architecture. He withdraws after three years.
1976 Graduates from the journalism program at Istanbul University.
1982 Publishes first novel, *Cevdet Bey ve Oğulları* ("Cevdet Bey and Sons"), as the outcome of winning a literary prize. The story, written in the mode of historical realism, revolves around three generations of a wealthy Istanbul family from the late Ottoman Empire to 1970s Republican Turkey. Has not appeared in English translation.
1983 *Sessiz Ev/Silent House* marks the beginning of Pamuk's experimentation with literary form. While conveying a multigenerational saga, the novel relies on modernist techniques such as multiperspectivalism and stream of consciousness. English translation: 2012.
1985 *Beyaz Kale/The White Castle*, a literary deconstruction of the Orientalist binary opposition between East and West. Although predominantly set in seventeenth-century Ottoman Istanbul, the novel adopts postmodern literary techniques, including doubles, unreliable narrators, and metafiction. His first novel to be translated into English, in 1990. Pamuk becomes a visiting scholar at Columbia University, during which time he writes most of *Kara Kitap/The Black Book*.
1990 A complex lover/beloved story that animates Istanbul, *The Black Book* relies on intertextuality, multigenre narration, passing, and Borgesian literary techniques. Literary themes of mystical Islam, or Sufism, predominate. English translation: 1994, retranslated in 2006.
1994 *Yeni Hayat/The New Life*, a quest novel that further develops the intersection of postmodernism and Sufism, and situates a mysterious absent text at the center of the plot. Adopts motifs of conspiracism. English translation: 1998.
1998 A novel of Islamic book arts, *Benim Adım Kırmızı/My Name Is Red*, set in the sixteenth-century Ottoman Istanbul context of a

miniaturists' guild, further experiments with the innovative techniques Pamuk had earlier introduced. English translation: 2001.

1999 *Öteki Renkler/Other Colors*, a collection of commentary, belles lettres, memoir, essays, and a short story. English translation: 2007.

2002 A political critique of Turkish secularism, *Kar/Snow* is set in the small border town of Kars and engages themes of ideology, representation, and reality in the context of state secularism, Kurdish insurgency, and the rise of political Islam. English translation: 2004.

2003 *İstanbul: Hatıralar ve Şehir/Istanbul: Memories and the City* presents a portrait of the novelist's childhood and youth interwoven with the city's cultural history. English translation: 2005.

2006 Awarded the Nobel Prize in Literature. Begins teaching literature courses every fall semester at Columbia University, New York.

2008 *Masumiyet Müzesi/The Museum of Innocence* focuses on personal and historic objects in the context of an obsessive Istanbul romance. The novel becomes the basis for a series of related projects, including a museum, museum catalog, and the screenplay for a video documentary. English translation: 2009.

2009 Delivers the Charles Eliot Norton Lectures at Harvard University. The six lectures form the basis of *The Naïve and Sentimental Novelist*, published in 2010.

2012 The Museum of Innocence, the actual museum described in the eponymous novel, opens in Istanbul. Publishes *The Innocence of Objects* (glossy museum catalog).

2015 *Kafamda bir Tuhaflık/A Strangeness in My Mind* traces the lifeworlds of Istanbul street vendors, particularly sellers of traditional Turkish boza, a fermented wheat drink. The novel provides a generational overview of the enfranchisement of Anatolian migrant laborer populations residing in Istanbul's *gecekondu* (shanties), which later become developed into modern apartment buildings. English translation 2015. Releases *The Innocence of Memories*, video documentary about the novel and museum (screenplay is published in 2018).

2016 *Kırmızı Saçlı Kadın/The Red-Haired Woman* explores iconic father-son mythologies in Eastern and Western traditions through a modern-day story that traces the position of a female protagonist navigating these relationships. English translation: 2017.

2019 Publishes *Balkon*, a collection of Istanbul photographs taken by Pamuk from the balcony of his writing studio overlooking the confluence of the Bosphorus and the Golden Horn as he was writing *A Strangeness in My Mind*.

2020 Publishes *Orange*, a collection of nighttime street photographs taken by Pamuk that traces the changing quality of light in Istanbul in recent decades from orange incandescent bulbs to bright surgical white light.

2021 Publishes *Veba Geceleri/Nights of Plague*, a suspenseful historical epic about a plague that ravages a fictional island of the Ottoman Empire in 1901. English translation: 2022.

2023 Delivers a series of four lectures at the Collège de France, Paris, under the title "The Paradox of the Novelist."

**Conversations with
Orhan Pamuk**

"One Should Seek to Be a People's Writer Rather Than an Elite Writer"

Nursel Duruel / 1982

From *Cumhuriyet*, "Seçkin yazar değil, vatandaş yazar olmanın yolu aranmanlı," December 30, 1982.

Nursel Duruel: The first impression one has after reading *Cevdet Bey and Sons* is the novel's distinct historical time, which moves gradually and becomes so tangible that we can almost touch it! Could you comment on that?

Orhan Pamuk: Maybe I've discovered the time of the "East" without realizing it! Furthermore, the characters in the novel—whether the good family man and merchant Cevdet Bey, the railway builder and engineer [Ömer], or the painter [Ahmet]—are consciously or unconsciously trying to break apart this "time" through politics, commerce, and intellect. Maybe because they were somewhat successful in doing so, it became difficult for me to place the youngest generation of my characters into that form of the novel. When I finished the novel four years ago, I said to myself, "Now I need other models of novel form." Jokes aside, I believe that this historical time in which the characters of the novel roam is still not fully foreign to us. Maybe in our country, too, most windmills are powered by machines, not water, but in our daily movements and basic human behavior, it seems as if the rules of our own time are very different than those of the West.

ND: You mentioned "other novel forms." The form of *Cevdet Bey and Sons* is not far from the form of the classical or traditional novel.

OP: Yes! That was a conscious decision. While writing the novel, I was largely under the influence of Lukács [in *Essays on Realism*]. This means I was aware that I was also under the influence of Tolstoy, Stendhal, and Mann. However, I will argue that *Cevdet Bey and Sons* contains some elements that traditional novels do not employ. I'm much more comfortable using modern novel techniques in the novel I'm currently finishing; but I would like to add that these techniques in themselves justify nothing. Many people rightly argue that it isn't enough to write like Balzac after Balzac. Furthermore, does it really take a lot of courage to say that writing like Woolf after Woolf or like Joyce after Joyce is also inadequate? The crux of the problem is to tear down all the techniques and styles to find your own form, but just considering that is frightening! Still one must try! Even if we don't succeed in the end, at least we can console ourselves by saying that we dared to seek the meaning in life specific to us, believing such meaning must exist, even though we couldn't find it. It's often been said that the novel is a mirror held up to society. But first, we must acknowledge that even Turkey no longer fits into the narrow frame of those old traditional mirrors. The Turkish novelist must find the mirror to hold up to his own reality! Then we'll understand that reality is not the old reality. In this way, the novel can fulfill its old task of reflection. I read somewhere that Carlos Fuentes said that a Latin American novelist must be both Balzac and [Michel] Butor. This statement seems accurate to me, if it means that a novelist who wants to reflect society must be experimental.

ND: *Cevdet Bey and Sons* spans a long period of time between 1905 and 1970. You must have done research to be able to talk about this period. How did you approach the material at hand?

OP: I've read a lot of memoirs and newspaper archives, but I never thought I'd use them in the novel. These sources are amusing, like the ones Rimbaud mentioned in the famous poem ["Voyelles"] where he found the color of vowels. I was not looking for details about the characters of my novel while reading the memoirs of former Ottoman pashas, the plans for national development that the authors self-published forty years ago, and old yellowing newspaper collections. For example, I thought I should mention the failed assassination of [Sultan] Abdülhamid in 1905 at the beginning of the novel. But if I hadn't found one particular detail, maybe I wouldn't have even put that in the novel: Two days after the event, a few pashas gathered in a mansion and told each other, laughing and joking, how scared they were when the bomb exploded! Sometimes such details seem more real to me than a bomb that killed forty people in the prime of life. The issue is finding such details by experiencing them, reading them, or making them up! I think, having found such a detail, the author should leave the rest to the reader's imagination.

ND: As a writer, where do you think you stand and where do you want to stand?

OP: I don't believe that producing literary works (I'm not talking about journalism) is a daunting task that demands great responsibilities toward society. Many of us kill the subjectivity that will give depth and flavor to our books with the coldness of an eminent statesman who controls everything. Dostoevsky said, "We all came out of Gogol's 'The Overcoat.'" It's as if the tradition of the Turkish writer says that we've come out of the kaftan of an acting statesman. I think that this moralistic attitude adopted by novelists—more than by our poets or short story writers—has led the author to adopt the paternalistic attitude of a superior person. Dostoevsky never saw himself as superior to his readers. Once this suffocating sense of responsibility is done away with, I know that every line we write will only increase the value of the work. If I knew that something would increase the value of my novels, I'd sit down to bargain with the devil. Distinguished writers who are ready to judge everyone but themselves and who belittle personal problems don't deign to do such things! I think from now on one should seek to be a people's writer rather than an elite writer. I don't think that for a single moment either Sait Faik or Orhan Veli [popular authors in Turkey] felt the false notion of being an elite writer. We take them seriously today because they didn't take themselves too seriously.

ND: You mentioned a novel you were finishing up.

OP: Yes, *Descendants of the Devil*. Although I tried rather different things in this novel, I can say that it is also a family saga, like *Cevdet Bey and Sons*. In these two novels, I accomplished my aims by narrating the decline of prominent families.

"I Wanted to Show How Everything Eventually Sinks into the Overwhelming Banality of the Dreary Thing Called Everyday Life"

Konur Ertop / 1983

From *Milliyet Sanat*, "Her şeyin, günlük hayat denilen sıkıcı şeyin kahredici bayalığına battığını göstermek istediğimi söyleyebilirim şimdi," June 15, 1983.

Konur Ertop: The first thing that stands out about your novel is its rich details and historical accuracy! Of course, these are not enough to build a whole novel. But you have created a work of art that is also important in this respect. Can you tell us about your writing process and how you structured your novel based on facts?

Orhan Pamuk: I had a structure in mind. I needed to find details to fit it. I read memoirs, scanned old newspaper collections, sifted through a pile of junk. That's how I found the details of this novel that I can call historical. Sometimes I also made them up! The important thing was whether these details could serve as suitable imagery for my purpose. Otherwise, I didn't expect to decipher any past event from such readings. Tolstoy taught me that what we call history is woven with absurd, meaningless, ridiculous details. Maybe now I can say that while collecting details for *Cevdet Bey and Sons*, I wanted to show how everything eventually sinks into the overwhelming banality of the dreary thing called everyday life. But that wasn't my only goal. If the things we call boring are arranged in a certain order, they both shine a light on the characters and are downright fun. I paid great attention to making it a fun book. If someone tells me that they had a laugh here or there while reading *Cevdet Bey and Sons*, I would be really happy.

KE: Did you know Cevdet Bey or any of his relatives?

OP: I didn't know who Cevdet Bey was at first! I do not say this because I look down on novels that have a strong autobiographical aspect—because there are great autobiographical novels that I love very much—I say this because I care about Cevdet Bey being born as an image in me, being theoretical. I had written the middle part of the book, but I had a feeling of incompleteness. Then I realized that I had to go back further, find the beginning of everything, and make it up. That's when I found the details I mentioned earlier. I recognized Cevdet Bey when I imagined a Muslim trader wandering among non-Muslim merchants in Sirkeci! Writing a novel is largely a job of finding such images; you must transform even people you know closely into images first. On the other hand, it can be said that I got to know the heroes of the middle and last generation of the book a little better. In fact, I tend to list off the books that inspired me to those who say that I'm an autobiographical novelist and state that I'm an autobiographical novelist to those who list the books that inspired me! If Kafka had been asked whether he knew Mr. Samsa, what would he have said? I don't know whether he would have recalled *Notes from Underground* and his dull family as well as his life as a civil servant.

KE: Could you explain in detail your own life and the environment you grew up in?

OP: You ask me to "explain." . . . I wouldn't dare to do that in a short conversation. But it's not hard to remember the details: Apartments, dark stairs, dusty, noisy radiators, moms and dads, grandmothers, meaningless snack kiosks, soccer players, aunts, uncles, the last trams, the doves napping between apartments, ugly and stupid chandeliers, books, cockroaches, traffic!

KE: Do you think *Cevdet Bey and Sons* has been understood correctly by its readers? Could you also specify the main theme of your book?

OP: I don't have much of an idea about how the book has been interpreted by its readers. Moreover, my opinion about the book changes frequently as well. Honestly, I was tired of the book when I finished writing it; I was bored, thinking that I was trying to write a nineteenth-century novel and it was a little late for that. On the other hand, I still care about the nineteenth-century novel because it reflects life directly, because I think it is more prone to objectivity. Few novelists, I think, can say what the main theme of their book is. While I was writing, I had many things in mind: time, daily life, history, Turkey, East-West, et cetera. I was trying to collect these thoughts as a whole, maybe I wanted the reader to get an image of what I said about this whole thing. I think that my novel has served its purpose when I hear that it entertains the reader and stimulates the urge to talk to others about the book.

KE: Can you talk about the journey of your novel? [The first award it received, how it was printed . . .]

OP: I wrote the novel between 1974 and 1978. In 1979, it received the Milliyet Publishers' Novel Award along with Mehmet Eroğlu's still unpublished novel. It took me three furious years before it could be published even after the January 24 decisions [to stabilize the economy after the 1980 coup]. At that time, my wife and I were planning to place an advertisement in literary magazines saying "Award-Winning Novel for Sale" to see whether anyone would consider publishing it. The thought of walking from door to door in Babıali [Istanbul publishers' district] was very dreary.

KE: What are you working on nowadays?

OP: I just finished writing a novel [*Silent House*]. I've been working on it for two and a half years. It will be published in November.

Orhan Pamuk from *Cevdet Bey* to *The White Castle*—"I Started Out with Lukács"

Fatih Özgüven / 1986

From *Yeni Gündem*, "Cevdet Bey'den Beyaz Kale'ye Orhan Pamuk–'Lukács'tan Çıktım Yola,'" August 11, 1986.

"In my mind was some sort of a family novel. I actually wrote the manuscript four times. The first draft was a much tighter and shorter novel. Then it started to grow. In fact, at that time, I had a desire to write a book that would include everything, I remember that. . . . Maybe you could call it a sense of totality. . . . That was my understanding of the novel at that time. I hadn't read Hegel that much, but by way of Marxism, I think there were traces of Hegelianism in my mind—I was influenced by ideas like everything constitutes a whole. The more I wrote, the stronger my desire for more unity and a sense of time, and the book took its current form. I can say that in terms of its techniques and choices it is intentionally written as a nineteenth-century novel."

Pamuk submitted this 587-page "novel of totality," the last line of which was written in December 1978, to the Milliyet Publishers' Novel Award that year with the title *Darkness and Light*. "I always had the idea of participating in this competition, but as the novel got longer, the deadlines passed, though I was able to catch the last one," adds Orhan Pamuk. Then, in April 1979, he received a phone call. Ülkü Tamer reported that Pamuk was cowinner of the award with Mehmet Eroğlu. The book was going to be published that autumn. However, it couldn't be published. In fact, it was not even published in the spring of '80, and when the January 24 decisions were announced the same year, Pamuk became deeply pessimistic about his novel. There was a slight conflict between him and Ülkü Tamer, the director of Karacan Publishing

House, who was set to publish the novel. After many discussions about withdrawing the book, resubmitting it, and then regretting it, Ülkü Tamer announced that he had decided to publish the book in the fall of '81, but he still failed to print it, and finally, in March '82, the hefty tome *Cevdet Bey and Sons* showed up in bookstores. Milliyet Publishers' Novel Award jury member Hilmi Yavuz said, "When I first picked it up, I thought, 'How am I going to read this book?' It appeared voluminous. But the book kept me reading, the author was not a novice at all, he knew about literature, his novel was a family novel in the tradition of Mann's *Buddenbrooks*." Another jury member, Selim İleri, who wrote the first review about the book, evaluated it by saying, "It was a novel that could exert its influence despite its heft. Telling a classical story in a classical structure with classical rules is a difficult task nowadays." (Selim İleri could not restrain himself from adding that Orhan Pamuk was most supported by Orhan Hançerlioğlu in the same competition, and that the approaching lunch hour hastened the decision to award the prize to two writers.)

While *Cevdet Bey*'s Karacan edition was selling slowly, reviews began to appear here and there. In the *Milliyet Sanat* literary magazine, Konur Ertop emphasized a theme that would become more evident later on, Orhan Pamuk's "meticulousness." "He must have prepared himself very well in order to produce such a successful work. . . . It seems that he is a good researcher," Ertop said. On the author's view that he wouldn't want to have written a novel whose value was based on such research, Ertop said: "Still, the reader will think that the book's veracity and its understanding of the reality of life stem from these 'truths.'" Following Fatma Akerson's "theoretical and respectable" article published in *Contemporary Criticism* that emphasized the strength of the theme/plot development in the novel, Fethi Naci wrote the first article that fully supported *Cevdet Bey*. He raised the young man to the level of "a great novelistic talent," and wrote that if it had been published in the years he was writing his [iconic] book *Türkiye'de Roman ve Toplumsal Değişme* ["The Novel and Social Change in Turkey"], he would have easily included it among his twenty favorite Turkish novels.

[. . .]

Descendants of the Devil!

This was the terrifying title Orhan Pamuk initially thought of for his second novel [. . .] which was eventually published under the beautiful title *Silent*

House. He described it as "a novel that was more personal, more mine." In this book, Pamuk was slowly weighing anchor from the waters of nineteenth-century literature and setting out toward the techniques and habits of the modern novel. Although it is again a family novel, Pamuk conceives of the family through the narratives of individuals surrounded by shared memories symbolized by the grandmother who never leaves her room. Pamuk embodied various tendencies in the characters without "overly emphasizing" the stream of consciousness and said that "play and fantasy dominated." The most important "contemporary" feature of the book is that it was written by a writer who felt that the contemporary novel is written through impressions rather than events. Hilmi Yavuz was of the opinion that "death in the historical perspective" was the main theme of the novel; others could be added.

[...]

On the other hand, Ahmet Kuyaş's astute analyses in his article "*Silent House* from the Perspective of the Historian" were not useful for the novelist Orhan Pamuk. Kuyaş underlined the symbolic qualities of the protagonists in the novel and presented the book as a more playful *Cevdet Bey*. However, Pamuk's taste in novels had changed. In his novel writing, he was concerned with "writing with joy and enthusiasm," rather than focusing on totality, and "the pleasure of telling the story through certain forms and methods."

[...]

The Story of the Shadow

The White Castle, one of whose first titles was "The Story of the Shadow," is the latest of Pamuk's three novels, whose sales rose as the number of pages decreased. Maybe it's a little early to talk about this novel right now, it's not yet clear what kind of a new beginning it represents in Orhan Pamuk's oeuvre. But a few observations can be made. Orhan Pamuk is not a skilled chameleon, for example. He takes up the "brothers" theme in the beginning of *Cevdet Bey* and transforms it into a "doubles" or "twins" theme, thus creating a topic that has interested him from the very beginning. Those who argue that he is a chameleon say that he is trying to impress us with his vast knowledge of history in this book. However, as he stated in an article in *Cumhuriyet Magazine*, the historical background he compiled from various sources is not important. In addition to the theme of "brothers," the question of "why we are the way we are" preoccupies the author intensely. I think Orhan Pamuk weaves all three of his novels within the framework of these two themes, one personal and private, the other more philosophical and cultural, by following a line from the Lukácsian novel to the style of the anonymous chronicler.

Orhan Pamuk: "Enigma Is Sovereign"

Judy Stone / 1994

From *Publishers Weekly* 241, no. 51, December 19, 1994.

Orhan Pamuk is nothing if not ambitious. All he wanted to do in his new novel, *The Black Book*, he says, was to write a huge, richly textured narrative that would capture the schizophrenic angst of Istanbul, a city in a country straddling two continents. He thus joined the search for an answer to the perennial Turkish question he defines as: "Are we European? Or are we Asian?"

Earlier in his career, with his third novel, *The White Castle* (Braziller, 1991) Pamuk had merged two themes: a culture in the mysterious process of change and men in the mysterious process of changing identity. These themes emerge again in *The Black Book*, out next month from Farrar, Straus and Giroux (1994).

Mysteries Abound

What better way to explore such mysteries than with a mystery? In *The Black Book*, a lawyer, Galip ("victorious") searches for his missing wife, Rüya ("dream"), and her half-brother, Jelal (a reference to the famous Sufi poet, Jelaleddin Rumi), a famous newspaper columnist and Galip's idol. The chapters alternate between Galip's third-person "investigation" and Jelal's first-person meditations, with each chapter preceded by quotations ranging from Sufi mystics to Lewis Carroll and Isak Dinesen. Two assassinations and three hundred odd pages later we are no closer to a solution of whodunit or why, but Galip has taken on Jelal's persona, churning out words of wisdom for the next day's fish wrapper. And the reader is left with a Golden Hornful of literary puzzles to ponder. [...]

Pamuk's latest work, *The New Life*, a "visionary road novel," has just been published in Turkey in an unprecedented first edition of fifty thousand copies; thirty-five thousand sold in the first ten days. The book is a bow to Dante's *La Vita Nuova* and, Pamuk says, "has affinities with German romanticism." The protagonist is a twenty-two-year-old youth who reads a book that changes his life.

Unbelievable Response

The Black Book sold seventy thousand copies, an "unbelievable" response in Turkey, Pamuk tells *PW* when we meet at his book-lined study in the old cosmopolitan Istanbul neighborhood of Nişantaşı, whose sights, sounds, and smells are vividly rendered in the novel.

"Initially, there were huge media attacks on me. The controversy went on for months, and I enjoyed it!" the tall, lean Pamuk declares in lightly accented English, with an impish look that his spectacles can't hide. "They criticized my long sentences and my style. Then they moved to another level, talking about postmodernism. Then there was a political response from leftists and fundamentalists. The fundamentalists claimed that since I use some basic Sufi material, I'm mocking it. I don't take that seriously. Then, I've been criticized for not being a proper Kemalist." (The reference is to Kemal Atatürk, who established the secular Turkish Republic in 1924, changed the alphabet from Ottoman Arabic to Latin, founded a system of public education, outlawed the fez, and gave voting rights to women.)

Pamuk doesn't take that charge seriously either, but he believes that it's necessary to know a little Turkish history in order to understand the complaint.

"The Turkish left has a very Kemalist tradition," Pamuk notes. "In a way, they want to protect the state because the state has been a progressive Westernizer, but in a way it's an antidemocratic force in Turkish history. All the Westernization attempts have been made by the state itself, not by the civil society. So the Turkish left found itself in a dilemma. If you want Westernization, you should defend the state, while on the other hand, leftism is meant to be antistate. Politically, I'm on the left, but that doesn't mean much. I'm antifundamentalist. That's the main danger here now."

Pamuk points out that he was the first person in Turkey to defend Salman Rushdie when the Ayatollah Khomeini issued a death sentence on the author.

Most Turkish intellectuals, explains Pamuk, whether conservative or leftist, hesitate to become involved in the controversy. "It's not because they are afraid," he says. "They think if the issue accelerates, we [writers] will lose. I don't agree, but I see their point."

At any rate, Pamuk has never been an outspokenly political writer. "I'm a literary person," he says. "Ten years ago, my friends used to criticize me for not being political enough. During the military coup in 1980, I was sitting here feeling guilty. Years before that, fascists and communists were killing each other in the streets. I stayed at home and wrote books. I always felt guilty because my friends were putting themselves in danger." [...]

Revenge of the Poor

[...] *The White Castle* may have been a reaction to the omnipresent question of identity. "What I'm trying to do here is to make a game of it and to show that it doesn't matter whether you are an Easterner or a Westerner. The worst way of reading or misreading the book would be to take very seriously the ideologies, the false consciousness, the stupidities that one has about these notions. The problem of East or West has been a huge weight for Turkish intellectuals."

In embroidering that theme, Pamuk's basic goal was to invent a literary language that would correspond to the texture of life in Istanbul. "I wanted to make you feel the terrors of living in this city, but not to describe it realistically. Imagine yourself walking in the streets of Istanbul, or crossing the Golden Horn on one of the bridges. Think about the images you see. All these sad faces, the huge traffic, the sense of history, more than two thousand years of history with Byzantine buildings converted into factories next to kitsch billboards. All this shabbiness. The book takes place just before the 1980 coup, when people were dying in the streets. I wanted to convey the idea of hopelessness, the idea of despair."

To weave that texture, Pamuk drew upon obscure stories he unearthed from traditional Sufi literature largely unknown to the Turkish public; from *The Arabian Nights*, folktales, anecdotes and murders from old newspapers, "believe it or not" columns, and scenes from American and Turkish movies.

"The book has an encyclopedic side," he says, "with all kinds of trivial knowledge about the past put together in a way that's not realistic but gives a sense that Mr. Pamuk is doing what Joyce has done for Dublin." He insists, however, that he was not "literally" inspired by Joyce.

As for the persistent theme of the doppelgänger, he insists, "That's not hard-core Pamuk."

Language comes before theme on his agenda, but he admires others who have played with that idea. He has read Freud and Jung on the doppelgänger themes "for fun," but he's never been in analysis himself. "I'm a straight Turk" he grins. [. . .]

A Normal Pursuit

[. . .] Victoria Holbrook [Pamuk's first English language translator] didn't have time to cope with the "dense and complex" pages of *The Black Book*, so Pamuk turned to Güneli Gün, an Ohio-based Turkish-American novelist. The translation took her two years. Since Turkish is an inflected language with the verb at the end of a sentence, Gün had to change the order of Pamuk's clauses and put them in logical and colloquial English while retaining his intricate effects. She says she would occasionally spend an entire day translating one of Pamuk's half-page-long sentences, working "until there was snap and style and sense to it." She also acknowledges the "scrupulous editing" of FSG [Farrar, Straus and Giroux] editors John Glusman and Robert Hemenway. And, she says, "Orhan doesn't worry about his holy word."

But Pamuk does like the "holy" words of a mystic poet: "Enigma is sovereign, so treat it carefully."

The Best Seller of Byzantium

Fernanda Eberstadt / 1997

From the *New York Times Magazine*, May 4, 1997, https://www.nytimes.com/1997/05/04/magazine/the-best-seller-of-byzantium.html.

At forty-four, Orhan Pamuk is, as he reminds you with a characteristic mixture of provocation and naïveté, "very famous." His novels—erudite, formally experimental yet compulsively readable—have won him an international esteem unprecedented for a Turk. (His sole predecessor, Yaşar Kemal, author of *Memed, My Hawk*, writes tales of the Anatolian outback.) His books have been translated into fifteen languages and are published by the most prestigious houses to critical glory: his latest novel, *The New Life*, just out from Farrar, Straus and Giroux, has been acclaimed by some American reviewers for the brilliance of its "postmodern metaphysics," "mesmerizing prose," and "Borgesian chiaroscuro."

But if Pamuk in the West enjoys a respectfully "literary" reputation, in his own country he is a rabble-rousing blockbuster. His five novels have each in turn sat at the top of the best seller list in Turkey—a nation not previously known for its serious readers. (*The New Life* at last tally had sold two hundred thousand copies.) Pirated editions of Pamuk's works are hawked from Istanbul street stalls; his appearance at Turkish human rights events attracts television crews; every morning he is in the newspapers being asked his opinion about the country's new Islamist prime minister or the threat of a military coup.

Pamuk's artistic accomplishment has been to play West against East, using the European novel's modernist tradition of formal experimentation in order to explore both his country's tangled Ottoman past and its contemporary politicoreligious extremes. His books, which interweave Proustian family sagas with dervish allegories and reportage on modern-day paramilitary cults, have roused a furor in Turkey.

Older Turkish intellectuals bred on Mustafa Kemal Atatürk's secularist dogma accuse him of playing with religion; Islamists accuse him of blasphemy; old-time leftists accuse him of cashing in. And meanwhile, Pamuk's new prominence in the Kurdish rights movement and his opposition to the police brutality and harsh penal codes that keep Turkey an authoritarian state threaten to alienate his popular audience. "Columnists write, 'He is a best seller; now he's selling his country,'" Pamuk says with amusement. "If you do something new in Turkey, they look at you as a pervert. The future can only come from America." Orhan Pamuk is singularly well positioned to become the chronicler of his country's imperial neuroses. Turkey, after all, is not a conventionally third world country but a superpower that once stretched from Baghdad to the gates of Vienna, and Pamuk's own family history exemplifies in microcosm Turkey's efficient transition from a multiethnic empire to a modern nation-state.

The Pamuks belonged to Turkey's French-educated haute bourgeoisie of civil servants, law professors, businessmen. Orhan's mother's family was an old Istanbul clan of textile manufacturers; his father's father was a civil engineer who made a fortune in the 1920s, when the new republic poured money into railroads. "Both Faulkner's grandfather and mine built railways," jokes Pamuk over a cup of tea in his office on a slushy January afternoon.

[...] In 1980, Turkey underwent one of its once-a-decade military coups, and Pamuk shelved a Conradian novel about a cadre of student revolutionaries who throw a bomb at the prime minister. Two years later—the same year that he married his wife, Aylin, an Ottoman historian from a White Russian family—his novel *Cevdet Bey and Sons* appeared, to enormous success. A second novel, *Silent House*, a multigenerational saga of an Ottoman-republican family, was published in France by Gallimard.

It was with his third novel that Orhan Pamuk won truly international fame. *The White Castle*, set in the 1690s at the outset of Ottoman decline, is an allegory of two look-alikes. A Venetian aristocrat, captured by pirates, is indentured to a Turkish inventor known only as Hoja (Master). Hoja, voracious for Western science, picks his Other's brain for knowledge of "them"—Westerners—and what "they" know. When Hoja and his Venetian servant, who have invented a war machine, join the sultan's army on its siege of a white castle in southern Poland, the men swap identities. Hoja escapes to Venice, while the Venetian retires to Anatolian exile. Or does he? Who is really who?

The White Castle introduces the doppelgänger theme that haunts Pamuk's work. "There's this other person who is always in a more genuine, more heartfelt, more hard-core place than you," Pamuk explains.

"Even his failures are more authentic. You love him and you also want to kill him. These are my essential subjects: rivalry, jealousy, problems of domination and influence, revenge. Crucial but unworthy issues that come from growing up in an exclusively competitive childhood with a brother only eighteen months older than I, and also of living on the margins of Europe. Turning around this feeling of off-centeredness. Saying, no, I am at the center. My contribution to the doppelgänger problem was to give it an East-West tilt."

The New Life pushes even further the poignant, where-do-we-belong dialectic of isolationism and imitation that has plagued modern Turks. Its student hero has been transfigured by reading a book whose identity we never learn. In pursuit of the "new life" it reveals, he sets out on a bus ride across Turkey's Asian hinterland. Pamuk feelingly evokes the paranoid weirdness of provincial Turkey—like America, a big, sparsely populated country where housewives, self-made millionaires, and retired colonels meet in messianic conspiracies.

[. . .] Pamuk and I are sitting on matching chintz armchair and sofa, facing the city. We have been talking for four days straight, ten, eleven hours a day. Sometimes we snatch a pot of tea from the kitchen, a handful of anise rusks. The KGB interrogation-style schedule is a tribute to Pamuk's compulsiveness: when his weary interviewer suggests a break, Pamuk says, "No, no, let's continue work." He is no stranger to obsessiveness, he admits—it's the demon that keeps him productive.

"Look, I work seven days a week, from nine in the morning till eight at night. I have the titles of the next eight novels I want to write. I feel myself pitiable, degraded on a day that I don't write. Turks—who are all born poets, God is whispering in their ear—have a dismissive phrase: he works like a clerk. I have turned this insult around: I am proud to say that I work like a clerk."

Pamuk claims he has no social life, rarely goes out, avoids the nights of raki drinking that are a staple of Istanbul literary life.

"I am not a worshipper of pagan happiness. I don't have a sunny family life; I prefer to be here in my office. Recently I discovered Elias Canetti, who says: 'It's not that I don't care about going to parties or meeting girls—it's that the impact is too great. After one party, I can't work for two weeks.' The more uneventful the life, the more material there is. Events kill the imagination. You know Flaubert said, 'The fewer erections, the better the writing.'"

What substitutes for live encounters is the world of books—for Pamuk, the "great consolation." His reading is feverish, encyclopedic; he crossquestions visitors about favorite authors like a boy trading baseball cards. The contemporary American section of his library looks like a plugged-in

New Yorker's shelves—not just one but three volumes each by Mona Simpson, Harold Brodkey, Nicholson Baker.

Turkish intellectuals, while extolling Pamuk's technical virtuosity, frequently remark that his novels are "bookish." The translator Yurdanur Salman complains that Pamuk's fiction is "dry, cerebral, not a juicy, organic text." The Turkish literary critic Jale Parla notes, "His source of inspiration has been more literature than life."

Are European novels unreservedly part of his inheritance, I ask Pamuk, or does he read Joyce and Flaubert with more ambivalence than, say, an American might? Those in the "provinces" of world culture suffer from a "double consciousness," Pamuk answers. "In movie houses in Istanbul, growing up, we devoured Hollywood dramas as guides to etiquette. There would be a love scene in a restaurant, and someone in the back row would shout, 'Look, they're eating peaches with a knife and fork!' And the whole audience would go, 'Aha!'

"Things in Turkey are not shiny like in the West. There is a feeling of being off the track, forgotten. I have given so much time and energy to exploring that sadness of feeling that the life lived elsewhere is more mythic, more real than your own pale, shabby imitation-life."

This provincial curse of isolation is especially potent in the Turks' case because they were deliberately cut off from their own formidable history. After the Ottoman defeat in the First World War and the consequent dismemberment of the empire, Kemal Atatürk created the new republic in the West's image. All "Eastern" traces, including religion, were banned as backward. Atatürk outlawed the dervish sects, introduced the Latin alphabet, and purged Turkish of its Arabic and Persian words. As a result, contemporary Turks cannot read their own classical texts, including a poem a hundred years old.

On the upside, Atatürk made a proud nation of a conquered remnant, offering the sole proof of a secular Muslim democracy. On the downside, he left a people with an enduring identity crisis. "Mentally trying to join another civilization, whether because of technology or a military defeat, is painful," says Pamuk. "I was raised in a community that considered itself to be Western, while the rest of the country did not seem to be. Religion [Islam] for us was low culture." His sole encounter with Islam, growing up, was being taken to the mosque by the maid. "It was a place where the servants met to gossip, and I was so Westernized I felt naked taking off my shoes."

This back-and-forth of having believed yourself to be Western, then realizing you're different; your naïve way of ignoring these differences, then eventually trying to establish your own place—this is not some metaphysical gymnastic. The whole country is suffering through the same dilemma. The simplest municipal problem—how to design streetlights or parking meters—becomes part of the East-West debate. Then you understand that this transition state has been going on for two hundred years; it is a way of life and will be for years to come."

[. . .] It is Orhan Pamuk's novelistic mission both to capture the geographical schism in the Turkish soul and to reconcile it, planting Arabic and Persian words, images and stories in a Western form. His enterprise is by no means instinctual: "I have three generations of positivist blood in me; the geography of my literary heritage began with Henry James. Hegel defines 'the contingent' as that which exists but is not necessary. In my early twenties I kicked out of my fictional project anything with Islamic origins. It was only later I realized that classical Sufi literature not only existed but was necessary. I like Faulkner's describing how in his twenties he tried to write French novels, and in his thirties he turned to Mississippi. I, too, finally understood that my huge stem of a civilization was interesting, and that the whole tradition was still alive in Istanbul. To search out this civilization in broken walls, in broken faces, became my highest challenge."

[. . .] Pamuk, too, is involved in his own trial. This second trial involves a recently issued anthology of articles, each of which on its original publication was charged with breaking a law. Now more than a thousand people, including Orhan, have declared themselves "editors," making the anthology's publication "the largest act of civil disobedience in Turkey." If its participants are jailed, many of Turkey's most popular soap operas, music programs and newspapers will shut down.

[. . .] "Turkey is a savage country; there is no understanding for other religious, ethnic, linguistic communities. If Jesus Christ were a Turkish policeman, he would be corrupted within ten months. Every day shameful scandals are exposed in the newspapers, but nothing changes. I want to live in a society in which people don't get arrested for their thoughts."

I ask him, as dusk falls on the marine expanse of lighthouses and minarets, if he might live elsewhere—expecting, I guess, for Pamuk to swear, if I forget thee, O Istanbul, let my right hand wither. I am surprised by his alacrity. Yes, he could easily move to New York or Paris. "With guilty conscience, but it's an author's job to transfer his work. I admire James Joyce in Trieste, carrying within himself the dramatic weight of Ireland. All of us Turkish intellectuals have moments of exile, feeling estranged by the coups or by this new fundamentalism. My first thought is always, how will I take my library?"

Turkish Interview Excerpts from *Öteki Renkler* (*Other Colors: Essays and a Story*)

Various / 1982–1999

From *Öteki Renkler*, Istanbul: İletişim Yayınları, 1999. Translated from the Turkish by Ezgi Üstündağ.

On Writing *Cevdet Bey and Sons*

From "Every Author's Dream Is to Discover a Completely New Form"
Serpil Eryılmaz / 1987
Türkiye Postası, "Her edebiyatçının rüyası yepyeni bir biçim bulmaktır," November 20, 1987.

Orhan Pamuk: There are some facets of every writer's literary persona—I mean in the individual style he develops—that originate not from the world around him or his literary abilities but from the small details, habits, and coincidences that make up his existence. I wanted my first novel to be about a family, and while I was working on it my family would always bring up this old house next to the apartment building in which I grew up. I also remember that house. It was in ruins, and apparently my family used to live there. I'd only seen the roof of that house from the top of my apartment building. I daydreamed about that house. I knew the house existed in the 1930s. This small detail from my life, this daydream enabled me to write about people living in the 1930s whom I'd never met. As you sit at a table, it's these small details that suddenly occur to you from which novels are born. Because at that same moment, you have other ideas, too. For one reason or another, one idea surpasses another until you've finally accumulated enough little parts to start working on your novel. After going through this process, I realized that

I would have to read sources from 1934 if I wanted to write a novel set in 1934. I actually enjoyed reading them, including copies of *Demiryol* [literally "Railroad"] magazine, old newspapers, gossipy books, novels about socialites. *Cevdet Bey and Sons* is therefore both a novel about my family and the story of another family born of research and my imagination.

From Other Colors, *"Cevdet Bey and Sons"*
Orhan Pamuk / 1999

Orhan Pamuk: My family is very present throughout *Cevdet Bey and Sons*: Many years ago my own grandfather had built a railroad and lived in Nişantaşı, first in an old stone house and then in a structure he had built that would soon be called Pamuk Apartments. We lived with my grandmother, uncles, and aunt in an apartment building much like the one described in the novel. I also lived for many years in the Pamuk Apartments, where I wrote part of *The Black Book* and which inspired that same novel. Unlike Cevdet Bey, I didn't have any shopkeepers in my family. But the small occurrences and rituals of family life, like lunch on the Feast of Sacrifice, trips to Beyoğlu and walks to Maçka, bickering during Sunday car rides to the Bosphorus, disagreements with family members, relations with friends and neighbors, these were all drawn from my family. This novel was also inspired by other works: after reading Thomas Mann's *Buddenbrooks*, I knew I could tell my story across multiple generations. [. . .] *Cevdet Bey* is the product of both my desire to write an epic family novel and to record Istanbul's story from the last years of the Ottoman Empire through the first fifty years of the Republic.

On Writing *Silent House*

From Other Colors, *"Silent House"*
Orhan Pamuk / 1999

Orhan Pamuk: One of the many sources of inspiration for *Silent House* was my grandfather's letters to my grandmother. My aunt Türkan Rado had mentioned these letters to me. My grandfather went to Berlin at the turn of the century to study law. Prior to his departure, he got engaged to my grandmother Nikfal. While he studied law in Berlin, my grandfather wrote frequently to his fiancée in Istanbul. The style of these letters is not unlike the manner in which Selahattin tutored Fatma. The letters are full of thoughts like, "Here they're debating whether or not women should have the right to vote, what do you think, what do you think about women's rights, they have this and that in Europe, how do you feel about that?" I know my grandmother's responses ranged from indifference to "it's sinful, it's forbidden." She was a painfully practical person with no interest in papers or books. Just like Fatma in the novel. *Silent House* began to come together after I imagined their unhappy relationship. And all the youth in the novel, the drag racing, drinking, going to the discotheque, loitering on the beach were inspired by my friends in the Bayramoğlu Beach neighborhood in the 1970s. For a short time, we spent our summers there. I grew up among and was close with these young people who were not too mischievous save for destroying their fathers' cars drag racing. I remembered them fondly as I wrote this novel.

From "Orhan Pamuk: 'Protagonists Should Serve the Novel Not the Novelist'"
Ülkü Demirtepe / 1984
Sanat Olayı, "'Roman kahramanları yazarın değil, romanın hizmetinde olmalı,'" February 1984.

Ülkü Demirtepe: You've experimented with a new style in *Silent House*. Could you explain how you decided on this new style?

Orhan Pamuk: By playing around with the wording and the language itself, researching ways to make sentence structure parallel thought patterns, trying to squeeze different tenses into one sentence. . . . In Turkey, writers innovating language and style are belittled as "incomprehensible" or just "not worth comprehending." Part of the reason for this may also be that such innovative writers have seldom been awarded prizes for challenging their readers.

[. . .]

ÜD: Has Selahattin from *Silent House* been relegated to the past or is he alive today?

OP: Doctor Selahattin's gravestone indicates he died in 1942. If you're asking about modernizers like Selahattin as intellectuals, there are fewer of them today who aim to radically transform their country's culture. [. . .]

The story in *Silent House* is told through the thoughts of each of its characters. When I penned a character's consciousness, I didn't limit myself to that character's vocabulary. I knew that limiting myself in this way would make it more difficult for me to convey these streams of consciousness. Most importantly, it is important to realize that we don't think with words, for words reside somewhere between the tongue and the brain: they occasionally come to mind and then leave. With the stream of consciousness technique in *Silent House* I wasn't trying to take a perfect snapshot of the characters' minds as they are. Without removing myself completely from the story, I try to convey the little thoughts floating around in the characters' minds. An important issue was to do away with those infuriating "he thought, she thought" phrases, which only make novels repetitive and monotonous. (If only I could find an elegant way to get rid of "Ahmet said, Mehmet said" phrases, too!) My goal was to devise a manner of narrating, a language that could convey what was going on inside my characters' minds. But unlike a provincial naturalist writer who tries to perfectly capture a chaotic marketplace on paper, it was never my intention to produce a written snapshot of human consciousness.

On Writing *The White Castle*

From "Part History, Part Fable"
Ayça Atikoğlu / 1985
Milliyet, "Yarı tarih, yarı masal," July 24, 1985.

Orhan Pamuk: One of the most attractive aspects of writing a novel is researching a different form, a new style of storytelling for each novel. *Silent House* is not at all like *Cevdet Bey and Sons*, and this novel [*The White Castle*] is not at all like either of them. When its brevity, tone, dimensions, and tempo are considered, in terms of form it recalls what the Europeans call *la nouvelle*.

From "Aspiring to the Novel Is Not a Common Thing for Turks"
Celal Üster / 1985
Cumhuriyet, "Türkün romana özenmesi, Türke özgü davranış değil," October 17, 1985.

Orhan Pamuk: Yes, this novel concerns itself with history. But it doesn't do this to describe a historical period but rather to tell a story. I simply placed a story that I already had in mind into this time period. This setting could have been thirty to forty years before the Mehmet the Hunter period

[Sultan Mehmed IV, r. 1648–1687] or even a century after. In the world and in Turkey, we are used to equating historical novels with works like *War and Peace* that attempt to convey and dramatize the social issues of an entire period with Shakespearean characters. *The White Castle* is not that kind of a novel. It was set in the past to add color to a particular story, not to convey the social issues of this historical period.

From "A Journey into the Secrets of Identity"
  Celal Özcan / 1990
  Bizim Almanca, "Benliğin gizlerine yolculuk," December 1990.

Celal Özcan: You adapted the East and West into a motif of twin siblings. Is this a reflection of the notion that these two cultures are entirely separate and irreconcilable?

Orhan Pamuk: At the heart of the book lies the story of the twins. In both Eastern and Western culture, for example in the works of German author Hoffmann [E. T. A. Hoffmann, 1776–1822] or in *The Thousand and One Nights* in Eastern culture, twins appear frequently and manifest as the doppelgänger motif. I playfully incorporated this theme within the identity conflict we were just discussing. The fact that my characters look like one another or see each other as if in a mirror is not an allusion to current issues but arises from turning an eternal identity problem into a game. The subject of my book is not how close or how far the East and West are from one another. Rudyard Kipling wrote verses like "East Is East, West Is West." My book may have been written to dispel these cliché notions. This book does not want the East to be the East nor the West to be the West.

CÖ: Does the relationship between the slave and his master have a dimension to it other than the relationship between the East and the West?

OP: There's this dimension: The camaraderie of two people locked up together in a house who are trying to impress a ruler, a sultan whom they find to be less intelligent than themselves with their scientific and cultural formations. Their relationship becomes sadomasochistic at times. It definitely progresses through moments of violence, hate, and strong sadomasochism. For me, the most important aspect of the book is that no matter how historical it may seem, it's full of those concrete instances that I can feel in my soul and one can still witness today—of worry, wasting time, discovering the dark ways of the world, and of people entering the most secret parts of their souls by torturing each other. Perhaps the East-West conflict I mention at the beginning of this book transcends any quests for identity and is really what makes these characters worth writing a book about. The relationship between the master and his slave inherently alludes to the East-West conflict, but more importantly it's a thirty-year relationship between two desperate yet ambitious people who live alone and under pressure in their violent surroundings, and that story is much more enjoyable to tell.

On Writing *The Black Book*

From "I Pull Rabbits Out of Hats"
Mete Çubukçu / 1990
Nokta, "Şapkadan tavşan çıkarıyorum," April 1, 1990.

Orhan Pamuk: All of my books are born of the previous book. From a detail, a sentence. From the youths in *Cevdet Bey* emerged, in a sense, *Silent House*. *The White Castle* originated with the historian Faruk [Darvınoğlu] from *Silent House*. *The Black Book* was born out of the dreamlike setting and some of the historical scenes, what I would call the dark scenes of mysterious blue nights, in *The White Castle*.

[...]

Newspaper columnists are an important part of my life. I began reading columns when I was twelve years old. I assigned great importance to them. They determined the direction of my political and daily world. I believe columnists in Turkey hold a special place that is rarely granted to those in other parts of the world. They are professors of everything. They give meaning to their readers' worldviews and captivate their readers. Reading a columnist's daily piece is a habit that meets a person's deep-seated needs. These people who, in some ways, construct our world eventually attain a sort of divine status.

From "Every Author's Dream Is to Discover a Completely New Form"
Serpil Eryılmaz / 1987
Türkiye Postası, "Her edebiyatçının rüyası yepyeni bir biçim bulmaktır," November 20, 1987.

Orhan Pamuk: In the novel there is a newspaper columnist. Toward the end of his life, this columnist begins to lose his mind. I needed to include some of the columns he wrote as he was losing it. I, now, am trying to write the way a columnist who is going mad might write. I really enjoy this, because in general, a novelist tends to write pages that connect past and future events. A novel is, of course, something with a beginning and an end. The columns I plan on inserting in this new novel will, in some sense, help the story progress. But at the same time, they will give me the freedom to imagine how I would write if I began to lose my mind.

From Other Colors, *"The Black Book"*
 Orhan Pamuk / 1999

Orhan Pamuk: I could say that what I've done with *The Black Book* is to discover a story structure befitting the violence, colors, and chaos of daily life in Istanbul. To me, the novel's long sentences, the dizzying, long, baroque sentences that seem to go in circles around themselves, seem to come straight out of the city's chaos, its history, and its current wealth, its indecisiveness and energy. *The Black Book* was written with the excitement of saying everything about Istanbul at once and so the book tries to say a lot of different things at the same time. Bringing *The Thousand and One Nights* to life in Istanbul is another goal of the novel. I wanted to write about Istanbul in the way I see and experience it: as a place that has yet to lose its mystery. When I was writing the book, I knew Western critics would say, "Pamuk has done with Istanbul what James Joyce did with Dublin." That is exactly what they said. But I do not share Joyce's goals: this comparison is accurate insofar as it refers to a love for the city's topography, its details, its shops and history. My goal is to create a personal encyclopedia of Istanbul . . . at its heart resides once again Nişantaşı apartment life, and real places like Alaaddin's Shop. From this point, the novel opens up to Beyoğlu and the entirety of Istanbul. And from there, to the East's storytelling traditions, mystical tales, parables, Rumi [1207–1273] and Sheikh Galip [1757–1799]. I had Sheikh Galip's *Hüsn-ü Aşk* [*Beauty and Love*, published 1825] in mind as I described Rüya and Galip's love and Galip's wanderings through Istanbul. But beyond all this, what *The Black Book* really does is describe my childhood and living in Nişantaşı in the 1970s and what it's like to live in Istanbul, walk through its streets. *The Black Book* is the history of my own life, the stores and things I love, Alaaddin's still-open store, the Nişantaşı police station, Taksim Square and Beyoğlu, and all the personal memories that reside in these places, and it's also an attempt to embrace Istanbul and its entire history. Where these two meet is the shady region where I believe my fears, love of life, and occasional mystery or personal paranoias reside.

From "Orhan Pamuk Discusses The Black Book*"*
Hami Çağdaş / 1990
Gösteri, "Orhan Pamuk *Kara Kitap*'ı anlatıyor," April 1990.

Orhan Pamuk: All the events in *The Black Book* were juxtaposed after being extracted one by one from the dark corners of memory. The arm of an old, broken baby doll is nothing by itself; what's interesting to us is how it manages to carve a place out in our memory. Departing from that point, at my own leisure I can enter a garden and show the reader everything I want him or her to see. Because memory, like an antique shop, is chock-full of items recalling every past era, it is a treasure trove for every writer trying to escape "linear" storytelling. In addition, it's a shelter, an indispensable fortress on which a writer can ground his own talents.

On Writing *The New Life*

From Other Colors, *"The New Life"*
Orhan Pamuk / 1999

Orhan Pamuk: I began working on *The New Life* rather unexpectedly, while I was in the middle of another novel. I was writing the novel that would eventually become *My Name Is Red*. I had been invited to a writers' festival in Australia, and I arrived there after a long flight. They put me up in a motel with other writers. I went to the beach with the neurologist Oliver Sacks and the poet Miroslav Holub. A long, endless shore, a leaden sky, and an almost-leaden sea. The weather was calm and overcast. I was at the edge of a continent that, as a child flipping through atlases, I had thought looked like a horse's head. Sacks, the neurologist, dove into the sea's "nerves" in his flippers and goggles and was gone. Holub, the poet, wandered off looking for pebbles and seashells and disappeared. And I was left alone on the endless shore. It was a mystical moment. Oddly enough, I thought to myself, "I am a writer!" I was very happy with being alive, being there, being in the world. That evening, they threw us writers a big party. I was tired and I did not go. From the hotel veranda, through the trees and the leaves, I was listening to the sounds of amusement, watching the lights coming from that distant garden. For me, observing fun from the sidelines symbolizes a writer's attitude toward life itself. At that moment, in the half-darkness Oliver

Sacks walked out of the door of the neighboring room. I told him I could not sleep because of my insomnia and the long flight. He brought a sleeping pill from his room. "I can't sleep either; let's split this," he said. "I never take sleeping pills," I said. It was like I told him I never did drugs. "I don't take them either," Sacks said. "But they do the trick for jet lag."

He was a neurologist, so I took the medication he had in his palm, thanked him, went to my room, swallowed the pill, went to bed, and optimistically awaited sleep. But sleep never came. In addition to the thought of "being a writer," I longed for "purity," authenticity. I lay in bed in the dark and thought about my life. I felt that only writing about happiness and something good would relax me. I rose from bed like a sleepwalker, grabbed the empty notebook I always carried in my bag, sat at the table in the big room and began writing: "I read a book one day, and my whole life was changed!" I had had this sentence in mind my entire life. I had always wanted to write a novel that began with that line. Its protagonist would be like me. The reader would not find out what the he had read, but only what happened to him after he had read that book. And the reader would take what he or she had learned and deduce what book the young man had read. I wrote the book's first paragraph that night in the hotel room in this manner and soon after got stuck. But the book had gotten me excited. I took a break from *Red* and wrote this novel as it came to me, staying true to its form, and finished it in two years.

From "Orhan Pamuk Discusses People Caught in a Whirlpool of Melancholy and Violence"
    Mürşit Balabanlılar / 1994
    Tempo, "Orhan Pamuk hüznün ve şiddetin girdabındaki insanımızı anlatıyor,"
    October 15, 1994.

Orhan Pamuk: I didn't place life's complex mysteries at the center of this book. Instead, I focused on the protagonist being tossed around by this mystery. For this reason, as a central Orhan Pamuk theme, I can say that the mystery in this book cannot be directly identified but is omnipresent, and that it also enters our minds from time to time before vanishing like the blurry objects we see through a moving bus window. What was important was not to identify or run after that thing at the depths but to wander among its clues by sensing them, like the half-awake passenger of a long bus trip. Perhaps the foundational idea of this book is affect. That's why I can say this book is close to poetry, which is especially close to the world of affect and is more poetic and lyrical.

[...]

Mürşit Balabanlılar: In this book you play around considerably with the ideas of travel, time, and watches . . .

OP: The watch names that Dr. Fine assigns to the spies he hires to follow his son around—all of these topics are personal interests of mine. . . . Maybe it's something I picked up from Tanpınar [Turkish modernist author Ahmet Hamdi Tanpınar, 1901–1962], but it's also something I learned from the anxiety surrounding "time" shared by authors like Faulkner, Virginia Woolf, or Joyce in modernist literature. And it's also based on the provincial watchmakers' stores I encountered while writing the screenplay for *The Secret Face*. . . . This is also about the importance Turks have attached to watches over the last one hundred fifty years. A Swiss watch manufacturer once said that "Turks are our biggest customers." Indeed, watches are special objects for us (for instance, praying five times a day, the call to prayer, et cetera). The watch itself is a fetish, enough to be a milestone in Islamic culture. For example, watches are most frequently given to newly circumcised boys. A child finishes school, graduates first in their class, and we reward them with a watch. This is not the case in other cultures. On the other hand, we're also not a punctual people. It's as though we're trying to find consolation in the belief that we can use watches to achieve the Western world's certainty and mathematical precision, which we have been unable to attain. It has been further internalized through its association with religion and prayer times.

From "The Caramel Taste of the 'Absolute'. . ."
Fatma Oran / 1994
Cumhuriyet Kitap, "'Mutlak'ın karamela tadı . . . ," October 20, 1994.

Fatma Oran: A single book completely changes the life of the novel's protagonist.

Orhan Pamuk: Reading a single book and having your entire life changed is, in my opinion, a classic theme particular to countries like ours. You know, a little bit before "modern life"; it's something that evokes a time when key words like magic, mystery, elixirs, or healing were part of daily life. On the other hand, it's something that someone like me sees frequently in his personal life: we've all encountered many individuals who have claimed "I read Georges Politzer's *Elementary Principles of Philosophy* and my entire world changed; I've been a Marxist ever since" or its Islamist variation. This reflects the mistaken notion that the secret of life and the world can be revealed to us in a short whisper: it's an essential part of our daily lives. In the same way, we always expect this: We're going to elect a prime minister into office and our entire lives are going to change. We're going to buy one lottery ticket and our lives are going to change. This is a hope for "salvation" that can be explained with this sort of magical, healing word. Yet we live in a world of unfortunate souls who are consoled by this sort of hope, and we ourselves are also like that. For this reason, the sentence "I read a book one day, and my whole life was changed," as a point of departure, merges with the bits of heartache, innocence, Kemalist fundamentalism, and religious fundamentalism that we all share; but we have always had this degree of naïveté and those who give us hope, from prime ministers to newspaper columnists, know full well that the masses seeking this hope are a little naïve, a little childlike.

From "The Mysterious Illusionist of Literature"
Hülya Vatansever / 1995
Elele, "Edebiyatın gizemli illüzyonisti," August 1995.

Orhan Pamuk: In the middle of the night, while you are still asleep, your bus pulls into a small town. The town's lights are dim, everything is hazy. The streets are empty. But from the bus's high windows you can see that one house's curtains are open. Maybe while you're there, your bus stops at a traffic light. And at that moment, amid all that activity, we find ourselves inside a house with open curtains on the backstreet of a town we have never visited, next to people who are smoking, reading the newspaper, or watching the news on television late at night in their pajamas before going to bed. All of us have experienced this feeling. This is one of the oddities introduced by modern technology. And sometimes we make eye contact and stare for a moment. At nearly one hundred kilometers an hour we dive into the most private or most absent-minded moments of people's lives, as though they're frozen in time. And this is one of the moments that life offers to remind us how many different lives, how many different individuals make up this world. We all gaze longingly at this other life as though we were staring at cans and tomatoes in a refrigerator. We compare our own lives with theirs. In one way or another we grow curious about that other life and want to be a part of it. We imagine being like or even becoming those people in there. The allure of other lives shows us how specific and unique our own lives are.

From "I'm Making Fun of Myself and the Reader"
Doğan Hızlan / 1994
Hürriyet, "Kendimi ve okuru sarakaya alıyorum," October 24, 1994.

Orhan Pamuk: I'm interested in Sufi mysticism as a literary source. I haven't been able to embrace Sufism as a disciplined set of attitudes and behaviors designed to cultivate my soul. I view Sufi literature as a literary treasure trove. As someone who was raised by a Republican family, I feel exceedingly Cartesian and Western-influenced in my rationality whenever I sit at my table to write. This rationalism is at the center of my existence. But on the other hand, as much as I can, I try to open my soul to other books, other texts. I don't view those texts as something to exploit but actually get pleasure from reading them. The soul is affected whenever one feels pleasure. And my rationalist eye is still active at these moments when my soul is affected. Perhaps my books are created in the push and pull between these two poles.

On Writing *My Name Is Red*

From "A New Orhan Pamuk in The New Life*"*
Ayça Atikoğlu / 1994
Milliyet, "*Yeni Hayat*'la yeni bir Orhan Pamuk," October 11, 1994.

Orhan Pamuk: The first person to read *My Name Is Red* carefully was the Director of Topkapı Palace, Filiz Çağman. When I started working on the book, Ms. Çağman was the head of the palace library. Before I started writing the book, I spoke with her at length. Ms. Çağman taught me that, as is apparent in their finished works, the miniaturists began painting a horse from its hooves and that this in turn meant that the miniaturists had memorized how to paint a horse. Ms. Çağman and I met at Topkapı Palace one Sunday before *My Name Is Red* was published and went over the novel page by page. We worked until a late hour. It was completely dark and the crowds had left the palace-museum.... We stepped out into the courtyard of the palace's school. The entire area was deserted, dark, and eerie. The leaves, breeze, and chill of autumn.... Shadows hit the walls of the treasury I wrote about in my book. We stopped and stared in silence for quite some time.... Holding pages from the unpublished book in our hands. You know how for some things we think to ourselves, "It was all worth it just for this." . . .

Writing *My Name Is Red* was worth it just for that windy, dark Sunday afternoon at the palace.

From "Writing Novels Gives the Pleasure of Watching Events from Above, from a Balcony"
Fatma Oran / 1999
Cumhuriyet Kitap, "Roman yazmak, olaylara bir yukarıdan, bir balkondan bakmanın zevkini taşır," January 14, 1999.

Orhan Pamuk: This is what I'm most proud of: When I began imagining this novel, I only had a limited understanding of and appreciation for Islamic miniature art. Being able to differentiate between these images by period and style requires, in my opinion, great patience and that, in turn, is impossible without a true love of the art. Initially, learning how to love these pictures is the most difficult. [. . .] At the Metropolitan Museum in New York, the miniatures, especially those from Iran, are displayed better, so one can put one's head closer to the pages, get closer to the images, the display cases are designed for that. I would look at the miniatures for hours. I would get bored with some of them, some of them had a playfulness, a forcefulness about them; but I would learn to love them after hours and hours of staring. I learned to labor before these pictures. At first this is a little bit like starting to read a book in a language you don't know with a bad dictionary; you only get a little bit out of it, the hours pass and nothing happens. Even worse, there are people who understand and have conquered this material and you envy the and believe you'll never be able to attain their level of knowledge or feel their pleasure. On the other hand, there is a certain degree of pride at play; this bizarre and at first glance unappreciable, difficult, closed, perspectiveless art with Eastern figures—whom you initially do not know how to approach or appreciate—with their narrow eyes and "foreign" clothing, but whom later, when you look and see their faces, learn to appreciate. I learned to love them only after years of studying this culture. What I am most proud of is not that I read a lot of books about them but that after ten years, I finally learned to love them.
[. . .]
My book's actual hero is the heard-but-not-seen storyteller and the novel's most tragic aspect is this character's terrible demise. I also feel like the storyteller; that is, I feel as though I'm under pressure. Don't write this, don't write that, if you write this be sure to say this, it will upset your mother, it

will upset your father, it will upset the government, it will upset your publisher, it will upset the newspaper, it will upset everyone; fingers will wag and, no matter what you do, they will always find a way to criticize. "Good God!" you think to yourself at first; but on the other hand, you think, I am going to write something that will upset every single one of them but will be so beautiful, they'll have to respect me. Writing a novel in a limited, superficial democracy such as ours is what makes me feel like I'm playing the role of the storyteller; in other words, it's not merely political barriers but also taboos, family ties, religious prohibitions, the government, and a whole slew of things that make life difficult for a novelist. Writing a historical novel, from this perspective, is like wanting to change one's wardrobe.

From *"Interview on* My Name Is Red*"*
Enver Ercan / 1999
Varlık, "*Benim Adım Kırmızı üzerine söyleşi*," March 1999.

Orhan Pamuk: *My Name Is Red* examines this idea: "If Shirin fell in love with Hüsrev just by looking at a picture of him, Hüsrev's picture must have really been painted in the style of a Western portrait." Because Islamic miniatures usually depict the general beauty of the human form. Shirin was able to look at this particular picture on the street and recognize Hüsrev (as though she had seen a passport photo). In that period, hundreds of pictures of sultans, khans, and Tamerlane were painted but we still don't know what their faces actually looked like because these are all based on a single, general image of a sultan or khan. Of course, sometimes the image resembles its subject in some way. But how much of a resemblance is there? Is that slight resemblance really enough to fall in love with?

From *"A Novelist Can Do Injustice to History"*
Nihal Bengisu / 1999
Aksiyon, "Romancı tarihe haksızlık edebilir," February 20, 1999.

Orhan Pamuk: One group of readers had the desire to see the Persian and Ottoman illustrations mentioned in the book. This was quite natural because the miniaturists were describing the illustrations through my words. I enjoyed describing those illustrations very much. Because I wrote this book as much to capture the images in words as I did to get the reader interested in them. Now I am anxious because some of the readers who were curious about the miniatures were disappointed when they saw them. We, like most of the world, were educated in post-Renaissance Western art and those works have captured our imaginations almost entirely. For this reason, miniatures, for those who have never studied them, seem boring and even primitive. At the same time, this is the central theme of my book.

[. . .]

There is a connection between the art of miniatures and the way my book is written. But there is something even more important: if studied closely, the individuals depicted in the miniatures are both turned inward, looking at the picture, and outward, looking back at the viewer. When Hüsrev and Shirin meet, they never actually see one another, in such a way that each gazes at the other, because their bodies are half turned toward us. As they tell their stories, my characters address one another in addition to the reader. They say both, "I am a picture and this is what I represent," and, "But look, reader, I'm also speaking to you." The miniatures remind us constantly that they are pictures. The reader is also aware that they are reading a novel.

Similarly, the female characters are also more than aware that the reader is invading their private affairs. They speak to you, on the one hand, and, at the same time, they try to clean up themselves and their surroundings and not say anything impolite. Women are not comfortable with being watched; they are not exhibitionists. Therefore, they pull the peeping reader into their lives as a confidant, thus transforming his status from infidel trespasser to friend and create an entirely new dimension.

"The Illuminator's Ink Is Red"
Oral Çalışlar / 1998
Cumhuriyet Dergi, "Nakkaşın mürekkebi kırmızı," December 20, 1998.

Orhan Pamuk: The experiences of the family in *My Name Is Red* are based loosely upon my own family's experiences. My mother's name is also Shekure and I have an older brother named Shevket. You will also meet an Orhan in the book. At one point, my father was not staying with us (the father in the novel has also left and not returned). Me, my mother, and my older brother were on our own. Just like in the book, my brother and I would fight. The topic was the return of our estranged father, just like the one in *My Name Is Red*. My mother struggled to make us obey her. As we see a few times in *My Name Is Red*, she would yell angrily at us. But the similarities end there.

[. . .]

Of course Shekure resembles my mother in some ways. The way she scolded my older brother and dominated us, for example. She was a woman who knew what she was doing, dominant and strong. At least she appeared that way. That is the extent of the character's resemblance to my mother. This is almost only a postmodern similarity. Seeming identical, yet being completely different. Of course, there is an ironic discrepancy in the time periods they inhabit. It's as though I tacked my mother's name onto a totally different era and setting. On the other hand, her strength is the knowledge that her desires contradict one another and that despite this knowledge, she is able to avoid becoming frantic. Her very optimistic approach to her inner turmoil, knowing that these contradictions would sort themselves out . . . Shekure has desires that are diametrically opposed to one another. Although she knows this, she does not get caught up in worry. She takes solace in the fact that life is constructed upon such contradictions and instead considers herself fortunate for everything in her life, because she knows that eventually an option will emerge.

[. . .]

Throughout my youth, from the age of seven to nineteen, I wanted to be a painter. I was the black sheep of my family because I drew pictures. Back then, they sold these primitive pocketbooks about Ottoman art. I used to copy the Ottoman miniatures in those books. I did this with a sort of instinctive curiosity. As a thirteen-year-old middle school student, I knew the stylistic differences between the sixteenth-century Miniaturist Osman and the eighteenth-century Ottoman artist Levni. I purchased and pored over books on this subject, in which I had a special interest. I contemplated writing a book about miniaturists for many years. At one point, this book had the form of a single miniaturist's life story, but eventually I abandoned that idea. Indeed, I myself have been living somewhat like a miniaturist for twenty-four years. If the miniaturists in my book spend their lives—until they go blind—bent over a worktable, then I myself have also been bent over some sort of a worktable for the last twenty-four years. Sometimes you can write; sometimes you cannot. Sometimes you feel discouraged and cannot do anything. Sometimes you write for three days straight and then toss it all out. Sometimes darkness, like swirling black clouds, sets in and sometimes you rejoice and feel delighted. Eventually, you will put out everything you have worked on. Because I'm also familiar with how groups of writers interact with one another, I thought I should include in my book jealousy, joy, acknowledgment of one's work, hope, and fury to capture the "life of an artist," not just that of a miniaturist.

[...]

If you ask me, at its core, this book depicts the fear of being forgotten and the horror of artistic amnesia. For better or for worse, over two hundred fifty years from the time of Tamerlane till the end of the sixteenth century—after that, Western influences changed everything—pictures influenced by Iran were drawn in the Ottoman Empire. Painting miniatures somewhat covertly defies the Islamic ban on drawing pictures. Nobody was able to question these illustrations because they were ordered by sultans, shahs, khans, princes, pashas. Nobody even saw them. Indeed, for the most part, they remained in books. Shahs were the most enamored with this art form. Some even consorted with the likes of Shah Tahmasp [1524–1576], eventually going so far as to become miniaturists themselves. Later, this elegant tradition disappeared altogether, pushed out by both the cruelty and the merciless strength of history and the power and attractiveness of the Western portrait and its associated aesthetics. My book is actually about the tragedy and grief associated with this amnesia. All these sorrows and grievances are rooted in the restrictions and misery of human existence.

Sense of the City: Istanbul

BBC Editorial Board / 2003

From *BBC News*, August 7, 2003, http://news.bbc.co.uk/2/hi/europe/3131585.stm.

The BBC is asking novelists who have a profound understanding of the city they live in to reflect on the fiction it has produced and the various works of literature set there.

"When I was writing my book, I was thinking that probably critics would write, 'Pamuk did to Istanbul what James Joyce did to Dublin.' As I was writing, imagining the book as a modern, ambitious book, of course I had in mind James Joyce—what James Joyce did to Dublin. To sum it up, what he did for me was this: he considered his city, as I consider Istanbul, to be on the margins of Europe, not at the center. Of course if you lived in that corner of the world you would be obsessed with all the anxieties of nationalism; your country is important, your city is important.

"So if you have that feeling then what you have to do is pull out your city, make it look and read like Paris or London, Balzac's Paris or Dickens's London so that it will find its place in world literature. City life, urban life, living in big cities, in fact, is living in a galaxy of unimportant, random, stupid, absurd images. But your look gives a strange, mysterious meaning to these little details of streets, asphalt or cobblestone roads, advertisements, letters, all the little details of bus stops, or chimneys, windows. All these things constitute a texture of a city, and each city in that fashion is very different. You cannot give the image of a city with a postcard. But, in fact, with a taste from that texture, that is what I did.

"The French author Gérard de Nerval [1808–1855], who was a little bit depressive, a poet, came and wrote a big, thick, strange book called *Voyage en Orient* [1851]. It is an ambitious, strange, sometimes colorful book, but some sections of it are wonderful. Then his friend, Theophile Gautier [1811–1872], he wrote about Istanbul in an interesting manner.

"But the best book written about Istanbul is by an Italian children's writer, Edmondo de Amicis [1846–1908]—a travel book—for grown-ups. But it was so successful that it was translated from Italian into many languages, for example, his chapter about the dogs of Istanbul, or the streets of Istanbul, these are the best writings on Istanbul.

"So many people came, but some of them missed the whole point. Some of them got some of it, but most of the foreigners saw and paid attention to the exotic rather than the random. They missed the texture. They paid attention to monuments and looked for the exotic and the strange, and, in fact, added a color of their own, which sometimes is not there.

"If you have a vision of a city as a main hero, characters, in a way, are also instruments for you to see the city rather than their inner depths. And the inner depths of the characters are also deduced from the city, as in Dostoevsky. Then it's impossible to distinguish the character from the city, the city from the character. You have all these perspectives moving around in the city, and to imagine them in our mind's eye gives a correct and precise image of the city.

"There's another thing, and that is the sounds—things that you hear in each city that are different. In Western cities the sound of the subway or metro is very particular and it stays in your spirit, and whenever you hear it in a film, suddenly all the memories of the city wake up in you. In Istanbul it's the 'vvvvoooooot' sirens of the boats, the 'chck' from the chimney, waves of the Bosphorus hitting the quays along with the seagulls and old-fashioned little boats 'putu putu putu' kind of thing. These are the things that immediately, if I close my eyes and you give it to me in another corner of the world, make Istanbul suddenly appear in my mind's eye."

"I Was Not a Political Person"

Alexander Star / 2004

From the *New York Times*, August 15, 2004, https://www.nytimes.com/2004/08/15/books/interview-orhan-pamuk-i-was-not-a-political-person.html.

Alexander Star: In your novel, Turkey is a somewhat surreal country, where secular nationalists and theocrats compete to impose what seem to be equally dubious ideas of how to force people to be free. Is this the Turkey you know?

Orhan Pamuk: Well, that gap between my characters' consciousness and the country's poetic reality is perhaps the essential tension of my novel. I wanted to go and explore both worlds and write about them as they are—the Westernized intellectual's worldview coming to terms with the poorest, most forgotten, and perhaps most ignored part of the country. The most angry part, too.

AS: A key concern in *Snow* is the desire of many Muslim women to wear headscarves to school—an issue that raises delicate questions about where you draw the line between, say, the tolerance of religion and the imposition of religion. The current Turkish government has, controversially, attempted to assist the graduates of religious schools. Do you feel that is a legitimate cause for them?

OP: Look, I'm a writer. I try to focus on these issues not from the point of view of a statesman but from the point of view of a person who tries to understand the pain and suffering of others. I don't think there is any set formula to solve these problems. Anyone who believes there is a simple solution to these problems is a fool—and probably will soon end up being part of the problem. I think literature can approach these problems because you can go into more shady areas, areas where no one is right and no one has the right to say what is right. That's what makes writing novels interesting. It's what makes writing a political novel today interesting.

AS: And yet your novel expresses a lot of anxiety over whether it's possible to fully understand the misery and humiliation of people living in unfamiliar circumstances.

OP: Spiritually and morally, I am close to my central character. As he goes to the poorest sections of Turkish society, he falls into the traps of representation—talking in the name of the others, for the most poor. He realizes these issues are problematic. In fact, they may sometimes end up being immoral: the problem of representing the poor, the unrepresented, even in literature, is morally dubious. So in this political novel, my little contribution—if there is any, I have to be modest—is to turn it around a bit and make the problem of representation a part of the fiction too.

AS: How did you come to write a political novel?

OP: I was not a political person when I began writing twenty years ago. The previous generation of Turkish authors were too political, morally too much involved. They were essentially writing what Nabokov would call social commentary. I used to believe, and still believe, that that kind of politics only damages your art. Twenty years ago, twenty-five years ago, I had a radical belief only in what Henry James would call the grand art of the novel. But later, as I began to get known both inside and outside of Turkey, people began to ask political questions and demand political commentaries. Which I did because I sincerely felt that the Turkish state was damaging democracy, human rights, and the country. So I did things outside of my books.

AS: Such as?

OP: Write petitions, attend political meetings, but essentially make commentaries outside of my books. This made me a bit notorious, and I began to get involved in a sort of political war against the Turkish state and the establishment, which ten years ago was more partial to nationalists. Anyway, I said to myself, Why don't I once write a political novel and get all of this off my chest?

AS: Did you have trouble publishing *Snow* in Turkey? How was it received by Islamists and others?

OP: Before the publication of the book I told my friends and my publisher that I was finishing an outspoken political novel. Shall we show this to lawyers? And they said, No, no, no, now that Turkey is hoping to get in touch with Europe and now that you're nationally—internationally—"famous," you don't need to do that. OK. And after some time I gave my publishers the book. Here is the book, I said. And a week later they called me and said they'd read the book, loved the book, but they wanted my permission to show it to a lawyer. They were worried that the public prosecutor might open a case or confiscate the book before its publication. The first printing was one hundred thousand copies. They were essentially worried about the economic side of the thing. For example, they hid the book in a corner, so if it were confiscated, they could keep some copies for themselves. But none of these pessimistic things happened. In fact, the country seriously discussed the book. Half of the political Islamists and people who backed the army attacked me. On the other hand, I survived. Nothing happened to me. And in fact it worked the way I hoped it would. Some of those radical Islamists criticized the book with very simplistic ideas, such as "You're trying to describe Islamists but you have to know that an Islamist would never have sex with a woman without getting married." On the other hand, more liberal Islamists were pleased that at least the harassment they had been exposed to by the Turkish Army is mentioned.

AS: When George Bush was in Istanbul recently for the NATO summit, he referred to you as a "great writer" who has helped bridge the divide between East and West. Citing your own statements about how people around the world are very much alike, he defended American efforts to help people in the Middle East enjoy their "birthright of freedom." Did you think he understood what you meant?

OP: I think George Bush put a lot of distance between East and West with this war. He made the whole Islamic community unnecessarily angry with the United States, and in fact with the West. This will pave the way to lots of horrors and inflict cruel and unnecessary pain on lots of people. It will raise the tension between East and West. These are things I never hoped would happen. In my books I always looked for a sort of harmony between the so-called East and West. In short, what I wrote in my books for years was misquoted and used as a sort of apology for what had been done. And what had been done was a cruel thing.

AS: Is the novel as a form something you think is alive and well in the Middle East or the non-Western world more broadly? Or do you feel you're doing something rather unusual?

OP: No, the art of the novel is well. It's surviving. It has lots of elasticity. I'm sure it will continue to live in the West, in the United States and Europe. But it will have a very strange and new future in countries like China and India, where now there is an unprecedented rise of the middle classes. Legitimizing the power of these new middle classes creates problems of identity both in China and in India. This involves their nationalism when they are faced with the distinct identity of Europe and the West, and their Occidentalism when they are faced with the resistance of their poor people. I think the new modern novel that will come from the East, from that part of the world, will again raise these tensions of East-West modernity and the slippery nature of these rising middle classes in China and India. And also in Turkey, of course.

AS: In *Snow*, the radical Islamist Blue remarks at one point that the best thing America's given the world is Marlboro Red. Would you agree with that?

OP: I used to smoke them a lot when I was young. We distribute our personal pleasures in our characters. That's one of the joys of writing fiction.

The Most Hated Turk

Peer Teuwsen / 2005

From *Tages-Anzeiger*, "Der meistgehasste Türke," February 5, 2005. Translated from the German by Johanna Schuster-Craig.

Orhan Pamuk is a brilliant writer. And a Turk. Since the publication of his latest book, *Snow*, he is hated in his homeland like no other. A conversation about nationalism and Turkish inferiority complexes.

The man who divided the country makes coffee. The view from the window of his office in Cihangir, Istanbul's intellectual neighborhood, looks out over the Golden Horn on the Bosphorus. Gulls screech, ships blast their horns, [there are] traffic jams on both land and sea. It is one of the last days of the year, and the sun has faded. Orhan Pamuk, the most famous and the most widely read living Turkish writer, serves the coffee with lots of sugar and sits on a wooden chair; he offers his visitor an armchair.

The fifty-four-year-old, who is regularly mentioned as a Nobel Prize contender, has written a book that was recently translated into English, which, in the English-speaking world, has been met with an enthusiastic reception. Margaret Atwood and John Updike are singing its praises. So far none of Pamuk's novels has taken place so close to the present moment. With *Snow*, Orhan Pamuk has placed himself in the eye of the storm, in the midst of the Turkish civil war between Islamists and secularists; in the midst of this decisive battle, at the end of which stands [Turkey's] accession to the European Union and thus to the West.

Snow tells the story of the poet Ka, who returns to his homeland after twelve years in Frankfurt with a newspaper assignment to write about a strange series of suicides in a small Anatolian town called Kars. But the actual purpose of his trip is to see his childhood sweetheart Ipek. Ka is one of the last who still manages to enter the city before it is cut off by snow from the outside world. The city is in chaos, which finds its climax one night in the local theater. And Ka gets caught in the crossfire of Westerners and

Islamists who woo the stranger forcefully and try to win him over for their cause. But the poet Ka is like a whirling vortex: he can't make decisions, he's always searching, he remains elusive. *Snow* thus becomes a plea to understand the fundamentalists, but to remain distant from them.

Whoever writes this kind of a book is suspect from both sides. Pamuk has been insulted and regularly receives death threats. "I make people uncomfortable," he says and opens the conversation. He speaks quickly, he responds to criticism cattily, he gets wound up. This is what you have to understand. It's completely different to be a writer in Turkey than it is to be one in Switzerland.

Peer Teuwsen: Mr. Pamuk, I've rarely met anyone who incurs so much wrath. Why is that?

Orhan Pamuk: Tough question. I am publicly critical of Turkish nationalism, which many of the nationalists here can't bear. And also the fact that I fly around the world promoting my books, giving an interview in New York one day and in Tokyo or Helsinki the next—and don't wave around the Turkish flag like an Olympic gold medal winner while doing so, but rather am critical—that drives many Turks crazy. Most Turks have simply not yet overcome the fact that they've lost an empire. And now these people think that the whole world has conspired against the Turks. These are understandable feelings, a melancholy that I described in my book *Istanbul*. But today, a hundred years later, the Turks should be able to knock on Europe's door with self-confidence. I detest these nationalists who say everyone hates the Turks. And they detest me.

PT: It could even be described as hate. Your compatriot, the writer Hilmi Yavuz, calls you a "spy for the West"; an "imperialistic intellectual." And he is not alone. Why such harsh words?

OP: Listen, I'll end this conversation right now if you mention those names. I do not comment on that. I do not concern myself with such mediocre people.

PT: I'm just surprised that these things are said. Their tone would be impossible in Switzerland. And if one reads your book, which sets these ideologies next to each other without playing them against each other, it's even less understandable.

OP: You take these guys seriously; that's a mistake. These ultranationalists—with the same vulgar behavior and the same evil grins—would have also attacked Virginia Woolf, Marcel Proust, or Thomas Mann as members of the bourgeoisie. These people can't hurt me anymore. Before, when I was still insecure and unknown, that would have been different. But I've managed to leave these people behind me.

PT: Nevertheless, it is interesting that you incur such hatred.

OP: Turkey is a strange country. There are people here who write five hundred-page books about "the secret Jews" in Turkey—and I am supposedly one of them—who say that the Jew is this way, pure anti-Semitism, terrible. There's nothing like this in any other country. And this now that Turkey is under particular scrutiny because of the attempted accession to the European Union and the Iraq War.

PT: They get upset. But this criticism has nothing to do with your work, for which you've received a lot of international recognition.

OP: Yes, I am upset because the people who attack me in this very vulgar way don't read my books. They have never learned to read critical books. They are fascinated that I am an international success, that I have been translated into thirty-four languages. They build themselves up on what I've done. But that's part of being internationally famous.

PT: Where does this nationalism come from?

OP: I don't know. I'm just surprised that these people don't realize how wonderful it is that we are approaching Europe. The alternative is a dictatorship, either religious or military. When this doesn't happen, that's progress. But instead of rejoicing, these people always talk about Cyprus!

PT: It seems to me that Turkey sees the EU a bit like a savior, like a drug. Isn't that dangerous?

OP: The EU concerns me very little, to me it's about freedom of speech, an open society, democracy—these things I dream of earnestly. But we will get these things: the reforms that Turkey has made in the last three years are enormous. I know, of course, that this was done mainly because one otherwise won't get into the EU and one receives no money from international organizations.

PT: You don't fear that on the long road to the EU there could be disappointments?

OP: Today 80 percent of the Turks want to enter the EU. You're not allowed to disappoint them.

PT: Maybe you trigger so many emotions because you made fun of nationalism and religion a bit in your last book.

OP: Of course. I can understand that my readers will be disappointed. After *My Name Is Red*, readers probably expected me to tell them another wonderful, sugar-coated, sparkling fairy tale. And now I show up with the topics that most people here would rather forget because they interfere with their view of the world: the rise of political Islam; the fact that 70 percent of women in this country wear headscarves because it's their culture. Eighty percent of my readers are Westernized middle-class women who despise political Islam. The ruling elite in this country doesn't want to understand the conservatives and the political Islamists. They don't realize that understanding the other person is a fundamental requirement for building a nation. "No," they say to themselves, "the nation is built by the army; we don't understand them—so we bomb them."

PT: You want to understand the political Islamists and secularists, but you also make fun of them. In *Snow*, for example, a Muslim girl hangs herself with her own headscarf.

OP: I don't make fun of that, no. But I have a strong sense of irony about ideologies and nationalism. And an ironic sense of violence. This unexpected irony that comes from my pen is the reason why I write my books. I do not write realistic social studies. I'm just trying to look at ideologies from a different point of view. Ninety-nine percent of people in *Snow* live a hard life, but I'm not Chekhov or Gorky. I'm not saying: "Oh, these poor people." I have to see it ironically—irony provides distance, it's the precondition that makes understanding possible. But there is also sympathy in my book. The problem is I can't represent these people. But I also write that.

PT: Your protagonist is a ghost, he wavers between ideologies, can't be understood, he belongs to neither side.

OP: Yes, in that sense he is not unlike me. I am like him. I might agree with a political Islamist and simultaneously agree with a Jacobin Turkish secularist. I'm not alone in this. Ninety percent of Turks know these doubts. Friends told me that in this book, the ideas of the political Islamists had never been depicted so precisely, so wisely and justly. If the Islamist Blue says in the book he doesn't want to imitate the West, then I say he's right. Why should everyone wear the same Western clothes? But it's also true that without the military the 80 percent who are political Islamists would suppress or even murder the 20 percent who are leftist intellectuals. In Turkey arguments have to finally count, but you still throw your opponent in jail because he's a "traitor"—which isn't really a convincing argument.

PT: So you're somebody that doesn't always know what your own opinion is about things.

OP: No—I do know. But you can't write a good novel with an opinion, you need at least two convincing positions that contradict each other. An opinion produces at the most an essay or a political statement. A good novel is a dance of different standpoints. That's what they did in the political novels of the fifties and sixties, they didn't want to send a message. My message is a completely different message, not a political one.

PT: What?

OP: That you can be happy and not have to worry about politics.

PT: Are you joking?

OP: No, this is what I firmly believe. My protagonist Ka just wants to get his girl and then flee this city where people are tormenting and torturing each other.

PT: There's probably no coincidence that Ka reminds one of K., Kafka's protagonist.

OP: Of course there's not: he can't penetrate into the heart of things, he is distant, he never belongs to anything or anyone. In this sense he is Kafkaesque. But then he goes further. He sees that all these nationalists, be they Kurds or Turks, have so much in common: intolerance, identity crises, a damning attitude toward us, the Europeans, because nobody cares about them, they're nobodies. This city is simultaneously a real one and an imaginary one. Just recently, a journalist from the BBC was there, because of my book. And I asked him if he had spoken with the people from Kars about my book. He said only: "Oh, the people there hate you." [*They laugh*] It's strange, right? They don't want others to see their poverty. That's exactly what happened with my books. Initially I told the Turks stories about themselves. Today my readers are afraid because, thanks to the numerous translations of these stories, I also tell the stories abroad. The Turks don't want one of their own to tell strangers the truth about them.

It's the sign of a huge identity crisis.

PT: The Turks are suffering from an inferiority complex about Europe.

OP: Yes, it's terrible. I'll tell you a story. My Finnish translator loved *Snow* so much that she wanted to travel to Kars. I helped her do so. But she is not a typical Anatolian: she is blonde, fit, thin. That's why the whole city knew, a minute after she arrived, that she was the translator of this book. A teahouse door opens, and a young man calls out to her: "Wait! I want to talk to you." She sits down, the man is very nervous, and he has only one question, which seems to be very important to him: "What do the Europeans think about us?"

PT: Even Atatürk took off his fez when he traveled to Paris.

OP: Ninety percent of Turks want to show when they are in Europe that they are as civilized as the Europeans. And if Pamuk says they are still not like them, then they don't like that at all.

PT: But that's exactly what the EU is doing now. It says to Turkey: You still need to work very hard if you want to be as good as we are.

OP: Exactly, and that is very dangerous. The EU sees itself as civilized and measures others who want to enter according to their own standards. As two men do when comparing their members: very enticing, but also very debasing for the one who has a smaller one.

PT: Would you also read from your book in Kars?

OP: Yes, in thirty years, perhaps when the country is reconciled with its past, when it can bear my irony, when the economic misery is no longer as bad. Today I would not travel there; that'd be too dangerous. I understand that anyone who rarely reads may be hurt by this book. But I am a novelist. And now we're getting into the crux of the matter. Writing novels is a Western invention, and I'm doing this in a country which for a long time didn't have novels. This was also Stendhal and Voltaire's problem. One of them said: "They are making fun of us; they are not French." There is a long tradition of writers who did not meet expectations, but rather kept distant from their own people. We have many writers who are proud to be Turkish.

PT: What is "Turkish"?

OP: Turkish is another word for "confused." But once again: These people who are so proud of being more Turkish than others aren't being read.

PT: They say the same about you.

OP: Yes, but my books are bought, and theirs aren't—that can be measured. But congratulations, I've had the impression during this conversation that I wasn't sitting across from a European, but rather from a Turkish journalist.

PT: Do I look Turkish?

OP: No, but you have a feel for this disgusting nationalism that has been haunting this country for the last two or three years. And you've managed to provoke me, thank you.

PT: But I'm still not quite finished. How can the Turks then reconcile themselves [with the past]?

OP: It's all about one thing: Today Turks earn an average of four thousand euros per year; a European earns nine times as much. This degradation must be addressed, and then the consequences like nationalism and fanaticism will dissolve by themselves. Therefore, we need to join [the EU]. You see, our past is changing with our present. What happens now changes the past. Your relationship with the country can be compared with your relationship to your family. You have to live with it. Both say: there are atrocities happening, but nobody else should know about them.

PT: And you talk about it anyway. Do you just want to get in trouble?

OP: Yes, everyone should do that. Thirty thousand Kurds were killed here. And a million Armenians. And almost nobody dares to mention it. So I do it. And this is why they hate me.

PT: I still need one last answer. In Kars, pictures of the Swiss Alps hang everywhere. Why?

OP: That's very journalistic, that's just how it is. It's just a beautiful picture of a beautiful landscape that they've found. It looks better than a bare wall.

PT: What is your image of Switzerland?

OP: As a seven-year-old I lived in Geneva. Our apartment opened on to a back courtyard of a Suchard factory. There was always the scent of chocolate in the air. And a beggar played music in the courtyard. My mother would wrap a few coins in paper and throw them down to him. A beggar who played music—that was something I first saw in Switzerland. Aha, in Switzerland the beggars work for their money; in Turkey they show physical disabilities to get money. For me, this was the first difference between East and West. My impression—that we do not belong to the West—was very strong.

"One's Novels Can Be Seen as the Milestones in the Development of One's Spirit"

Ángel Gurría-Quintana / 2005

From the *Paris Review*, "Orhan Pamuk, the Art of Fiction No. 187," no. 175, Fall/Winter 2005, https://www.theparisreview.org/interviews/5587/the-art-of-fiction-no-187-orhan-pamuk.

Ángel Gurría-Quintana: How do you feel about giving interviews?

Orhan Pamuk: I sometimes feel nervous because I give stupid answers to certain pointless questions. It happens in Turkish as much as in English. I speak bad Turkish and utter stupid sentences. I have been attacked in Turkey more for my interviews than for my books. Political polemicists and columnists do not read novels there.

ÁGQ: You've generally received a positive response to your books in Europe and the United States. What is your critical reception in Turkey?

OP: The good years are over now. When I was publishing my first books, the previous generation of authors was fading away, so I was welcomed because I was a new author.

ÁGQ: When you say the previous generation, whom do you have in mind?

OP: The authors who felt a social responsibility, authors who felt that literature serves morality and politics. They were flat realists, not experimental. Like authors in so many poor countries, they wasted their talent on trying to serve their nation. I did not want to be like them, because even in my youth I had enjoyed Faulkner, Virginia Woolf, Proust—I had never aspired to the social realist model of Steinbeck and Gorky. The literature produced in the sixties and seventies was becoming outmoded, so I was welcomed as an author of the new generation.

After the midnineties, when my books began to sell in amounts that no one in Turkey had ever dreamed of, my honeymoon years with the Turkish press and intellectuals were over. From then on, critical reception was mostly a reaction to the publicity and sales, rather than the content of my books. Now, unfortunately, I am notorious for my political comments—most of which are picked up from international interviews and shamelessly manipulated by some Turkish nationalist journalists to make me look more radical and politically foolish than I really am.

ÁGQ: So there is a hostile reaction to your popularity?

OP: My strong opinion is that it's a sort of punishment for my sales figures and political comments. But I don't want to continue saying this, because I sound defensive. I may be misrepresenting the whole picture.

ÁGQ: Where do you write?

OP: I have always thought that the place where you sleep or the place you share with your partner should be separate from the place where you write. The domestic rituals and details somehow kill the imagination. They kill the demon in me. The domestic, tame daily routine makes the longing for the other world, which the imagination needs to operate, fade away. So for years I always had an office or a little place outside the house to work in. I always had different flats.

But once I spent half a semester in the US while my ex-wife was doing her PhD at Columbia University. We were living in an apartment for married students and didn't have any space, so I had to sleep and write in the same place. Reminders of family life were all around. This upset me. In the mornings I used to say goodbye to my wife like someone going to work. I'd leave the house, walk around a few blocks, and come back like a person arriving at the office. Ten years ago I found a flat overlooking the Bosphorus with a view of the old city. It has, perhaps, one of the best views of Istanbul. It is a twenty-five-minute walk from where I live. It is full of books and my desk looks out on to the view. Every day I spend, on average, some ten hours there.

ÁGQ: Ten hours a day?

OP: Yes, I'm a hard worker. I enjoy it. People say I'm ambitious, and maybe there's truth in that too. But I'm in love with what I do. I enjoy sitting at my desk like a child playing with his toys. It's work, essentially, but it's fun and games also.

ÁGQ: Orhan, your namesake and the narrator of *Snow* describes himself as a clerk who sits down at the same time every day. Do you have the same discipline for writing?

OP: I was underlining the clerical nature of the novelist as opposed to that of the poet, who has an immensely prestigious tradition in Turkey. To be a poet is a popular and respected thing. Most of the Ottoman sultans and statesmen were poets. But not in the way we understand poets now. For hundreds of years it was a way of establishing yourself as an intellectual. Most of these people used to collect their poems in manuscripts called divans. In fact, Ottoman court poetry is called divan poetry. Half of the Ottoman statesmen produced divans. It was a sophisticated and educated way of writing things, with many rules and rituals. Very conventional and very repetitive. After Western ideas came to Turkey, this legacy was combined with the romantic and modern idea of the poet as a person who burns for truth. It added extra weight to the prestige of the poet. On the other hand, a novelist is essentially a person who covers distance through his patience, slowly, like an ant. A novelist impresses us, not by his demonic and romantic vision but by his patience.

ÁGQ: [. . .] Would you say that writing prose has become easier for you over time?

OP: Unfortunately not. Sometimes I feel my character should enter a room and I still don't know how to make him enter. I may have more self-confidence, which sometimes can be unhelpful because then you're not experimenting, you just write what comes to the tip of your pen. I've been writing fiction for the last thirty years, so I should think that I've improved a bit. And yet I still sometimes come to a dead end where I thought there never would be one. A character cannot enter a room, and I don't know what to do. Still! After thirty years.

The division of a book into chapters is very important for my way of thinking. When writing a novel, if I know the whole story line in advance—and most of the time I do—I divide it into chapters and think up the details of what I'd like to happen in each. I don't necessarily start with the first chapter and write all the others in order. When I'm blocked, which is not a grave thing for me, I continue with whatever takes my fancy. I may write from the first to the fifth chapter, then if I'm not enjoying it I skip to number fifteen and continue from there.

ÁGQ: Do you mean that you map out the entire book in advance?

OP: Everything. *My Name Is Red*, for instance, has many characters, and to each character I assigned a certain number of chapters. When I was writing, sometimes I wanted to continue "being" one of the characters. So when I finished writing one of Shekure's chapters, perhaps chapter seven, I skipped to chapter eleven, which is her again. I liked being Shekure. Skipping from one character or persona to another can be depressing. But the final chapter I always write at the end. That is definite. I like to tease myself, ask myself what the ending should be. I can only execute the ending once. Toward the end, before finishing, I stop and rewrite most of the early chapters.

ÁGQ: [. . .] Did you already have your first novel in mind when you decided to quit? Is that why you did it?

OP: As far as I remember, I wanted to be a novelist before I knew what to write. In fact, when I did start writing I had two or three false starts. I still have the notebooks. But after about six months I started a major novel project that ultimately got published as *Cevdet Bey and Sons*.

ÁGQ: That hasn't been translated into English.

OP: It is essentially a family saga, like *The Forsyte Saga* or Thomas Mann's *Buddenbrooks*. Not long after I finished it I began to regret having written something so outmoded, a very nineteenth-century novel. I regretted writing it because, around the age of twenty-five or twenty-six, I began to impose on myself the idea that I should be a modern author. By the time the novel was finally published, when I was thirty, my writing had become much more experimental.

ÁGQ: When you say you wanted to be more modern, experimental, did you have a model in mind?

OP: At that time, the great writers for me were no longer Tolstoy, Dostoevsky, Stendhal, or Thomas Mann. My heroes were Virginia Woolf and Faulkner. Now I would add Proust and Nabokov to that list.

ÁGQ: The opening line of *The New Life* is "I read a book one day and my whole life was changed." Has a book had that effect on you?

OP: *The Sound and the Fury* was very important to me when I was twenty-one or twenty-two. I bought a copy of the Penguin edition. It was hard to understand, especially with my poor English. But there was a wonderful translation of the book into Turkish, so I would put the Turkish and the English together on the table and read half a paragraph from one and then go back to the other. That book left a mark on me. The residue was the voice that I developed. I soon began to write in the first-person singular. Most of the time I feel better when I'm impersonating someone else rather than writing in the third person.

ÁGQ: You say it took years to get your first novel published?

OP: In my twenties I did not have any literary friendships; I didn't belong to any literary group in Istanbul. The only way to get my first book published was to submit it to a literary competition for unpublished manuscripts in Turkey. I did that and won the prize, which was to be published by a big, good publisher. At the time, Turkey's economy was in a bad state. They said, yes, we'll give you a contract, but they delayed the novel's publication.

ÁGQ: Did your second novel go more easily—more quickly?

OP: The second book was a political book. Not propaganda. I was already writing it while I waited for the first book to appear. I had given that book some two and a half years. Suddenly, one night there was a military coup. This was in 1980. The next day the would-be publisher of the first book, the *Cevdet Bey* book, said he wasn't going to publish it, even though we had a contract. I realized that even if I finished my second book—the political book—that day, I would not be able to publish it for five or six years because the military would not allow it. So my thoughts ran as follows: At the age of twenty-two I said I was going to be a novelist and wrote for seven years hoping to get something published in Turkey . . . and nothing. Now I'm almost thirty and there's no possibility of publishing anything. I still have the two hundred fifty pages of that unfinished political novel in one of my drawers.

Immediately after the military coup, because I didn't want to get depressed, I started a third book—the book to which you referred, *Silent House*. That's what I was working on in 1982 when the first book was finally published. *Cevdet* was well received, which meant that I could publish the book I was then writing. So the third book I wrote was the second to be published

ÁGQ: What made your novel unpublishable under the military regime?

OP: The characters were young upper-class Marxists. Their fathers and mothers would go to summer resorts, and they had big spacious rich houses and enjoyed being Marxists. They would fight and be jealous of each other and plot to blow up the prime minister.

ÁGQ: Gilded revolutionary circles?

OP: Upper-class youngsters with rich people's habits, pretending to be ultraradical. But I was not making a moral judgment about that. Rather, I was romanticizing my youth, in a way. The idea of throwing a bomb at the prime minister would have been enough to get the book banned.

So I didn't finish it. And you change as you write books. You cannot assume the same persona again. You cannot continue as before. Each book an author writes represents a period in his development. One's novels can be seen as the milestones in the development of one's spirit. So you cannot go back. Once the elasticity of fiction is dead, you cannot move it again.

ÁGQ: When you are experimenting with ideas, how do you choose the form of your novels? Do you start with an image, with a first sentence?

OP: There is no constant formula. But I make it my business not to write two novels in the same mode. I try to change everything. This is why so many of my readers tell me, I liked this novel of yours, it's a shame you didn't write other novels like that, or, I never enjoyed one of your novels until you wrote that one—I've heard that especially about *The Black Book*. In fact I hate to hear this. It's fun, and a challenge, to experiment with form and style, and language and mood and persona, and to think about each book differently.

The subject matter of a book may come to me from various sources. With *My Name Is Red*, I wanted to write about my ambition to become a painter. I had a false start; I began to write a monographic book focused on one painter. Then I turned the painter into various painters working together in an atelier. The point of view changed, because now there were other painters talking. At first I was thinking of writing about a contemporary painter, but then I thought this Turkish painter might be too derivative, too influenced by the West, so I went back in time to write about miniaturists. That was how I found my subject. Some subjects also necessitate certain formal innovations or storytelling strategies. Sometimes, for example, you've just seen something, or read something, or been to a movie, or read a newspaper article, and then you think, I'll make a potato speak, or a dog, or a tree. Once you get the idea you start thinking about symmetry and continuity in the novel. And you feel, Wonderful, no one's done this before.

Finally, I think of things for years. I may have ideas and then I tell them to my close friends. I keep lots of notebooks for possible novels I may write. Sometimes I don't write them, but if I open a notebook and begin taking notes for it, it is likely that I will write that novel. So when I'm finishing one novel my heart may be set on one of these projects; and two months after finishing one I start writing the other.

ÁGQ: Many novelists will never discuss a work in progress. Do you also keep that a secret?

OP: I never discuss the story. On formal occasions, when people ask what I'm writing, I have a one-sentence stock reply: A novel that takes place in contemporary Turkey. I open up to very few people and only when I know they won't hurt me. What I do is talk about the gimmicks—I'm going to make a cloud speak, for instance. I like to see how people react to them. It is a childish thing. I did this a lot when writing *Istanbul*. My mind is like that of a little playful child, trying to show his daddy how clever he is.

ÁGQ: The word gimmick has a negative connotation.

OP: You begin with a gimmick, but if you believe in its literary and moral seriousness, in the end it turns into serious literary invention. It becomes a literary statement.

ÁGQ: Critics often characterize your novels as postmodern. It seems to me, however, that you draw your narrative tricks principally from traditional sources. You quote, for instance, from *The Thousand and One Nights* and other classic texts in the Eastern tradition.

OP: That began with *The Black Book*, though I had read Borges and Calvino earlier. I went with my wife to the United States in 1985, and there I first encountered the prominence and the immense richness of American culture. As a Turk coming from the Middle East, trying to establish himself as an author, I felt intimidated. So I regressed, went back to my "roots." I realized that my generation had to invent a modern national literature.

Borges and Calvino liberated me. The connotation of traditional Islamic literature was so reactionary, so political, and used by conservatives in such old-fashioned and foolish ways, that I never thought I could do anything with that material. But once I was in the United States, I realized I could go back to that material with a Calvinoesque or Borgesian mind frame. I had to begin by making a strong distinction between the religious and literary connotations of Islamic literature, so that I could easily appropriate its wealth of games, gimmicks, and parables. Turkey had a sophisticated tradition of highly refined ornamental literature. But then the socially committed writers emptied our literature of its innovative content.

There are lots of allegories that repeat themselves in the various oral storytelling traditions—of China, India, Persia. I decided to use them and set them in contemporary Istanbul. It's an experiment—put everything together, like a Dadaist collage; *The Black Book* has this quality.

Sometimes all these sources are fused together and something new emerges. So I set all these rewritten stories in Istanbul, added a detective plot, and out came *The Black Book*. But at its source was the full strength of American culture and my desire to be a serious experimental writer. I could not write a social commentary about Turkey's problems—I was intimidated by them. So I had to try something else.

ÁGQ: Were you ever interested in doing social commentary through literature?

OP: No. I was reacting to the older generation of novelists, especially in the eighties. I say this with all due respect, but their subject matter was very narrow and parochial.

ÁGQ: Let's go back to before *The Black Book*. What inspired you to write *The White Castle*. It's the first book where you employ a theme that recurs throughout the rest of your novels—impersonation. Why do you think this idea of becoming somebody else crops up so often in your fiction?

OP: It's a very personal thing. I have a very competitive brother who is only eighteen months older than me. In a way, he was my father—my Freudian father, so to speak. It was he who became my alter ego, the representation of authority. On the other hand, we also had a competitive and brotherly comradeship. A very complicated relationship. I wrote extensively about this in *Istanbul*. I was a typical Turkish boy, good at soccer and enthusiastic about all sorts of games and competitions. He was very successful in school, better than me. I felt jealousy toward him, and he was jealous of me too. He was the reasonable and responsible person, the one our superiors addressed.

While I was paying attention to games, he paid attention to rules. We were competing all the time. And I fancied being him, that kind of thing. It set a model. Envy, jealousy—these are heartfelt themes for me. I always worry about how much my brother's strength or his success might have influenced me. This is an essential part of my spirit. I am aware of that, so I put some distance between me and those feelings. I know they are bad, so I have a civilized person's determination to fight them. I'm not saying I'm a victim of jealousy. But this is the galaxy of nerve points that I try to deal with all the time. And of course, in the end, it becomes the subject matter of all my stories. In *The White Castle*, for instance, the almost sadomasochistic relationship between the two main characters is based on my relationship with my brother.

On the other hand, this theme of impersonation is reflected in the fragility Turkey feels when faced with Western culture. After writing *The White Castle*, I realized that this jealousy—the anxiety about being influenced by someone else—resembles Turkey's position when it looks West. You know, aspiring to become Westernized and then being accused of not being authentic enough. Trying to grab the spirit of Europe and then feeling guilty about the imitative drive. The ups and downs of this mood are reminiscent of the relationship between competitive brothers.

ÁGQ: Do you believe the constant confrontation between Turkey's Eastern and Western impulses will ever be peacefully resolved?

OP: I'm an optimist. Turkey should not worry about having two spirits, belonging to two different cultures, having two souls. Schizophrenia makes you intelligent. You may lose your relation with reality—I'm a fiction writer, so I don't think that's such a bad thing—but you shouldn't worry about your schizophrenia. If you worry too much about one part of you killing the other, you'll be left with a single spirit. That is worse than having the sickness. This is my theory. I try to propagate it in Turkish politics, among Turkish politicians who demand that the country should have one consistent soul—that it should belong to either the East or the West or be nationalistic. I'm critical of that monistic outlook.

ÁGQ: How does that go down in Turkey?

OP: The more the idea of a democratic, liberal Turkey is established, the more my thinking is accepted. Turkey can join the European Union only with this vision. It's a way of fighting against nationalism, of fighting the rhetoric of Us against Them.

ÁGQ: And yet in Istanbul, in the way you romanticize the city, you seem to mourn the loss of the Ottoman Empire.

OP: I'm not mourning the Ottoman Empire. I'm a Westernizer. I'm pleased that the Westernization process took place. I'm just criticizing the limited way in which the ruling elite—meaning both the bureaucracy and the new rich—had conceived of Westernization. They lacked the confidence necessary to create a national culture rich in its own symbols and rituals. They did not strive to create an Istanbul culture that would be an organic combination of East and West; they just put Western and Eastern things together. There was, of course, a strong local Ottoman culture, but that was fading away little by little. What they had to do, and could not possibly do enough, was invent a strong local culture, which would be a combination—not an imitation—of the Eastern past and the Western present. I try to do the same kind of thing in my books. Probably new generations will do it, and entering the European Union will not destroy Turkish identity but make it flourish and give us more freedom and self-confidence to invent a new Turkish culture. Slavishly imitating the West or slavishly imitating the old, dead Ottoman culture is not the solution. You have to do something with these things and shouldn't have anxiety about belonging to one of them too much.

ÁGQ: In Istanbul, however, you do seem to identify with the foreign, Western gaze over your own city.

OP: But I also explain why a Westernized Turkish intellectual can identify with the Western gaze—the making of Istanbul is a process of identification with the West. There is always this dichotomy, and you can easily identify with the Eastern anger too. Everyone is sometimes a Westerner and sometimes an Easterner—in fact a constant combination of the two. I like Edward Said's idea of Orientalism, but since Turkey was never a colony, the romanticizing of Turkey was never a problem for Turks. Western man did not humiliate the Turk in the same way he humiliated the Arab or Indian. Istanbul was invaded only for two years and the enemy boats left as they came, so this did not leave a deep scar in the spirit of the nation. What left a deep scar was the loss of the Ottoman Empire, so I don't have that anxiety, that feeling that Westerners look down on me. Though after the founding of the Republic, there was a sort of intimidation because Turks wanted to Westernize but couldn't go far enough, which left a feeling of cultural inferiority that we have to address and that I occasionally may have.

On the other hand, the scars are not as deep as [those of] other nations that were occupied for two hundred years, colonized. Turks were never suppressed by Western powers. The suppression that Turks suffered was self-inflicted; we erased our own history because it was practical. In that suppression there is a sense of fragility. But that self-imposed Westernization also brought isolation. Indians saw their oppressors face-to-face. Turks were strangely isolated from the Western world they emulated. In the 1950s and even 1960s, when a foreigner came to stay at the Istanbul Hilton it would be noted in all the newspapers.

ÁGQ: Do you believe that there is a canon or that one should even exist? We have heard of a Western canon, but what about a non-Western canon?

OP: Yes, there is another canon. It should be explored, developed, shared, criticized, and then accepted. Right now the so-called Eastern canon is in ruins. The glorious texts are all around but there is no will to put them together. From the Persian classics, through to all the Indian, Chinese, and Japanese texts, these things should be assessed critically. As it is now, the canon is in the hands of Western scholars. That is the center of distribution and communication.

ÁGQ: The novel is a very Western cultural form. Does it have any place in the Eastern tradition?

OP: The modern novel, dissociated from the epic form, is essentially a non-Oriental thing, because the novelist is a person who does not belong to a community, who does not share the basic instincts of community, and who is thinking and judging with a different culture than the one he is experiencing. Once his consciousness is different from that of the community he belongs to, he is an outsider, a loner. And the richness of this text comes from that outsider's voyeuristic vision.

Once you develop the habit of looking at the world like that and writing about it in this fashion, you have the desire to disassociate from the community. This is the model I was thinking about in *Snow*.

ÁGQ: *Snow* is your most political book yet published. How did you conceive of it?

OP: When I started becoming famous in Turkey in the mid-1990s, at a time when the war against Kurdish guerillas was strong, the old leftist authors and the new modern liberals wanted me to help them, to sign petitions—they began to ask me to do political things unrelated to my books.

Soon the establishment counterattacked with a campaign of character assassination. They began calling me names. I was very angry. After a while I wondered, What if I wrote a political novel in which I explored my own spiritual dilemmas—coming from an upper-middle-class family and feeling responsible for those who had no political representation? I believed in the art of the novel. It is a strange thing how that makes you an outsider. I told myself then, I will write a political novel. I started to write it as soon as I finished *My Name Is Red*.

ÁGQ: Why did you set it in the small town of Kars?

OP: It is notoriously one of the coldest towns in Turkey. And one of the poorest. In the early eighties, the whole front page of one of the major newspapers was about the poverty of Kars. Someone had calculated that you could buy the entire town for around a million dollars. The political climate was difficult when I wanted to go there. The vicinity of the town is mostly populated by Kurds, but the center is a combination of Kurds, people from Azerbaijan, Turks, and all other sorts. There used to be Russians and Germans too. There are religious differences as well, Shia and Sunni. The war the Turkish government was waging against the Kurdish guerillas was so fierce that it was impossible to go as a tourist. I knew I could not simply go there as a novelist, so I asked a newspaper editor with whom I'd been in touch for a press pass to visit the area. He is influential and he personally called the mayor and the police chief to let them know I was coming.

As soon as I had arrived I visited the mayor and shook hands with the police chief so that they wouldn't pick me up on the street. Actually, some of the police who didn't know I was there did pick me up and carried me off, probably with the intention of torturing me. Immediately I gave names—I know the mayor, I know the chief. . . . I was a suspicious character. Because even though Turkey is theoretically a free country, any foreigner used to be suspect until about 1999. Hopefully things are much easier today.

Most of the people and places in the book are based on a real counterpart. For instance, the local newspaper that sells two hundred fifty-two copies is real. I went to Kars with a camera and a video recorder. I was filming everything and then going back to Istanbul and showing it to my friends. Everyone thought I was a bit crazy. There were other things that actually occurred. Like the conversation I describe with the editor of the little newspaper who tells Ka what he did the previous day, and Ka asks how he knew, and he reveals he's been listening to the police's walkie-talkies and the police were following Ka all the time. That is real. And they were following me too.

The local anchorman put me on TV and said, "Our famous author is writing an article for the national newspaper"—that was a very important thing. Municipal elections were coming up so the people of Kars opened their doors to me. They all wanted to say something to the national newspaper, to let the government know how poor they were. They did not know I was going to put them in a novel. They thought I was going to put them in an article. I must confess, this was cynical and cruel of me. Though I was actually thinking of writing an article about it too.

Four years passed. I went back and forth. There was a little coffee shop where I occasionally used to write and take notes. A photographer friend of mine, whom I had invited to come along because Kars is a beautiful place when it snows, overheard a conversation in the little coffee shop. People were talking among themselves while I wrote some notes, saying, What kind of an article is he writing? It's been three years, enough time to write a novel. They had caught on to me.

ÁGQ: What was the reaction to the book?

OP: In Turkey, both conservatives—or political Islamists—and secularists were upset. Not to the point of banning the book or hurting me. But they were upset and wrote about it in the daily national newspapers. The secularists were upset because I wrote that the cost of being a secular radical in Turkey is that you forget that you also have to be a democrat. The power of the secularists in Turkey comes from the army. This destroys Turkey's democracy and culture of tolerance. Once you have so much army involvement in political culture, people lose their self-confidence and rely on the army to solve all their problems. People usually say, "The country and the economy are a mess; let's call in the army to clean it up." But just as they cleaned, so did they destroy the culture of tolerance. Lots of suspects were tortured; one hundred thousand people were jailed. This paves the way for new military coups. There was a new one about every ten years. So I was critical of the secularists for this. They also didn't like that I portrayed Islamists as human beings.

The political Islamists were upset because I wrote about an Islamist who had enjoyed sex before marriage. It was that kind of simplistic thing. Islamists are always suspicious of me because I don't come from their culture and because I have the language, attitude, and even gestures of a more Westernized and privileged person. They have their own problems of representation and ask, "How can he write about us anyway? He doesn't understand." This I also included in parts of the novel.

But I don't want to exaggerate. I survived. They all read the book. They may have become angry, but it is a sign of growing liberal attitudes that they accepted me and my book as they are. The reaction of the people of Kars was also divided. Some said, "Yes, that is how it is." Others, usually Turkish nationalists, were nervous about my mentions of Armenians. That TV anchorman, for instance, put my book in a symbolic black bag and mailed it to me and said in a press conference that I was doing Armenian propaganda—which is, of course, preposterous. We have such a parochial, nationalistic culture.

ÁGQ: [. . .] For whom, then, are you writing?

OP: As life gets shorter, you ask yourself that question more often. I've written seven novels. I would love to write another seven novels before I die. But then, life is short. What about enjoying it more? Sometimes I have to really force myself [to ask,] "Why am I doing it? What is the meaning of all of it?" First, as I said, it's an instinct to be alone in a room. Second, there's an almost boyish competitive side in me that wants to attempt to write a nice book again. I believe less and less in eternity for authors. We are reading very few of the books written two hundred years ago. Things are changing so fast that today's books will probably be forgotten in a hundred years. Very few will be read. In two hundred years, perhaps five books written today will be alive. Am I sure I'm writing one of those five? But is that the meaning of writing? Why should I be worrying about being read two hundred years later? Shouldn't I be worried about living more? Do I need the consolation that I will be read in the future? I think of all these things, and I continue to write. I don't know why. But I never give up. This belief that your books will have an effect in the future is the only consolation you have to get pleasure in this life.

ÁGQ: You are a best-selling author in Turkey, but the books you sell at home are outnumbered by your sales abroad. You have been translated into forty languages. Do you now think about a wider global readership when writing? Are you now writing for a different audience?

OP: I am aware that my audience is no longer an exclusively national audience. But even when I began writing, I may have been reaching for a wider group of readers. My father used to say behind the backs of some of his Turkish author friends that they were "only addressing the national audience." There is a problem of being aware of one's readership, whether it is national or international. I cannot avoid this problem now. My last two books averaged more than half a million readers all over the world. I cannot deny that I am aware of their existence. On the other hand, I never feel that I do things to satisfy them. I also believe that my readers would sense it if I did. I've made it my business, from the very beginning, that whenever I sense a reader's expectations I run away. Even the composition of my sentences—I prepare the reader for something and then I surprise him. Perhaps that's why I love long sentences.

ÁGQ: To most non-Turkish readers, the originality of your writing has much to do with its Turkish setting. But how would you distinguish your work in a Turkish context?

OP: There is the problem of what Harold Bloom called "the anxiety of influence." Like all authors I had it when I was young. In my early thirties I kept thinking that I might have been too much influenced by Tolstoy or Thomas Mann—I aimed for that kind of gentle, aristocratic prose in my first novel.

But it ultimately occurred to me that although I may have been derivative in my techniques, the fact that I was operating in this part of the world, so far away from Europe—or at least it seemed so at the time—and trying to attract such a different audience in such a different cultural and historical climate, it would grant me originality, even if it was cheaply earned. But it is also a tough job, since such techniques do not translate or travel so easily. The formula for originality is very simple—put together two things that were not together before. Look at *Istanbul*, an essay about the city and about how certain foreign authors—Flaubert, Nerval, Gautier—viewed the city, and how their views influenced a certain group of Turkish writers. Combined with this essay on the invention of Istanbul's romantic landscape is an autobiography. No one had done this before. Take risks and you will come up with something new. I tried with *Istanbul* to make an original book. I don't know if it succeeded. *The Black Book* was like that too—combine a nostalgic Proustian world with Islamic allegories, stories, and tricks, then set them all in Istanbul and see what happens.

ÁGQ: [. . .] How Turkish do you feel yourself to be, then?

OP: First, I'm a born Turk. I'm happy with that. Internationally, I am perceived to be more Turkish than I actually see myself. I am known as a Turkish author. When Proust writes about love, he is seen as someone talking about universal love. Especially at the beginning, when I wrote about love, people would say that I was writing about Turkish love. When my work began to be translated, Turks were proud of it. They claimed me as their own. I was more of a Turk for them. Once you get to be internationally known, your Turkishness is underlined internationally, then your Turkishness is underlined by Turks themselves, who reclaim you. Your sense of national identity becomes something that others manipulate. It is imposed by other people.

Now they are more worried about the international representation of Turkey than about my art. This causes more and more problems in my country. Through what they read in the popular press, a lot of people who don't know my books are beginning to worry about what I say to the outside world about Turkey. Literature is made of good and bad, demons and angels, and more and more they are only worried about my demons.

Orhan Pamuk and the Turkish Paradox

Der Spiegel / 2005

From *Der Spiegel*, Frankfurt Book Fair Special, October 21, 2005, https://www.spiegel.de/international/spiegel/frankfurt-book-fair-special-orhan-pamuk-and-the-turkish-paradox-a-380858.html.

Der Spiegel: Mr. Pamuk, you were awarded the German Book Trade's Peace Prize in recognition of both your literary works and your political activities. Which of the two pleases you more?

Orhan Pamuk: I think it's a bit ironic that both Turks and Germans place so much emphasis on the political side of this prize. It's almost as if they were saying that appreciation for the literary quality of my novels isn't something to be proud of. How fortunate that my most recent novel is deliberately political.

DS: And why did *Snow* become a distinctly political novel?

OP: Well, I've been expressing my views on politics for some time now, but in newspapers and magazines, not in novels. This kind of thing gives you notoriety at home. You begin striking back, and the whole thing begins to escalate. At some point I asked myself: Why don't I just put my political visions into a book, just to get them off my chest?

DS: [. . .] Istanbul has remained your city to this day. You have a tremendous view from your office, where you write. At your feet lies the great bridge that spans the Bosphorus, linking Europe and Asia. How do you feel when you work here?

OP: I'm happy. I sometimes joke that I am the first writer of historical fiction who can look out his window and point to the objects in his novels. I have a view of the entrance to the Bosphorus, the old city, Hagia Sophia, the Blue Mosque; in fact, I see all the mosques. It's an extremely privileged view, as I know, and I like to say that, as Istanbul's storyteller, I've earned it.

DS: Many see you today as Turkey's leading intellectual. Isn't it paradoxical that you never wanted to be part of the cultural establishment, and yet you've become its most important representative?

OP: I can say quite honestly that I don't regret it. After my country was so tormented by politics and I developed an international reputation, journalists from all over the world began talking to me about my country's problems. It was inevitable, something one cannot escape.

DS: You are an avowed supporter of Turkey joining the European Union. Do you think that your highly critical novel *Snow* has been of much service to this effort?

OP: I know exactly what you're trying to say. In Holland a friend said to me: "You know, I used to be in favor of Turkey's accession, but now I've read your novel and I'm horrified. Is it really that dismal in your country?" My answer to him was that it's a historical novel.

DS: But it takes place in the 1990s!

OP: Exactly. A lot has happened since then. Just the hope of someday being able to join the EU has changed the legal situation in Turkey. In my imagination, the events in the novel happened in the early 1990s, when there was great concern that Islamic fundamentalists could assume power. That's why I said that it's a historical novel.

DS: [. . .] What is the most important difference between Europe and Turkey?

OP: The bloody years of war and all the atrocities in European history have taught the Europeans that secular politics free of religious hatred is mainly a question of peace. This concept is not anchored in the same way in the consciousness of Turks, which has to do with the fact that the secular was forced upon us by the army. But that attitude has since changed.

DS: The protagonist in your novel, Ka, calls himself an atheist. Would you say the same thing about yourself?

OP: The problem I have with this term stems from the fact that many prominent intellectuals made such a drama out of it in the past. My religion is complicated. Literature is my true religion. After all, I come from a completely nonreligious family.

DS: Do you consider yourself a Muslim?

OP: I consider myself a person who comes from a Muslim culture. In any case, I would not say that I'm an atheist. So I'm a Muslim who associates historical and cultural identification with this religion. I do not believe in a personal connection to God; that's where it gets transcendental. I identify with my culture, but I am happy to be living on a tolerant, intellectual island where I can deal with Dostoevsky and Sartre, both great influences for me.

DS: Do you keep a regular diary?

OP: I very much enjoy reading other writers' diaries, mainly because it makes me ask myself: Are they like you? How do they think? I have never liked diaries that are published during an author's lifetime. Writing my own diary is the best form of remembrance, but only for my own use. I need these notes; it's like an impulse. I need a moment of time for myself every day, like a child playing with his things. When I travel, I routinely find a quiet place, open my diary, and write something in it. It has its own kind of magic. It gives me the feeling of having accomplished something. On days when I don't have time for this, I feel tortured. A nicely filled page, whether it'll be published today or in fifty years, gives me the feeling of being a good boy.

DS: Why did your Turkish publisher hesitate to publish the original version of *Snow* three years ago?

OP: The legal situation then was completely different than it is today. Someone thought it might be a good idea to show the book to an attorney first. We weren't sure how the public prosecutor's office would react to the portrayal in the novel. Criticizing the military is considered morally reprehensible, because it involves such a tremendously important issue as secularization. The attorney assured us that most of the material in the novel was OK.

DS: Didn't you hesitate to address the Kurdish question or the issue of Armenians?

OP: I was already talking about these topics, which can easily get you into trouble in Turkey, outside of my books. Let me put it this way: Not just Dostoevsky but many great authors of the nineteenth century wrote under conditions of strict censorship. The great thing about the novel, about the art of writing a novel, is that you can write about anything. All you have to say is that it's fiction. That was the case with *Snow*. No one reacted the way some feared they would.

DS: But you have been and continue to be the target of physical attacks in Turkey.

OP: When Turkey began approaching the EU, I wasn't the only one who worried that the dark stain in Turkey's history—or rather the history of the Ottoman Empire—could become a problem one day. In other words, what happened to the Armenians in World War I. That's why I couldn't leave the issue untouched. I alluded to the fact—but certainly didn't intend it as an erudite remark—that this is difficult to talk about in Turkey.

DS: [...] Namely the fact that hundreds of thousands of Armenians were killed in what is now Turkey?

OP: This remark of mine resulted in a powerful explosion. When something that explosive is kept hidden away, a tension builds within that must ultimately be released.

DS: And you consistently avoided referring to it directly as "genocide." In fact, you never even used the word.

OP: Because I didn't want to. In fact, the word "genocide" was first used in the Turkish newspapers in an attempt to attack me, even though I didn't even use the expression. And then it was quoted by the Europeans. What could I have done? After people suddenly began talking about something that used to be taboo and a real hate campaign developed against me, I could hardly stand up and say: I never even said that!

DS: That was when you moved to New York for a while. Were you fleeing, in a sense?

OP: You tend to overdramatize things. It's your job. I was invited by Columbia University, where I had once studied on a scholarship. So I stayed for a while, that's all.

DS: Are you worried about the trial you will face in December for "public denigration of Turkish identity?"

OP: I must respect the laws and the legal system of my country. In that respect, I do take it seriously. However, I do not expect that the matter will have significant legal consequences for me. I'm not terribly concerned about it.

DS: So you don't expect to be sent to prison?

OP: Absolutely not.

DS: Isn't having been in prison at least once a sort of badge of honor for a Turkish author?

OP: Wouldn't it be an even greater honor to be the first Turkish writer who had never been there? Isn't that much better? Better for Turkey and better for the author?

DS: Do you believe that Turkish Prime Minister Recep Tayyip Erdoğan has been sufficiently supportive of you?

OP: Well, Erdoğan didn't support me when I was having some big problems.

DS: He expressed his regret over the charges.

OP: Sure, when it reached the international level. He wants to see Turkey in the EU. Besides, you mustn't forget that this man was also imprisoned, merely for having quoted a few poems.

DS: Do you see Erdoğan as a dedicated reformer or as an Islamist who hides his true intentions well?

OP: I see him as an organizer first, a perfect organizer. He's a tough guy. His form of Islam—the typical fundamentalist Middle Eastern rhetoric—was quite common in Turkey ten years ago. From there, he moved to a highly remarkable standpoint, namely the desire to move Turkey forward in the direction of Europe, supported by Islamists, former Islamists, a few secularists and 70 percent of the Turkish population. If you ask me whether that sounds like a contradiction, I say: No, great changes in the direction of peace have often come from people who were no great advocates of peace to begin with.

DS: How strong is the idea of Europe in Turkey?

OP: Just think of how elated the nation was recently over the news that negotiations had begun with the EU. This country, with its political intolerance, as I have described it, is now prepared to march forward, to break with its taboo about the Armenians and is making great strides with respect to human rights and freedom of speech so that it can join the European Union. This alone shows how powerful the European idea is.

DS: What would happen to the Turkish identity if Turkey actually became a member of the EU one day?

OP: Of course we Turks would lose a part of this identity, just as Europe would lose a part of its own. It would also be a different Europe then. Accepting Turkey into the EU is an ambitious political endeavor of historical proportions. Europe would become a strong, multireligious unit. It would gain the strength of seventy million Turks who also happen to be Muslims. This isn't dangerous in the least, since Turks want peace. They are prepared to become true Europeans.

DS: Are you proud to be a Turk?

OP: Of course. I am proud to be a Turk, and to write in Turkish about Turkey—and to have been translated into about forty languages. But I don't want to politicize things by dramatizing them.

DS: Can you reveal to us what you plan to say when you accept the peace prize?

OP: What I would like to do is define Europe through its great art of the novel.

Nobel Foundation Telephone Interview with Orhan Pamuk

Adam Smith / 2006

From nobelprize.org, October 12, 2006, https://www.nobelprize.org/prizes/literature/2006/pamuk/interview/.

Adam Smith: Hello, may I speak to Orhan Pamuk, please? Hello?
Orhan Pamuk: Hello.
AS: Hello, may I speak to Orhan Pamuk, please?
OP: Speaking.
AS: Oh, my name is Adam Smith, and I'm calling from the official website of the Nobel Foundation in Stockholm.
OP: Yes.
AS: We have a tradition of recording very short conversations with Nobel Laureates immediately after the announcements.
OP: OK.
AS: So, first of all, many, many congratulations on being awarded . . .
OP: Oh, thank you very much. It's such a great honor.
AS: I gather you're in New York. What were you doing when you received the news?
OP: Oh, I was sleeping and thinking that, in an hour probably, they will announce the Nobel Prize, and then someone would maybe tell me who won it. And then I'm thinking, so what am I going to do, what's today's work? And I'm a little bit sleepy. And then the phone call, and then I'm, "Oh, it's already half past seven." You know, this is New York and I don't know the light, so I don't feel pretty. . . . And I answered, and they said I won the Nobel Prize.
AS: That's an extraordinary phone call to receive. There was an enormous cheer that went up at the press conference when they announced the prize.
OP: Really, oh that's great. I'm very happy to hear this. This is great.

AS: We've recorded it on the website so you can, when finally you get off the phone, you can go and relive the moment.

OP: And also I saw so many journalists you know, wanted me to have it, so I'm pleased about that. I'm very pleased about all these details. Thank you very much, sir.

AS: You're the first ever Turkish writer to be awarded a Nobel Prize for Literature. Does that give the award a special significance for you?

OP: Well, unfortunately, that makes the thing very precious in Turkey, which is good for Turkey of course, getting this prize, but makes it more extra-sensitive and political, and it somehow tends to make it as a sort of a burden.

AS: Yes, because it's been quite a public year for you.

OP: Yes.

AS: So I imagine this will add to that. The citation for the award refers particularly to your "quest for the melancholic soul of [your] native city," and there's an extremely long tradition of writing about Istanbul, and in praise of Istanbul. Could you describe, briefly, what it is about the city that has acted as such a strong draw for people's imagination over the years?

OP: Well, it was at the edge of Europe, but different. So it was the closest "other." And it was really both close and, in a way, other. Mysterious, strange, uncompromising, and totally un-European in ways, although in its spirit there was such a great place for Europe [*words unclear*].

AS: And referring to the phrase "melancholic soul," how would you describe Istanbul to those who've never seen it?

OP: I would say that it's one of the early modern cities where modernity decayed earlier than expected. I would say that the ruins of the past gave the city its melancholy, along with its poverty. But then I would also say that it's now recovering from this melancholy, hopefully.

AS: And another facet of your writing that was particularly emphasized in the citation, from the Committee, is the way that you deal with the interactions between different cultures. And of course it's a cliché to say that Turkey lies at the crossroads between East and West, but it does presumably offer the perfect vantage point from which to view the cross-cultural interface?

OP: This meeting of East and West and clash of civilizations, this is unfortunately one of the most dangerous and horrific ideas that have been produced in the last twenty years, and is now serving for . . . This fanciful idea is now unfortunately getting to be real, and this theory is serving the clash of civilizations and the deaths of so many people.

AS: Because historically there has really been much more mixing of cultures than is popularly supposed.

OP: Culture is mix. Culture means a mix of things from other sources. And my town, Istanbul, was this kind of mix. Istanbul, in fact, and my work, is a testimony to the fact that East and West combine cultures gracefully, or sometimes in an anarchic way, came together, and that is what we should search for. This is getting to be a good interview by the way.

AS: Thank you, that's very kind of you. Many of your characters might be said to embody multiple cultural influences. I mean your writing indicates that they're far from uniformly either Eastern or Western; it's a mix.

OP: Yes.

AS: Do you write solely in Turkish?

OP: Yes. I think I wrote some six or seven articles in English, in international magazines, in the *Times Literary Supplement*, in the *Village Voice*.

AS: So there are presumably . . .

OP: But of course I'm a Turkish writer, essentially, and live in the language. Language is me, in a way. Really, I feel it.

AS: Right, and there are ideas that you can express in Turkish, I assume, that would be very hard to capture in other languages?

OP: Exactly. Because thinking is composed of two things: language and images, and then yeah, half of thinking is the language. I agree, yes sir, please ask the question.

AS: Well, could you give an example of a concept that . . .

OP: Wow! I can of course, but not on the day that I have received the Nobel Prize.

AS: That's fair enough; you don't really have to answer any questions on the day you receive the Nobel Prize.

OP: Yeah, OK.

AS: You can say anything you like.

OP: OK, thank you very much, sir.

AS: So then an easy question. I mean the award will encourage a lot of new readers to dip into your work for the first time. Where would you recommend they start? What would you suggest to people, and also . . .

OP: Oh, depending on the reader of course. The reader who buys books because the writer has received the Nobel Prize should start with *My Name Is Red*. The reader who has already read that book should continue with *The Black Book*. The reader who is interested in more contemporary issues and politics should go ahead with *Snow*, so forth and so on.

AS: Wonderful, wonderful. And if your readers are lucky enough to be able to read in multiple languages, but can't manage Turkish, do you have a recommendation for which language most excellently captures the spirit?

OP: Of course English is the world's language now, and that's the language I've been checking my books with, and I'm proud with my translators and I'm also confident. So, basically English translations.

AS: OK, thank you very much.

OP: Thanks, as you see I'm a dutiful good boy. I did my homework very well now.

AS: Very well indeed! No, I'm thrilled with your cooperation. Thank you very much.

OP: Bye-bye. I have to hang up now because my agent is calling and others, so many responsibilities that I have to address.

AS: Of course, quite so, thank you for spending the time. See you soon, bye-bye.

OP: OK, bye-bye.

Nobel Prize in Literature Interview: Orhan Pamuk

Horace Engdahl / 2006

From nobelprize.org, December 6, 2006, https://www.nobelprize.org/prizes/literature/2006/pamuk/interview/.

Horace Engdahl: That book [*The White Castle*] won you international fame.
Orhan Pamuk: *The White Castle* was published in 1985 [in Turkish], and when it was published I was in the United States, at Columbia University in New York. [...] It's very typical of the non-Western person coming to the main cultural centers of Western civilization—say London, Paris, or New York—and then having a sort of anxiety about his cultural identity. And I lived these things when I faced the immense richness of American libraries and culture. Then I began to ask myself, What is Turkish culture? [...] And at that time I used to think that Turkey's cultural roles, identity, should only be a sort of an ultra-Occidentalism. There, at the age of thirty-two, I began to read old Sufi allegories, the classic texts of Islamic mysticism—most of them are classical Persian texts—with an eye on Borges and Calvino. [...] They opened a secular way of looking at classical Islamic heritage.
[...]
HE: Yes, I mean, it's amazing, the richness of the oriental material that you bring into especially *The Black Book*. I mean, it's overwhelming for a Western reader. [...] It's true that more than once when you read *The White Castle* and *The Black Book* you think of Calvino for instance, *Invisible Cities*, which I suppose you must have liked. But still there's a lot of it that is very unexpected to the Western reader and it has to do, of course, with the Sufi tradition and also with the writings of Rumi, especially.
OP: There is also an influence of *Arabian Nights* or as the Turks call it *The Thousand and One Nights*. I think that book [...] as a sort of a book which

comes from the Indian tradition going through Arabic and Persian influences, and then as a sort of ocean of stories, which was given a shape and an understanding and elevated to a higher stature by the French and English orientalists, was also behind *The Black Book*. The idea of constantly telling stories, the idea of a person who is in deep trouble, but who cannot face that—his troubles, problems—who instead of addressing the question gives you another story.

[. . .]

HE: In *The Black Book* there's also, for a Western reader, this magic of fluid identities that sometimes even borders on metempsychosis. Is this something that came to you during the writing? Because you have the element, of course, in *The White Castle*, but it's so much more poetic in *The Black Book*.

OP: I like the idea that the boundaries of human personality are not strong. My understanding of human nature is not Freudian, but I think that there are no essences of, there are no characters or essences. [. . .] I believe that we constantly change, and these are dear ideas which in my novels, perhaps, I combine with my country's—Turkey's—history. That of, you know, having two souls, two spirits, that of believing in national harmony with these two sides, while on the other hand, keeping an eye on the fact that there is almost always a dramatic tension with two sides of our personality.

[. . .]

HE: [. . .] If I may come to address the question of your role as a writer, you've been saying something in interviews that I have read about how much you value isolation, that what really makes you write is that you can retire into a room. [. . .] This of course brings to mind the famous passage in one of Montaigne's essays where he talks about his *arrière-boutique*, the secret room you always have to keep behind the shop that you never let anybody into and where things like your wife, your children, your father, your mother, your country doesn't exist for you anymore. Where you're absolutely alone.

OP: Montaigne invented first for the Western, French and Western, civilization the idea of a solitary person who reads books on his own, passes judgment on his own, who believes his idea and his reasoning and then has a deep conviction of brotherhood of humanity, of all the persons in the world because we share the same mind. And he, I think, paved the way for not only the Enlightenment and glorification or proliferation of Western thoughts but this idea which I cherish, that of the solitary person who [is] not necessarily political, but who at the back of his room reads, writes, and produces something that had never been thought before entirely. That is the beginnings of perhaps the uniqueness, the cult of personality in Western civilization, the uniqueness of the character and the consequence of these thoughts are style, style in literature. [. . .]

My idea of a writer is not a person, a social person, a person who expresses himself in society or in a community, but a person who for this or that reason, tragically or with joy, who leaves the community, the society, the group, the tribe, the nation that he or she belongs to, and with some sort of an instinct that he doesn't want to understand, goes to a room and writes there. There he explores perhaps first the inner depths of his soul, but then comes out with something new, which he will address to all humanity because the essential idea being that we are all, we have the same kind of minds. [. . .]

HE: Yes, I think you can see in Montaigne how this idea emerges when he has a friend, you know, Étienne de La Boétie, and—

OP: He wrote very well about friendship.

HE: Yes, when the friend dies, he has to find someone else and that is, eventually, the reader.

OP: I see, I agree, yes.

HE: That's how it happens, and this has to be an anonymous reader. It's very important because earlier everybody writes for people they know. They have an addressee that is known that is socially close, so to speak, but from this moment on it's anybody.

OP: Yes, and modernity was invented with this idea that we are not, yes, we are not writing for one particular person. But then we're addressing a sort of other in a room, but with a nonexistent readership.

HE: And the book is calling forth someone who would be this person, able to understand.

OP: I have all my life played around with the idea of the reader looking over my text over my shoulder, sometimes talking with them, which upset my readers sometimes, sometimes openly addressing them, sometimes playing around with their expectations, sometimes pulling the reader into the story, sometimes also introducing myself or a person who is very like me as also, figures who talk with the reader.

HE: You use your own name.

OP: Yes, [. . .] then obviously they are characters who are very close to me, maybe someone, a fictional realistic portrait of me.

HE: But not quite you, yet.

OP: Yes. We have to be elusive to continue in this art of fiction, we should never give up everything, but we should continue to give up something from the inner depths of our spirit, from our heart. I believe the power of fiction comes from also, not only from that, but of course also from frankness, from honesty, from telling the truth, which your friends suspect that you will never tell, be not politically but spiritually brave and believe that a student, a person like you, a person who may be thirty years, forty years younger but who may experience the same thing either in your country or in another corner of the world, will share the sentiments, these little details, that you would think that's only personal and should be neglected, will address the hearts of every reader.

HE: Yes, on the other hand, one has to ask oneself at some point whether this possibility of sharing is universal. I mean you deny the clash of civilizations, right, and of course what you show in your writing is how things go around and return from unexpected directions, and things that you believed to be foreign are actually very close to yourself, and vice versa. On the other hand, I, as a Western reader, a Nordic reader, have to ask myself if there is something in your books that you believe is difficult for a Northerner or a Westerner to understand. Let me point to one rather peculiar detail in one of your books. In *Istanbul*, when you speak about some famous travelogues written by French poets in the nineteenth century, Gérard de Nerval's *Voyage en Orient*. I've read that book; it's a marvelous book, I mean it's a marvelous description of what he calls Constantinople. At the beginning of his visit to Constantinople he goes out to look at the sultan, you know, and you have picked this up, and the sultan is leaving his carriage and Nerval believes that he meets the eye of the sultan. Do you remember that?

OP: Yes.

HE: And he feels such pity for the sultan, and it's almost a spontaneous brotherhood that emerges between these two men in a matter of seconds, you know, when he thinks through what must be this man's existence with his slave women and all that sort of thing. But you deny the possibility of Nerval catching the sultan's eye, and I must ask myself, "Why?" and is that not a way of telling us that "No, you don't quite understand"?

OP: The detail that comes across in other travel books as well, that everyone goes to [see] the sultan [who] is going around and you can see him only on Fridays, and they'll go there and they'll say, "Oh we came eye to eye and we had a little sort of a spiritual moment of understanding," which I thought was a bit of a cliché. [. . .] And then of course there were most of these in the mid-nineteenth century, French visitors are writing for the newspapers, *feuilletons* now, and then you have to be, you know, it's like "Our reporter came face-to-face with the sultan and they had a moment of understanding," which is good, which is good. But also, on the other hand, there is this very Western idea that, not Muslim or Eastern, that you come eye to eye and then, Dostoevsky also has passages like that, then our storyteller, be it a reporter or a novelist or a Gérard de Nerval or a traveler, begins to put himself in the shoes of this other person, which is a great invention, which is the beginnings of the art of the novel.

I strongly believe that what makes the art of the novel continue with all its glory is that it is about compassion, understanding others, people who are not like us. It is about the human being's desire to put itself, himself, herself in the place of the other that's strange, even as strange as the Ottoman sultan. And he wants to understand this person, that is the beginning of putting a frame into the world and thinking that we can understand each other, that it's very interesting to understand the Other.

"No One Drives Me into Exile"

Der Spiegel / 2007

From *Der Spiegel*, May 2, 2007, https://www.spiegel.de/international/world/spiegel-interview-with-orhan-pamuk-no-one-drives-me-into-exile-a-480550.html.

Der Spiegel: Mr. Pamuk, you are traveling to Germany this week to complete the book tour you canceled in February. Why did you cancel all your engagements so suddenly at the time?
Orhan Pamuk: The murder of my friend Hrant Dink came as a great shock to me. Many writers and intellectuals were deeply depressed over this assassination. It awakened the fear that in Turkey we are returning to the dark days of the 1970s, when so many people were killed and when murder was used for political ends. In that situation, my preference was to travel to the United States. I wanted to gain some distance from the tragic event by going abroad.
DS: Many interpreted your sudden departure as a decision to flee.
OP: I received threats. But my cancellation had nothing to do with any lack of confidence in the German security officials. However, I would have been asked constantly about the death threats during my book tour. As a result, they would have acquired a significance they do not deserve.
DS: Critical authors might even fear for their lives in Turkey. How endangered do you feel?
OP: I have hired a bodyguard, on the recommendation of my friends and the government. It's outrageous, having to live like this.
DS: [. . .] But on your book tour you plan to introduce Istanbul, a portrait of your home city, which was especially honored during the awarding of the Nobel Prize.
OP: Yes, I talk about my childhood in the book, the days of post-Ottoman melancholy, when Turkey was still very, very far away from Europe, both culturally and economically. Back then, the city had nothing of the modernity it had always longed for, but instead stood on the ruins of lost Otto-

man glory. It was more of a gloomy mood, a feeling of sadness and isolation, not just of individuals but of an entire city, a sort of collective resignation.

DS: Are you describing your own feelings about life in the book?

OP: When I describe Istanbul, I am also writing about myself. When I was a boy I was a complete prisoner of the melancholic introspection we call *hüzün*. It may have something to do with the fact that the history of my family is a story of decline, not unlike the family Thomas Mann describes in *Buddenbrooks*. We owned a large house when I was born, but both it and our fortune were later lost. In this respect, my personal story coincides with the mourning of the loss of Ottoman wealth.

DS: Your book ends in 1972. Istanbul today is considered the most modern city in the Islamic world. Is this the Istanbul you have dreamed about—cosmopolitan and Western?

OP: The Western Istanbul, as visitors see it, only makes up about 10 percent of the city and its population. Istanbul is certainly in the process of transforming itself into an attractive cultural, tourist, and financial center. But there are also millions of sad stories in this giant sea of immigration, poverty, misery and contradictions. So much anger, frustration, and fury. Turkey's political and ethnic problems are concentrated here. Fortunately, however, these conflicts are no longer dealt with so brutally.

DS: You say this, even though you were even summoned before a court for writing a critical sentence about the Turkish massacres of the Armenians in 1915?

OP: We are still fighting for complete freedom of expression. But there is no comparison to the Turkey of my childhood, when certain topics were only discussed in a whisper and most things were swept under the rug. At that time, Armenians and Greeks on the street were told: "Speak Turkish, citizen!" Nowadays almost everything is discussed openly.

DS: Is Istanbul truly a bridge between cultures, between East and West?

OP: That's a cliché, as far as I am concerned. It also annoys me to be constantly reduced to the role of a bridge builder. I don't have the right to be the representative of a culture, a political constellation, a certain ethnic group or history. Because I have now been translated into more than forty-five languages, I am considered a representative of Turkey. But I don't want that role. I am a writer.

DS: What role does Islam play for you?

OP: I think it's horrible that we Turks are always seen under the aspect of Islam first. I am constantly asked about religion, and almost always with a negative undercurrent that makes me furious. True, most of my countrymen are Muslims. But if you truly wish to understand my country, you have to look at its history and our consistent orientation toward Europe. The Turks have a love-hate relationship with European culture. Turkey is part of Europe. [. . .]

DS: You often talk about craft and patience when you discuss writing—not unlike the painters of miniature paintings you portray in your book *My Name Is Red*.

OP: I certainly see myself more as a craftsman than as an artist. Of course, creativity and inspiration do play a role. True literature is more than just a story someone has told. It must provide the reader with the essence of the world on a moral, philosophical, and emotional level. I have tried to develop this inner truth in all my works. But without patience and the skill of a craftsman, even the greatest talent is wasted.

DS: [. . .] Do you feel, like the protagonist Ka in your novel *Snow*, that you too are a victim of politics?

OP: There are certainly similarities between him and me. But Ka is a pathetic version of me. He tries his luck as a poet, becomes frustrated, and hangs out abroad, in Germany. I am more successful, and no one drives me into exile, not even the nationalists—all difficulties aside. But in his attempts to understand people, in his moral pretense, in his fears and desires, his naïveté, but also in his perseverance, Ka is certainly similar to me.

DS: Because you are considered a perceptive observer of Turkish life, many saw your last two books in particular, *Snow* and *Istanbul*, as guides to understanding Turkey.

OP: It's very gratifying to me to see my works bringing people closer to my country. But it troubles me to be reduced to that. It is not my intention to explain Turkey, its culture and its problems. My literature has a universal concern: I want to bring people and their emotions closer to my readers, not explain Turkish politics.

DS: But you make no secret of your political views, and you have spoken out in favor of Turkey's acceptance into the European Union. Are you disappointed that your country still has no concrete outlook for accession?

OP: In any event, the Europe project is currently in the process of becoming a sad piece of history. Both sides are at fault. Some Europeans have, for example, exaggerated the human rights violations that still exist here and have sometimes even exploited them. The Turkish leadership, for its part, reacted too sensitively to reservations about us that were expressed in certain countries. Our establishment simply lacked self-confidence. Our elites were offended and made their disappointment known. This only increased reservations in Europe, where there are those who pounce on every excuse they can get. This rejection, in turn, has given Turkish nationalists a boost. It's a vicious circle.

DS: Have you also lost interest in Europe by now?

OP: I am disappointed and frustrated. But I remain convinced that Turkey's acceptance into the European Union would be beneficial for both sides. It would certainly be a gain for our democracy, our culture, and our economy.

DS: How far has Turkey come on its road to Europe?

OP: Seen from Mars, we're on the verge of joining. And I do believe that we will be part of Europe one day. But perhaps both sides should stew in their own juices for a while, to see how each of them does without the other.

DS: [. . .] In any event, there has been an alarming surge in Turkish nationalism.

OP: Yes, there is growing nationalism and ugly racism. This has something to do with Turkey's inability to deal with the Kurds . . .

DS: . . . Who still feel discriminated against . . .

OP: . . . but also with the humiliating EU negotiation process and the resulting frustration. The worst consequences of this nationalism are the curbs on freedom of opinion and hate campaigns against intellectuals. Pro-European intellectuals are being placed under great pressure.

DS: [. . .] You have expressed your political views less often since your trial. You used to place stronger emphasis on the writer's political role.

OP: It is one thing to express an opinion about politics, to open your mouth, when you are furious about a development. Censorship should never be allowed. One should be able to say anything. But I refuse to let politics be foisted on me. There has been far too much politics in my life in the last two years. I believe strongly in an author's moral responsibility. But his first obligation is to write good books.

"Novels Are Encyclopedias"

Carol Becker / 2007

From the *Brooklyn Rail*, "In Conversation: Orhan Pamuk with Carol Becker," February 6, 2008, https://brooklynrail.org/2008/02/express/orhan-pamuk-wih-carol-becker.

Carol Becker: I'd like to start by talking with you as a literary critic. It seems to me that there is an incredible sense of optimism in the way you write about other writers. In other words, through the works of European novelists, especially Dostoevsky, Thomas Mann, Kafka, and Joyce, you have gained your own insights about Europe and inevitably your love and devotion to the novel. In the essay "In Kars and Frankfurt," you wrote that "Mallarmé spoke the truth when he said, 'Everything in the world exists to be put into a book.' Without a doubt, the sort of book best equipped to absorb everything in the world is the novel." Similarly, in *The Black Book*, you have this wonderful phrase, "The world is a book." And in your marvelous introduction to *Tristram Shandy*, you talk about the novelist's ability to bring paradise into the present. Would you talk about the nature of the novel, and why you think it's capable of such vitality?

Orhan Pamuk: As we know, much to our despair, it's such a common cliché among the journalists; they always call me and say, "I am doing a piece in the arts page for a magazine, and the novel is dead. What do you think?" Most of the time when I was writing the essays that you just mentioned, part of me would get quite angry over these comments. I sometimes, with self-irony, would also say that I am a humble servant of this great art. The novel, beginning in the eighteenth century, began to take over all the previous literary forms. In fact, we can even say it was the early form of globalization. The world, in so many ways, is so culturally globalized that our ways of seeing it are very similar to the post-Renaissance, let's say from the invention of perspective in Italian and Dutch painting to the invention of photography and thereafter; we still see the world in a similar manner. We are likewise all globalized in our literary imagination, in the forms that we use, and I would say the literary globalization of the world had been completed years ago, when nobody was talking about globalization. With this, I imply that the art of the novel is well and kicking and that everyone from all over the world has access to and is using it. It is now a common heritage of humanity. It has what I would call an intense elasticity in that it can absorb national problems and represent national dramas, so that you can use and impose your particular understanding of this form into your corner of the world, or discuss your national debate, whatever it is, such that it will hold the nation together, because it is a text that everyone can argue with. Let me give you an example: I wrote *Snow*, a political novel, thinking everybody would be angry, and, yes, everyone was angry, but everyone was also reading, discussing, and talking about it. I think the art of the novel, as a form, is one of the great arts humanity has developed that has continuity, that changes and survives. Over the last twenty years, we have witnessed a return to the eighteenth-century Diderot kind of novel, which is a form that combines essays and novels together. Actually, I consider myself a sort of a representative of that "encyclopedic" novel. In other words, you can put anything into novels. Novels are encyclopedias. Mallarmé's words to that effect say that in the end, everything in the world, for the imaginative novelist or imaginative literary person, is in fact made to end up in a book. That's how I see the world as well, because I am a novelist, and I care about the informative, encyclopedic quality of the novel.

CB: You use a Stendhal quote from his *The Charterhouse of Parma* as the epigram for *Snow*. "Politics in the literary work are a pistol shot in the middle of a concert, a crude affair though one impossible to ignore. We are about to speak of very ugly matters." It's a great place to begin a political novel. Can you talk about why you think politics ruins the novel and why it is so difficult to create a really successful political novel?

OP: There are so many problems with the political novel.

CB: Of course, and yet you wrote one.

OP: I wrote one, right, but I don't think it is a great genre that produces masterpieces. It's rather a limited genre, despite the fact that Dostoevsky, Conrad, Stendhal, and a few others produced the best examples of it. Still, it's troubled by some inner contradictions. By that I mean when a novelist or an artist has heartfelt political agendas about prior political tension in some corner of the world where there is a highly dramatized and unstable political situation, he or she tends to interiorize these problems and desires to express them on a political level. But once the author commits himself or herself to those problems, he or she is not a good novelist, because they take sides. They can't identify with everyone. They often have clear-cut good guys and bad guys, white guys and black guys, and so on. Once someone is morally committed to a political stance, it is almost impossible, or it is very problematic, to produce a satisfying, aesthetically convincing and "beautiful," so to speak, novel. However, a few have managed to do that. Dostoevsky's *The Possessed*, sometimes translated as *The Demons*, is a great political novel in this sense. On the one hand, Dostoevsky had in him the quality of believing angrily, with energy, in a social cause, getting angry about everyone. He had a nasty side to his spirit. He also had the unique ability, even in his anger, to identify with the bad guys. So it's hard to be politically motivated and committed and write a novel that will not be damaged by the natural consequences of moral commitment, that is, inability to understand the "bad guy." That is the fragile moment of the political novel. Although there have been a few classics, I think it can never be a major genre.

CB: What I found so insightful was the notion that a writer or a novelist can break through what you define as "the confines of the self" by entering into the otherness of characters. And it would seem at this moment, when otherness is such a difficult issue in the world, that globally there would be a major reason to be a novelist. That was what I meant when I said there's an incredible sense of optimism in the way you write, and you managed to express it in *Snow*.

OP: Thank you.

CB: This is especially true with the character Blue, whom you made so attractive. But what really was interesting to me was not just that you were able to represent a radical Islamist, as you call him, as a sympathetic character, but that you were able to enter into the philosophical argument that a person like him would pursue. How did you do that?

OP: Well, at the heart of this great art of the novel that we're talking about lies the human capacity to identify with what we call the "other." The "other" is an academic word we use for people who are not like us; to talk about those who are not like us has been the problem of the last twenty years. So much has been written about "others" academically, but not in the form of the novel. I strongly feel that the art of the novel is based on the human capacity, though it's a limited capacity, to be able to identify with the "other." Only human beings can do this. It requires imagination, a sort of morality, a self-imposed goal of understanding this person who is different from us, which is a rarity. Once you begin to do that, you also imply or define a frame of understanding of a group, because a group is made of people sometimes like us and sometimes unlike us, and once you begin to identify yourself with those who are not like you, you inevitably begin to enlarge both your frame of mind and the frame of the group, you begin to see things differently. This is what Proust, Tolstoy, Dostoevsky, Thomas Mann, the great masters of this art have managed to develop; this human capacity, which I strongly believe is inherent in all human beings, such that all nations use it as their basis of communication. Now you're asking me, "How did you do that?" I don't know. The personal side of me doesn't want to explain it at all. Of course I have read a lot to understand the inner workings of the political Islamists, the rebels. But then I should also warn you that I have political Islamists in my part of the world, and they had so many affinities, say thirty years ago, with radical Marxists. Among the old-fashioned Marxists and political Islamists there is a continuity and repeated pattern of anti-Westernism, of parochialism and all sorts of conspiracy theories in place of logical thinking, especially nationalism disguised as anti-imperialism. Varieties of these thoughts and sentiments are shared by the Marxists and Islamists in many ways.

CB: [. . .] It's especially interesting because increasingly with young art students who want to manifest ideas and work between forms, it's a question of the appropriate form or inventing forms, which is a different matter altogether. They seem to be more and more interested in what form will best suit their ideas, concepts, or missions. In the future, with an increased availability of media and technology of all forms early on in the progression of an artist's education—film, video, animation, computer-generated images, and so on—we are going to see more of this overlap of form.

OP: I do have sympathy for that kind of representation, but I still believe young artists should not neglect the classical idea of craftsmanship. The hand should be trained before the mind, especially in painting. In the last hundred years or so, the idea of uniqueness and individuality is becoming more and more emphasized, so much so that we tend to think less of past art. Actually, the old masters were less self-centered than we are now. [. . .]

CB: [. . .] The Nobel speech "My Father's Suitcase," included in the recent book, is a beautiful tribute to your father. His temperament was such that you say, "He was too comfortable in his skin, too assured about the future ever to be gripped by the essential passions of literary creativity." He would say to you, "Life is not something to be earned, but enjoyed." In some sense, this is your explanation for why he did not pursue the sort of literary career that you have, even though he wrote. You present him as someone who didn't seem to have the hunger of disquietude necessary to give his life over to writing. Then also you present the wonderful notion that we don't really want to know the interior lives of our parents, that our own narcissism precludes our desire to understand them as anything other than our parents. Could you talk a bit more about your father?

OP: Well, on the one hand, my father's father was a very rich man, and that made life easier for him. He came from a secular Westernized family who had enjoyed the first two or three decades of the Modern Turkish Republic. They strongly believed in Turkish nationalism and Turkish Occidentalism, that is Westernization, which they thought of as a path toward civilization. That said, my father being the son of a very rich family, I strongly felt that he did not want to endure or live through the hardship of a literary life during the late 1940s to mid-'50s, when that life would have been very tough and it was considered a rich man's fancy to be a writer. On the other hand, he was an intelligent person who enjoyed books and had literary friends. He would also, behind their back but in a charming manner, mock them for only addressing a Turkish readership. Listening to my father—even at an early age—I had the impression that an author should address not national concerns, but all humanity. When he was bored with us at home, he would often travel to Paris, stay in hotel rooms, and fill pages and pages of notebooks, which he gave me just before he died. I remember him saying to me and my brother, with a laugh, "Well you guys have to work hard. I was privileged but there's no money left, children. Too bad." But he did this in such a graceful, kind manner that you liked the man for even saying it. He had an immense and excellent library and cared about Jean-Paul Sartre instead of pashas and saints in Turkey. It inspires me to think similarly, that I should take a modern writer as a secular saint, one I've decided I want to be like. My father had tremendous confidence in my brother and I, which we took for granted. I would draw a line and he would say, "Oh, this is genius!" Not because he really believed I was a genius, as I sometimes thought. He believed in himself so much that he thought only a genius's son could do such a thing. But he gave me the self-confidence that I needed.

CB: You have written about writers who were physically on the so-called periphery, like Borges, but who were in fact central in terms of their contribution. I would add Neruda or García Márquez to that group. Can you elaborate on the meaning of such categories?

OP: I lived practically all my life, except the last two or three years, in Istanbul. That is to say, especially in the 1950s, '60s, and '70s, we were living in the provinces. The center of the world is somewhere else. Even though we identify with and follow Westernization, we are not a part of it. That gives you a heavy sense of living on the sides, not at the center. V. S. Naipaul, though I may not agree with his politics, is a good observer of this kind of situation—what was academically called the postcolonial situation—although it doesn't quite apply to Turkey, as Turkey was never a Western colony. We Turks have never been victims of "imperialism." That makes the Turkish situation somewhat unique. But then being on the margins inspires you to go to the center. The cultural consequences of this kind of sentiment are an important part of my work. When a new book of mine is reviewed positively by the international press, especially in the first books, I had the impression that, say, my love scenes were considered to be about "Turkish love," while I thought I was writing about love in general. It seemed that when I wrote about love, it was about Turkish love. When Proust wrote about love, he wrote about love in general. All my life I fought against the impulse to impose my story, to make others accept my story, not to pigeon-hole me to an ethnic or national identity, but to accept my humanity as a part of a whole humanity, to accept my story as humankind's story.

CB: I'd like to ask you about the issue of freedom of expression. There is always the assumption that when artists and writers speak out politically, exposing the lies or the contradictions within their own society, they are somehow anti-American or anti-Turkish, while in fact if you are truly attempting to call attention to what is happening in your country, if you care enough to really do this, you are being the most patriotic. I remember being on picket lines during the antiwar movement during the 1960s, and people would yell out at me, "Go back to Russia!" I would think, "Go back to Russia? I don't come from Russia; I come from this country, and I'm trying to make a statement about this country." You talk quite elegantly about notions of the novelist's desire, ability, compulsion, and obligation to record the secret "shames" of his or her society, even though others want and need to keep them hidden while feeling betrayed when they are made visible. I've seen this in the United States, especially with the war in Iraq and in South Africa. In fact, when J. M. Coetzee's novel *Disgrace* came out, even though it was an accurate representation of part of the reality of the new South Africa, it was received by many in the ANC [African National Congress] government with negative criticism and accusations, which I know was very painful for him. You must have gone through the same experience.

OP: Well, firstly, political hardships have taught me not to pay attention to rhetorical figures or rhetorical maneuvering of political enemies. If they insult you on something, you shouldn't go back and say, "That's not the fact." We should not pay much attention to it. My mind is not concerned with the lies ultra-right-wingers tell about me in Turkey. Secondly, in a semirepressed society like South Africa, once you talk about things the establishment doesn't want you to talk about, they will use their power to misrepresent you. You cannot fight back. Even if you fight back, it's hard to convince the majority of the people that the accusations are untrue. You call them the establishment because they have the media, they have the army, and so on. This is not only in Turkey; it's everywhere. The definition of being critical is to say something to the establishment and to say something against the media. It has its costs. My point is that sometimes the political situation is so repressive that little things you say get grossly enlarged and distorted by the time they come back to you. Either you have to take a step back or wait for them to pass away. I did not really look for the political troubles I was forced into, but I felt that they fell into my lap, so to speak. I never sought them out. I see myself as a person who is writing in solitude all the time. I know that politics is a matter of community, of friends getting together, talking, drinking, living, thinking together, especially in my part of the world, but at the same time, the art of the novel implies that you become another person, someone who doesn't join the community so willingly.

CB: You mention this in "The Implied Author." All the work you have done has become so politicized that you've been thrust into the political arena, even though you'd rather lock yourself in your room and write. And yet, in your own terms, your involuntary political involvement has helped you to grow up at the expense of a certain childishness. How difficult was that realization?

OP: These are my words, but I'm not happy growing up.

CB: This I understand.

OP: I make it clear when I say creative thinking requires a sort of irresponsibility. By that I mean the seriousness and responsibility that society demands, which you impose on yourself and others, will vanish once you find yourself in a political situation. However, creativity also requires the kind of freedom of a child who does not consider the political consequences or any other consequences of his playfulness. In fact, new ideas come to us when we pay attention to this playful aspect, which is in some ways contradictory to politics.

CB: Do you have a sense of who your readers are in Turkey?

OP: My readers inside of Turkey and outside of Turkey are always the same, that of women and students who like to read novels and "intellectuals" who want to be updated on the scene about the recent creative writing. But that may be less true outside of Turkey. Ninety-five percent of men over thirty-five don't read novels in my part of the world. It's true in other places

as well. I have seen so many resentful attitudes that say, "I could have written novels, too. But there are more serious things to do in life." Or they say, "Mr. Pamuk, I don't like your political comments, but I respect you as a serious writer. Can you autograph this book for my wife?" But then students, or people who care about creativity and different ideas, about representing a nation and its problems, all the things that make a good intellectual student enthusiastic—all these people read my novels. Including women readers à la Madame Bovary. But this is not a Turkish situation. It's a global situation.
[...]

[*To the audience*] This is a fragment from my Nobel Prize acceptance speech, entitled "My Father's Suitcase": "As you know, the question we writers are asked most often, the favorite question, is: Why do you write? Here's an answer: I write because I have an innate need to write! I write because I can't do normal work like other people. I write because I want to read books like the ones I write. I write because I am angry at all of you, angry at everyone. I write because I love sitting in a room all day writing. I write because I can only partake in real life by changing it. I write because I want others, the whole world, to know what sort of life we lived, and continue to live, in Istanbul, in Turkey. I write because I love the smell of paper, pen, and ink. I write because I believe in literature, in the art of the novel, more than I believe in anything else. I write because it is a habit, a passion. I write because I am afraid of being forgotten. I write because I like the glory and interest that writing brings. I write to be alone. Perhaps I write because I hope to understand why I am so very, very angry at all of you, so very, very angry at everyone. I write because I like to be read. I write because once I have begun a novel, an essay, a page, I want to finish it. I write because everyone expects me to write. I write because I have a childish belief in the immortality of libraries, and in the way my books sit on the shelf. I write because it is exciting to turn all of life's beauties and riches into words. I write not to tell a story, but to compose a story. I write because I wish to escape from the foreboding that there is a place I must go but—just as in a dream—I can't quite get there. I write because I have never managed to be happy. I write to be happy."

Orhan Pamuk and Salman Rushdie on "Homeland"

Deborah Triesman / 2007

From the New Yorker Festival, October 5, 2007, https://www.youtube.com/watch?v=3VimE5_GKmQ.

Deborah Triesman: Orhan Pamuk, directly to my right, who won the Nobel Prize last year, has lived in Istanbul for most of his life. He is widely considered Turkey's leading novelist and literary spokesman. His bestselling novels, among them *My Name Is Red*, *The Black Book*, and *Snow*, which are almost exclusively set in Turkey, deal, among other things, with questions of culture, identity, and religion in Turkey, both historical and present. In a memoir, *Istanbul: Memories in the City*, and in his most recent collection of essays, *Other Colors*, he has produced loving and wistful portraits of his homeland. At the same time, he has a sometimes strained relationship with Turkey thanks to his honesty and outspokenness. He has come under attack sometimes by the press, sometimes by nationalist groups. In 2005, charges were filed against him for having referred publicly to the Armenian genocide in the Ottoman Empire. Those charges were eventually dropped, but the uproar left him sometimes in need of police protection in his own hometown.

Salman Rushdie, on the far side, was born in Bombay and educated in England and lived in Pakistan briefly before settling in London and then New York. His fourth novel, *The Satanic Verses*, which was inspired in part by the life of Muhammad, told the story of two Indian expatriates in Britain and was published in 1988. What followed is well known: the book was deemed blasphemous by Muslim communities around the world, riots ensued, it was banned in India, and Iran's Ayatollah Khomeini issued a fatwa calling for his murder. Rushdie spent years in hiding but continued to write, and over the next twenty years produced the acclaimed novels *The*

Moor's Last Sigh, The Ground Beneath Her Feet, and *Shalimar the Clown,* as well as a number of nonfiction works, among other honors too numerous to mention. He was made earlier this year a knight of the British Empire—Sir Salman. So, first, I am just curious to know generally what associations you each make with the idea of homeland. Are Turkey and India still homeland for you or have they become something else over the years?

Salman Rushdie: Yeah, I think there's a sense in which the place in which you grow up is a place that you think about as home, in a way you don't think about anywhere else. And for me, Bombay, which by the way I do not call Mumbai—Mumbai is an alien city occupying the same space as Bombay—Bombay is home. And not just Bombay in general but Bombay at a certain time. Because I think the city today is rather different than the city that I grew up in. And I still love it, but the feeling of home is also connected with its time as well as space. But yeah, I always have the feeling when going to India of coming home. Always. And part of that is linguistic, too, because I still speak Hindi and Urdu, and one of the things that happens when I go back is that the language is all there, but at the moment today, it's kind of half of it is packed away in the attic. But when you get there, it comes out. And so regaining the ability to inhabit your mother tongue is also part of the feeling of home.

Orhan Pamuk: Yes, of course. I'll give a similar answer, of course. My homeland is Turkey, especially Istanbul. I belong there. I wouldn't say that I'm out of home here, but it's probably so. And I also resist, whenever I'm outside of Turkey, everyone says, Oh, you're an exile. [. . .] I resist saying that I'm an exile, I can return back to Turkey whenever I want. [. . .] One thing portable about home is the language. I have the language with me. I can go to Mars, I can go to Siberia, I can go to Latin America . . . but I have the Turkish language with me and I carry it in my pocket, in my spirit, and I write with it, that it's my home, and I have a portable home with me all the time, and that's the Turkish language. I think I strongly belong to that, but then I don't evaluate everything about home with being home. I don't also say, This is home, and the rest of the world is phony and second rate. I don't say that. In fact, I'm aware of the "homeness" of the home when I'm outside of Turkey. One of my books, *The Black Book,* I wrote in the United States, and there I had the most radical anxiety of being a Turk. I had the most anxiety of my identity. Who am I? [. . .] And I realized what home was for the first time, radically, when I was away from home.

DT: [. . .] Your novels are set around the world and in different places, but India and Turkey are places that you return to over and over again in writing, whether you're there or not there. Are you just drawn in and compelled to write about these places?

SR: I think it's just that it's in the given of what I have as a writer, you know. [. . .] But I also wanted to say about what Orhan said, I also don't feel like an exile. There was only one moment in my life when I did feel like an exile. There was a period for reasons you've mentioned, a period of almost ten years, when I was not able to go to India. And during that time, it was the only time I've actually felt a sense of exile. And one of the reasons why I'm unusually proud of *The Moor's Last Sigh* is it's the only novel I wrote about India without being able to go to India. And when the people in India read it, they paid me the greatest compliment of all. Which is they said, Okay, so you sneaked back in, didn't you? [*Laughter*] Because otherwise, how do you know all this stuff? [. . .]

OP: I write about home because that's all I know. I write about Istanbul because that's where I spent fifty years. And when you ask me about humanity, I'll talk about humanity without forgetting that I'm only talking about Istanbul. But then that's the question, in fact. That when we are talking and referring back [to] and underlining our home, if we do exaggerate and dramatize that we are away from home—that there is a home and another world, and then there is a difference—then we begin to fall into the traps of representation. I write about Istanbul because I have come across humanity in Istanbul. My aim is not in fact to say that I'm going to describe Turks [. . .] I thought I was writing about humanity! Once I was outside of Turkey and began to get translated, everyone began to say that, Oh, he's writing about Turks in Istanbul. I thought I was writing about humanity. And this is a major concern I have about underlining writing about home. We all love our home, it's inevitable. [. . .] Now that I'm outside of home and they're asking me questions about home, or what home is, what it means to me, I don't want to underline a distinction between home and other places. Once you begin to do that, then you are out there to represent home.

[. . .]

SR: But the one sense in which it has become kind of problematic certainly to, I think, to writers from the third world more than to Western writers is this question—because it gets connected to this idea of authenticity, you know? American writers, European writers have always felt free to go live anywhere in the world they wanted to live. If F. Scott Fitzgerald lives on the Riviera, if Joyce lives in Trieste, if Hemingway lives in Paris, they don't somehow stop being American or Irish. If an Indian writer lives in London or New York, it's a problem. And not only that, there's also an expectation that if you're an Indian writer, you should only write about Indian material. Again, Western writers have always given themselves the freedom to write about anywhere they like, sometimes with questionable results. One need only think of John Updike's novel about Africa, *The Coup*, one of the worst novels ever written. [*Laughter*] But if Picasso wants to use African art as a model: fine. If an Indian writer wishes to use a Western source as inspiration: suspect. And so there is this double standard that that one has to deal with. In the case of India, this is a huge diaspora culture now. There are Indians everywhere and the Indian experience is

becoming a diaspora experience as well as a national experience. And there's no reason at all, it seems to me, why a writer living in Silicon Valley should not write an interesting novel about a village in India. [. . .] Look at this another way: we all leave home, you know. We all do. We all grow up in our parents' home and at some point we make a home of our own. So the idea of "home" is not singular; it's narrative. You have a home that is given to you and then you have a home or homes that you make. And people who never leave home are kind of sad. [*Laughter*].

OP: I disagree. I disagree.

SR: Finally! We disagree! [*Laughter*]

OP: [. . .] What counts is not staying at the same place. You may stay at the same place. [What counts is that] you would be uncomfortable at home. [. . .] You have a different, not "homely" mind: that's what counts. You have a different point of view, read different books, you have different criteria, you don't agree with the community. Then I think you are deeply at home. [. . .] I think you have a deeper sense of home if you have a set of values—which I do as an autodidact, from all the books I have read in my solitary reading hours—I derived values, literary images, in fact utopian visions that I should entertain my mind with. Then I judge my home, in fact write about home, with ideas that are not "homely." And then I manage, naïvely, I think, to pin down "home" better than the guys who had stayed there and thought the things [they] were required to think.

SR: There is a thing I've written about in the past [*Imaginary Homelands*] [. . .] it seems to me that in all human beings there are opposite impulses: there is the impulse to home and the impulse to away. There's the desire, the dream of roots and the dream of leaving. I think we all have that. We all have that feeling of comfort and solidity, an explicable existence, meaning that comes out of being in a place to which you feel you belong. But there's also a kind of exhilaration in the Self, and the discovery of the Other which we also all seek and respond to in the act of leaving. And I think what's happened, however, is that the dream of home, of roots, has been culturally privileged. We think of that as good—to belong and stay and inhabit the thing that you were accidentally born into. And that the dream of leaving, the deliberate chosen exit, is more problematic and sometimes suspect. But the thing is, interestingly to me, if you look at our artistic production, whether it's books or movies or whatever, it's those figures who we are excited about, the ones who go on the road: the tramp like Chaplin, the outlaw, the bandit, the criminal, the person who goes on the wrong side of the tracks, the "leaver" is actually what we dream about. It's as if we spend our nonimagining selves trying to construct ideas of home and place and belonging, and our imagining selves want to be these outlaws. Both those things are in us, in all of us.

DT: Going back to something Orhan was saying, in terms of your formation as writers, what was more important: where you came from or the international community of writing that you were discovering?

OP: I think it's both. The interesting thing about being a writer is that you get these universal, general ideas from books. You read them, you believe in them, they are very valuable; you want that back at home. They are attractive because "home" lacks them. [. . .] And they say, Well, you're getting all these European ideas from books, but this is Turkey. And then sometimes the other way around. [. . .] Of course, humanity wants both to control and command the universals and also belong to the particular. One thing about being in the West, or living at the center of the world, is that it's a privilege, say, once upon a time Balzac or French literature enjoyed—perhaps now English literature or English-speaking literature—that you are both at home *and* you are mastering the universals. Which is, if you look from my corner of the world, I get upset and angry about that. I want to fight against that: To some privileged authors home is where they can speak in the name of humanity [. . .] and also have this smell, colors of, the dirt of the little street. This only happens in countries that rule the world, so to speak, control the cultural world, so to speak. That makes it problematic.

SR: When I was starting out as a writer, I resisted the idea that because I came from India I had to write about India. My first novel was this unfortunate heap of shit [*laughs*] that was never published. [. . .] But it made me very profoundly rethink the business of being a writer, and it actually did take me back to beginnings. I thought: I'm going to go somewhere much closer to myself, somewhere much closer to a world that I know. And long before I knew what *Midnight's Children* was going to be about as a book, I thought I would write something about childhood. It didn't occur to me in my first conception that it would become this much larger fiction with public dimensions. I just thought I had to go closer to home in order to find out who I am as a writer, if anyone. For me that was the key that unlocked the door. [. . .]

DT: You resent sometimes being told that you're writing about Turkish love, not love in general, or Indian situations. Can you ever take a writer away from his country? Would you have a Borges without Argentina? Would you have a Proust without France, or a Faulkner without America?

OP: Of course not, but then you're hinting at the answer, you know—

SR: But that's a certain kind of writer. I mean as I say, you can have a Hemingway without America—

OP: But that implies that Americans have this imperial vision. You can feel it from every place: they don't need a visa [*laughter*] and then they have the money and they go and no one asks them, "Why are you here?" They accept it's natural for the Americans to be all around, while if I go, it's "So why are you here? Is this your first time?" I've been asked this question for the last twenty-five years so many times.

SR: [. . .] But it is this strange difference which has to do with the history of the world; it has to do with imperialism and colonialism and so on: The assumption is that Western writers can be writers of the world, whereas Eastern writers must be trapped in their region.

OP: It's not, unfortunately, an assumption. It's a fact. We have to fight against this fact and prove that it's an assumption.

SR: Yes, you replace the fact by a new fact. [. . .]

OP: Okay then my definition of home, which I've discovered just lately, is this: I had an event at the public library and someone said, "What's the difference between here and Istanbul?" And, you know, it just came to me—and I think that's the most instinctive reply that I have ever had about being home and outside of home. And my immediate answer was, "In Turkey, in Istanbul, I feel responsible about everything. Here, I don't feel responsible." [. . .] Here I don't feel at home because I left that responsibility behind. I am only here with my freedom and playfulness of being away from home. [. . .] And also at home, a writer in my part of the world, not necessarily Turkey, if you're a writer you're a professor of everything. You're responsible; you have to have information about everything and answer and address all the questions the nation the country has. While here there is more freedom that you're a writer: you write your books, you do your interviews, you promote your books, and the beauty of the book is what counts and that's it. Perhaps because of that, or perhaps, I haven't lived here enough to pick up enemies, or anger, or resentment. [. . .] Back in Turkey I feel responsible for everything and here, I'm a voyeur and it's a nice feeling.

SR: I'm very moved by Orhan's sense of responsibility. [*Laughter*]

OP: I feel responsible for you too, Salman, don't worry. [*Laughter*]

SR: I don't feel responsible for you. [*Laughter*] I've always felt completely irresponsible. You're kind of saying that by getting here and being able to shed that sense of responsibility, it's a kind of a liberation.

OP: Yes.

SR: I've always been in favor of a responsibility really, but this question about writers being expected to know everything, it's very bizarre. You know, I go around the place and I'm endlessly asked to solve the "Middle East problem."

OP: Yes, but they never ask you to solve the "American problem"! [. . .]

DT: On a different tack, you're both relatively secular people who come from countries in which religion is relatively central. Does that make you feel less at home in your own countries?

SR: No, because there's always a bunch of people who agree with you.

OP: Yeah, there's a strong secular history in both countries, I think, and religion is not so strong . . . it doesn't crush everything.

DT: Do you feel that you're put on one side of a wall that is splitting the country?

SR: [. . .] The fictional answer is that it doesn't matter whether you believe in something or not; if you're writing about people who do believe in something, you have to faithfully create that reality. You would be a very bad writer if you could not create a worldview other than your own in the mind of somebody you wanted to write about. Actually, when I'm writing fiction, my own, if you like, religious beliefs or lack of them, are kind of irrelevant. [. . .]

DT: You've also studied Islam and you're very knowledgeable—you're responsible for it—and it's played a central part in several of your books. And Orhan, your last novel, *Snow*, was about a secular person going into a very religious community, almost from a journalistic point of view. [. . .] Obviously these things are important even though they're not actually reflective of your life. . . .

OP: Writing novels is about our capacity to identify with people who are not like us. All my friends are telling me that I'm always writing autobiographical fiction. Some characters are autobiographical, but I do my best to identify with people with whom I don't politically, culturally agree. For example, in *Snow*, that you referred to, there is a character called Blue who is a sort of a radical Islamic fundamentalist. And I did my best to identify and show him, as Tolstoy says, as a good man, and that is, I wouldn't say a duty, but the joy and challenge of writing a novel. Theoretically, in a corner of your mind you have a set of values with which you judge this person—but when you're writing fiction you have to do your best to forget about these values. They may be "home" values, there may be values that you have imported, or that you want to forget about, but the essential thing is that it's best to be able to identify with people who disagree with you religiously, secularly, this or that way. [. . .] The problem is to find the right tone, the right voice. [. . .]

SR: [. . .] But I think the very interesting point that Orhan made about tone and form, it's very well illustrated by Kafka's novel about America. Kafka never came to America. His novel, which was posthumously given the title *Amerika* by Max Brod, which he himself, I think, wanted to call *The Stoker*. *Amerika* is a wonderful novel, which, kind of isn't about America at all, except that it takes place in a place called America. That ability to create a fictional space with a real name, it only works if you get technical aspects right. It's to do with tone, form, rhythm, language. It's not to do with "reality." The novel is not really a realistic form, and this is something which much contemporary literary criticism loses sight of. The novel is an imaginative form. It's a formalized dream. These things did not happen, these people did not live, these events were not so. To insist on the fictive nature of fiction is also to liberate you from the question of authenticity, and location, and roots. [. . .]

DT: Going back to your point—it's all fiction and it's invented regardless of where it's set—a problem you've both had is people taking you literally and reading your fiction as fact. [. . .] So you run up against this problem of a) people thinking you're writing as yourself, not as a narrator, and b) what you're writing about is actually happening. You have a certain audience that doesn't suspend their beliefs.

OP: Yes that's the point about being a writer: You write fiction and people judge you as if you're writing journalism and you have to answer all the questions in that manner. That is the interesting thing about fiction. The reader both knows it's fiction but judges it on reality.

SR: Given that the question you're most often asked as a writer is "How autobiographical is it?" I've developed a technique on book tours, which is to give opposite answers to consecutive journalists. "It's not autobiographical at all—it's just all kind of out of my head, and why would you imagine that it's autobiographical?" And to the next journalist I say, "It's totally autobiographical. Everything that happened in this book, happened either to myself or to close friends or family members." And these interviews appear on the same day, in the same city, and nobody ever notices that you've contradicted yourself. [*Laughter*] Which just shows that nobody reads interviews with writers. [*Laughter*]

DT: Do you ever have to think of yourself because of this as reporters in a sense? Do you feel you have to be faithful to the reality of the situation?

OP: If you underline the "home," the authenticity of your experience, then that this is something that no one else has lived [. . .], then yes, the question of authenticity or journalistic value, the realistic content of what you have written begins to go up. [. . .] But then the home is not the only criteria to judge the rest of the experience. We all feel obliged to pay attention to it, return to it. [. . .] James Joyce wrote *Ulysses* in Trieste, not in Dublin. We carry our homes with us, but that's the beginning. Then we invent things over it and continue. [. . .] Our work should not be based on realistic content. [. . .]

SR: On this subject of reportage, I think I have two things to say: one is that there's an aspect of the truth, what really happened, which is very energizing to a text. It's true that Joyce wrote *Ulysses* in Trieste, but he took with him the *Irish Times* of June 16 of Bloomsday. He carried it with him everywhere he wrote that book. And almost everything in that newspaper finds its way into the novel. [. . .]

The other issue is, if you like, a more kind of historical, political issue which is: There was a role for the nineteenth-century novel of bringing the news. When Dickens wrote about poor schools in the north of England, it did a great deal to hasten the reform of those schools, after *Nicholas Nickleby*. We don't so much see the novel as having that role now because there are much bigger information media available, faster. But I think the problem is that we live in an age where the truth is so trivialized, falsified, and simply hidden from us that the novel still has the role of bringing the truth. [. . .] So what happens is that if you simply are performing an act of remembering, this becomes at odds with official history and, therefore, becomes an action of reportage. And there is still a place for that in the contemporary novel. [. . .] So the question is how do you incorporate that material in such a way that it's properly integrated into the fictional architecture of an imaginative world. That's a very difficult question. [. . .]

DT: I know that what happens whenever we publish a piece of fiction in the *New Yorker* is that we get at least one letter from a reader saying, "You know, what a nice story, but unfortunately you have your facts wrong. Gruyère cheese doesn't smell, or that bridge is in Delhi not Calcutta."

SR: One of the great experiences of being published in the *New Yorker* is to have fiction fact-checked. [. . .] But there is something very beautiful about having fiction checked for factual inaccuracies.

A Conversation with the Nobel Prize-Winning Author of *The Museum of Innocence*

Bigthink.com / 2009

From bigthink.com, November 11, 2009, https://bigthink.com/videos/big-think-interview-with-orhan-pamuk/.

Big Think: What is your advice to aspiring novelists?

Orhan Pamuk: The strongest advice would be, don't ever listen to either my advice or anyone else's advice. You find your own—follow your own humors, you will find them. Just work hard and read hard.

BT: What insights into love does *The Museum of Innocence* draw upon?

OP: [. . .] My aim in this novel was not to put love on a pedestal and say, what a sweet thing it is, what a great thing it is. On the other hand, I look at it as almost a bad thing—or not bad thing—something that happens to us, to all of us. Then let's try to analyze it, see through it, and see how human minds and hearts—if you make a distinction between them—react to life. My, I can also simplify, my point of view is that lots of things are operating in our minds, in our spirit, in our blood, so to speak, when we are in love. And one thing that is important is that one part of our mind is seeing things clearly, knows that we are in love, that what we are doing in fact will not serve our love, but it will be in fact not good for getting or impressing the beloved. But we do those things. And when we are in love—and this is the essential point about my novel too—that we do things; one part of our minds observes with a bit of sadness and melancholy, thinking that this will not make us happy. This is one thing. The second thing that I focus on in the novel is to see analytically all the things that lovers do; that is, waiting for the phone to ring, resentment and anger, jealousy, finding yourself stupid or overanxiety, angers, expectations, and a lot of illusions, delusions, and how we cheat or how we misguide ourselves when we are in love. My character Kemal in *The Museum of Innocence* thinks that actually he is going to win over his beloved in two weeks, at most in two months, while he spends eight years running after her.

BT: How is love connected to the objects of everyday life?

OP: The book—at one point in the book, when my character is infatuated by love and feels what we popularly call love pain, he realizes that objects, things that are associated with his beloved—objects that they shared together in their happy times—have the power of consoling him, perhaps because they bring back the memories, the joyful memories they shared together. This we all know, more or less, from Proust's "madeleine." Or I'll give you an example of a movie ticket. Let's imagine that we have found a movie ticket in an old jacket pocket. We have already forgotten that we've been to that movie. We don't even remember we've been seeing that. But as soon as we have the ticket, we begin thinking, well, not only that we've seen the movie, but we remember scenes from the movie, because we have an object associated with those sensations and memories. All objects have that power, and when my character is badly in love and is not happy with his unrequited love, he begins to collect, or gather around, the objects that he had shared with his beloved. Later, after some time, he makes a museum of these objects. And my novel is in a way an annotated museum catalog. If you put the objects together and tell the story of each object, we have a novel. That was more or less the idea, how I composed this book. Then I'm also doing that; I'm also doing the museum. Maybe I should talk about it later more when I—my museum is also about objects that these lovers share, but also it's a city museum because they share the culture of Istanbul between 1975 until the end of the twentieth century. [. . .]

BT: Are museums a Western concept?

OP: I argue that collecting things is related to—getting attached to things is a universal human reaction to some trouble, trauma, whatever you may call it. In my novel it is of course love, and my infatuated lover is so troubled that he gets attached to things for various reasons. This is more or less the common passion in all collectors. But it is only the Western civilization that puts a collector's mania onto a pedestal, because museums were invented in the West.

First there were in the seventeenth and eighteenth centuries what they called *Wunderkammer*, or "cabinets of curiosities," to exhibit the power and taste of the princes or the elites or the rich people. Then when the Louvre was converted from a royal palace to a public sphere, a museum, then again it was a place for showing the power and sophistication of the ruling elites. But museums are also places for learning: you put together things, then you categorize and you produce information. Human information is in fact contained in things and the theory about their relationships. Once you put two or three, five objects in an exhibit in a museum, these objects tell a story. You ask yourself if you visit, "What's the relationship between them?" And that's a story. That's a theory.

Museums put collectors on pedestals, and making collections, getting attached to things, is not an embarrassing thing once museums legitimize your habit of collecting. But if there are no museums, then your habit of collecting, and also your collections, exhibits only your personal wounds. So I made this distinction toward the end of my *Museum of Innocence*, when my character—after my character decides to exhibit his immense collections that are related to his love. And my character also visits small museums of the world, five thousand of them, perhaps because he likes them. He likes the empty, melancholic old museums where no one goes. And I've been to so many of them all over the world just because I like the atmosphere inside, the melancholy atmosphere, the creaking of the parquet floor, the museum guides almost half-sleepy; even they're also impressed that you're here and looking at these objects no one comes for. There you feel the venture of a prince, a rich guy, a sad guy, a poor collector who thought that he would transcend history by his collection, by his objects. But then it's how successful—no one comes.

You feel that outside there is a time, modern times, that's going on, while inside the museum it's timelessness. These sensations I like. In fact, in the end we write novels because we just like these sensations. We want to immerse ourselves in these images. I like to—in fact, a part of the novel, or one part of the novel, is that I like, I very much like, to go out to forgotten, neglected museums of the world. And one of the reasons I wrote this novel was just to revisit them, to see them, to talk about them.

BT: What are some of the world's most neglected museums?

OP: Okay, I'll mention them. For example, Bagatti Valsecchi in Milano, one of the sources of my museum. In fact, when the book was published in Italy, I went there, had a reading there, trying to highlight the museum because this was a museum done in the mid-nineteenth century by two Italian aristocrats to represent fifteenth- and fourteenth-century Renaissance life in Italy. They had bought all the things, Renaissance things, from flea markets because they were cheap and available at that time, and converted their own homes into a museum. But then they were using these museum objects, old objects, real objects from the Renaissance, as their daily life objects. And I like museums where people think about their afterlife, their life after death, and slowly and slowly, before they die, convert their homes into museums. There are places like that—for example, Musée Gustave Moreau in Paris. Gustave Moreau, I think, is a classicist, a bit of a kitschy painter, but a great painter. But an interesting figure. Proust mentioned [that] so many writers, André Malraux, surrealists, were influenced by him. Why? Not because of the quality of his paintings, I think, but because of the idea of his museums. He comes from a well-to-do family, and toward the end of his life, he converted his studio, the house his family lived in all along for years, into a museum, calculating that after his death his studio and house will be a museum. And he was successful in that. Just because his museum was successful, we still know the name Gustave Moreau.

[...]

BT: As a now American-based author, what do you miss most about Istanbul?

OP: Probably I—it's a feeling of being at the periphery, not under Western eyes in our own way of life. But that is also changing. When I started writing thirty years ago, no one cared about Turkish culture or Turkish writers. But now Turkey is getting on the agenda. I like being out of the scene. The feeling of not living at the center of the world is a nice feeling. I perhaps complain about Turkey's being provincial, but I also, I confess, like being provincial, enjoy being out of the drama, enjoy being non-Western, et cetera.

BT: Is there any tension in your writing about Istanbul from the US?

OP: No. And in fact, there is joy about that. Don't forget that the greatest book about any city—a novel, *Ulysses*—was written by James Joyce in Trieste. In fact, you love it. You like that there is a sweet taste of longing when you write when you're away. And my *The Black Book*, which is the book in which I found my voice, I wrote more than half of it in New York, dreaming of Istanbul, just like I've always identified with James Joyce living in Trieste, dreaming of Dublin. That's no problem.

BT: Is it possible to be a global writer?

OP: Well, it may be. Maybe I am like that, perhaps, but I don't identify myself with that concept. That we should address all humanity, that writers should transcend their national audience, I agree with. In fact, it is a moral obligation not to write for the national audience, and it also makes you shift your point of view. But on the other hand, "global writer" is not, you know, aesthetically something I like, and I don't want to refer to myself as such.

BT: What are conditions like in Turkey today for a novelist?

OP: Good. The Turkish book industry is booming. No one—you would not be intimidated by free speech problems if you write a novel. Don't forget that Dostoevsky or Tolstoy wrote their novels when the tsar was reading and censoring. Most of the time you won't get in trouble for writing a novel. But political commentary, journalistic writing, outspoken Kurds, radicals, they're always in trouble. But what—free speech is—novels will not get you in trouble of free speech. But yes, political commentary radically criticizing the army, criticizing religion—so many things will still get you in trouble in Turkey. Sometimes legal trouble, sometimes maybe campaigns, death threats kind of trouble.

BT: Who are your heroes?

OP: Look, I don't want to see heroes around. I believe in a world where there are no heroes, and I've read and know humanity a lot. There are moments that I admire in a person, courage, intellect, hard work. These are the qualities I admire in an intellectual, in a writer, and there are so many people who have these things. Say I admire Noam Chomsky, or say I used to admire, when I was a teenager, Jean-Paul Sartre. I like outspoken public intellectuals, but on the other hand, then I also see their failures, their vanities. They're all human beings. My policy of looking at intellectuals—and they are most of the time people I admire—is to pay attention to what they did best and ignore their failures, because they all fail. We all—intellectuals, writers—in the end say something interesting. And pay attention to what they say. Then there are also uninteresting things they say, or just their failures. I don't care about that.

BT: What keeps you up at night?

OP: That—is it beautiful? Is it good enough? Is that chapter good? Now, unfortunately, will the museum be good enough? Is it good? It's always the idea that—its self-criticism worries me. Most of the time, and I mean . . . is it good enough? Is it interesting enough? Am I addressing—am I telling the truth? Am I authentic, or am I posing? This kind of thing upsets me. I'm very worried about being pretentious or inauthentic, or just writing for the sake of writing. So I am also a graphomaniac, I write all the time. Whenever I have a nervousness or tension, I pull out a notebook and write some things in it. I like that, and it calms me down. Sometimes I draw, sometimes I write, and that makes me happy.

Orhan Pamuk Interview: Painting and Literature

Charlie Rose / 2009

From the *Charlie Rose* program, November 28, 2009, https://charlierose.com/videos/13590.

Charlie Rose: Has art—has painting more influenced literature or literature more influenced painting?

Orhan Pamuk: I think they are intertwined. Painting taught literature to describe. [. . .] If you know how to see things, you know how to pick up details and make an integrated part of the story. Let's remember that the art of the novel as we know it today developed not earlier than mid-nineteenth century. Although *Don Quixote* was written at the end of the sixteenth century, novels as we know today were developed by Stendhal, Balzac, Zola, all of whom, if you leave aside Dickens in England, were heavily interested about painting, wrote about the painters of their time, wrote books, even, were friendly with painters, and impressionism was about to be developed some thirty, twenty years later. And they have learned, and so many scholars argue that to describe things, to see things—not only that, to see things as emblems of human trauma, human statues, class, gender, also to see things as defining a person's taste and refinement. This is Flaubert. Flaubert was also heavily interested in painting. Painting prepared grounds for the French—at least for the French—realistic novel, and from there on it was a global novel. I think the novel today was developed by the French and British in mid-nineteenth century and there was a lot of painting influence, and the writers who did that were heavily influenced by painters.

CR: Is one novel recognized as the first?

OP: I think Stendhal, Balzac were novelists, but I cannot pick, say, this one—for me, the greatest novel is *Anna Karenina*.

CR: Why *Anna Karenina*?

OP: I think this is not my personal opinion. It is the greatest novel. If you just say to yourself, "Why do you want to read it again?" You just want to read it again. Just this fall, I gave Norton lectures at Harvard University and these lectures you choose a subject, and I choose the art of the novel, and more than half of my examples are based on *Anna Karenina*. Why? It just gives you the feeling that, yes, life is like that. When I was writing this book, of course, I am, sort of a Hemingway kind of competitiveness I had was with *Anna Karenina*, that I think that every novel in the end should address this basic idea, feeling, sentiment, What is life like? Literary novels should address that. When we finish a novel, put it by the side, we say, "Is life like that? I think life is like that, or I did not notice life is like that." I think novels should address our basic sense of what are the values. Is it friendship? Is it history? Is it culture? Is it community? Is it ethical commitment to an idea? Or is it just happiness? What is happiness? I think old-fashioned novels did that. I think we should continue doing that. This novel aspires to do those things.

CR: Do you believe that novels will tell you more about a culture than history will tell you about a culture?

OP: I believe novels teach us details of a culture. Some novels are based on more fantasy and imagination. You cannot learn more about—we cannot have realistic information about a culture. But some novels, say Flaubert gives in *Madame Bovary* or *A Sentimental Education*, tells so much about French society of the mid-nineteenth century. Novels give us the period, but some novels do not choose to, say science fiction novels, detective novels, romances, they don't teach, or most historical novels do not teach us about history, but give us something about the period they are written. I think novels in the end are based on human experience. They convey their experience, and evaluation of that experience should be the novel. Novels also are democratic forms in the sense that you don't have to be an intellectual to enjoy a novel, although some novels...

CR: Because it's a story.

OP: It's a story—no, along with being a story, that they are based on little daily life observations. What do we see in a novel? Someone is drinking tea. I'm looking at my watch. The other guy is turning on a light, and we see something from the window.

CR: And a novelist has a gift that others don't—to see those things and understand the context and significance of what is daily and ordinary?

OP: A novelist should have—yes, in that line, two talents, to see those things in such a way that when he or she writes about them, you say, "Yes, that's how coffee feels. That's how when you see the fresh morning breeze, that's how it feels." The second thing pulls together all these little human intersections with light, so to speak, with life, light, verbs, sounds, colors in such a big organization that when you finish that organization, also embedded in a story, you have a sense of life. You say, "Well, that's my understanding of life, too." Proust—so many novelists, in fact, compared novels to cathedrals, that from these little observations you make a cathedral that suggests something deeper that is the center of the novel, the meaning of the novel, what the novel implies. The joyful, attractive thing about writing novels is that you don't have to be a professor, scholar, anything. You just pay attention to little details of human life, and then compose these details in such a way as to identify with the heroes, that you give such a deep understanding of life that can compete with philosophy or religion.

CR: What skills do you have now that you didn't have ten years ago, other than you have more experiences of living?

OP: Good. When I was writing my first novels, when I was twenty-three, I wanted to be a painter, and I stopped painting. And I said to my family, an upper middle-class family in Istanbul, I said, "I'm going to be a novelist." They said, "What? Who is going to read your novels? You don't know anything about life." Coming to your question, they were implying, my family and my friends, that novels are about human experience. When I finished this novel, I also said—after thirty-five years—at that time, I said, "Well, no, novels are about literature, about Kafka, [Samuel] Beckett. You have to be experimental. Kafka didn't live anything. He was just working in an insurance office. Novels should not be full of life." Now thirty-five years later, I think that now I agree that perhaps because I have life experience that novels should be full of a sense of life. But in order to be able to say it you have to be over fifty-five like me.

Orhan Pamuk Interview: Turkish Geopolitics

Charlie Rose / 2011

From the *Charlie Rose* program, May 13, 2011, https://charlierose.com/videos/18601.

Charlie Rose: Does it pain you at all that France has given you so many awards, that that country stands in the way, along with Germany and Holland, of Turkey joining the European Union?

Orhan Pamuk: [. . .] The question is painful, of course. That we, Turkish intellectuals, [. . .] generations of Turkish intellectuals, along with so, I say, Vietnamese intellectuals, Thailand intellectuals, Indian intellectuals, took France, the glorious French Revolution and the ideals of modernity, and imitated them for quite a long time. And then, it's sad to see that actually in the negotiation with joining the European Union, France is the country that resists Turkey most.

[. . .]

CR: But does Turkey prove that a country can be Islamic, plural, secular, democratic?

OP: That's what we are trying to prove, sir. But just because we haven't reached these ideals, it doesn't mean that you sense that this isn't possible, is a vain thing. I think, yes, I strongly think that Turkey will soon be a full democracy. It isn't now. [. . .] But we shouldn't lose our self-confidence in its direction.

[. . .]

CR: What does it feel like to be a man of international renown and to know that the power of the state can threaten you and put you in prison like everybody else?

OP: It's very bad, really. [. . .] In the end what's at stake is this. That I don't want to lose Turkey. I want to belong here. But I don't want to lose my free speech of criticizing Turkey. So it means that I have to balance it in a way that I move out of Turkey. I come back. I move out of Turkey. I come back. That also makes my visibilities too much and I'm upset by it, that I want to be—I want to be by myself. I am in this, in the last two months, I am busy with my museum [The Museum of Innocence], going inward and doing this strange thing because that is how I deeply express myself. I'm not a political commentator. I'm a, you know, novelist or artist.

CR: There is a problem with that argument, which is the following. Politics is about life. You write about life. Your observations are about life. You may very well understand the reason that human beings act in the way they do as much as any political scientist in the world. And we're all part of the debate of our time, about who we are [. . .] and what is the nature of the society we want to live in.

OP: Yes. And especially in countries like Turkey or countries where free speech is not developed, and democracy is always a bit crippled or problematic. [. . .] For me, the legitimization of a government or my critique of a government should be based on moral issues, not foreign policy issues.

CR: And what are those moral issues? [. . .]

OP: Free speech, democracy, these are the issues. Also what the government does in foreign policy one day, you know, these are not things that I'm following really.

Orhan Pamuk: *Silent House*

Diane Rehm / 2012

From *The Diane Rehm Show*, October 12, 2012, https://dianerehm.org/shows/2012-10-10/orhan-pamuk-silent-house.

Diane Rehm: Thanks for joining us. I'm Diane Rehm. In Orhan Pamuk's novel, *Silent House*, three siblings visit their grandmother in her decaying home in an old fishing village turned resort town. The year is 1980, and Turkey is on the verge of a military coup. While the grandchildren try to keep themselves busy on their summer vacation, they find themselves unable to escape the heightening political tension that's dividing the country. *Silent House* is the second novel Nobel Prize-winning author Orhan Pamuk ever published, but it's just now available in English translation. [...]

Orhan Pamuk: Good morning, Diane. It's so much fun to be again doing this show with you.

DR: I'm glad. *Silent House* was first published back in 1983. Describe the experience of revisiting one of your very early works.

OP: Yes. First, this is my second novel. I wrote it almost thirty years ago [...] and I saw that, in fact, so much has also changed around Istanbul. These neighborhoods that I described in the 1980s were at that time small. [...] As I was rereading my novel, I saw that all these neighborhoods, which I describe as being outside of Istanbul, are now part of a big city of fourteen million.

DR: But now, thinking about the writer who wrote that book back in 1983, in addition to seeing a changed place, did you see a different writer?

OP: I saw a more nervous, angry, resentful writer. Yes. And it's of course very much related to youthfulness. The problems of Turkey in my youth were even harder. More crushing, [...] demanding more moral commitment and political commitment from you. At that time Turkey was brutally politicized. I think the country's less political now, and at that time in the 1980s before the military coup, left-wing political groups or gangs were shooting right-wing political groups or gangs in the streets of Turkey, and all this, unfortunately, legitimized that military coup.

DR: And made you an angry young man.

OP: And everyone was angry. Everyone was angry, and then you understand that when there is no prospect of economic growth, and when you're living at the edge of Europe, and when you see that the country is not being run as was the case in 1980, in this novel, *Silent House*, there is a sense of frustration. People turning inward. There's a sense that terrible things have happened, while on the other hand, it has aspects of a family story, a family reunion, a family coming together.

[...]

DR: So *Silent House* was your second novel. But you wrote a book even before that . . . that was not published.

OP: Yes. We are planning to publish this . . . in the future. But we don't want to push too many of my early novels, because I'm working all the time. My next novel will be the new original novel that I'm finishing in Turkey [*A Strangeness in My Mind*].

DR: Now, would you consider *Silent House* a political novel or a novel about family?

OP: Both, of course. This is the story of an ambitious man [Selahattin] who is a military doctor. Westernization, Occidentalism, fancy ideas about Western reasoning, positivism all came to the late Ottoman Empire—and at that time, the Ottoman Empire was almost all of the Middle East—through the military, especially military doctors. [. . .] So anyway, my character believes in these ideas so much that he criticizes the sultan, after which he is exiled to this little fisherman's village with his wife [Fatma]. They live there for almost sixty years [. . .] and my novel starts as the generation of grandchildren visits the grandmother.

DR: Were you a member of a large family at the time?

OP: This novel is highly autobiographical like my first, still unpublished, novel [*Cevdet Bey and Sons*]. Perhaps my personal story can be summed up as such, that I come from a very crowded family of lots of uncles, cousins. I loved religious holidays, not because of its religion, but it's like Thanksgiving Day, all the family coming together, grandma, cooks, maids, uncles, playing in the garden, chatting, gossiping. There's a lot of that in my first two books because that's what I saw in my life. [. . .] I, like García Márquez, [write] kind of crowded families, little fights, family property fights and, unlike Márquez, lots of, I mean, he has lots of politics, politics about the future of the country, politics about resistance to the West, politics about this or that.

DR: So in this story, three grandchildren go to visit their grandmother, Fatma. Describe Fatma for us.

OP: Fatma is heavily based on my maternal and paternal grandmothers. They were both—perhaps the blood still continues with me—very solitary. They, especially my maternal grandmother, lived forty years alone in a huge mansion, not unlike in William Faulkner's short story "A Rose for Emily," almost in a gothic setting. My grandmother is living in a wooden old mansion where 90 percent of the building is not even used. My paternal grandmother also had a combination of butler and cook, and they were alone together, but their friendship was so interesting, something that you would see in Chekhov stories and plays.

[. . .]

DR: So Fatma is there with one character [Recep] who's very important in this novel. He is a tragic figure. He is a dwarf. He is a person who serves her, who is very faithful to her but is resented by the other children.

OP: Slightly resented, slightly protected. They also like him because he is protecting their grandma, giving them tips, advice, and clues on how to treat her. And of course there is also a dark secret in the family that I will not give away on this program. You will see that if you read the novel. But what was interesting for me was to do a sort of a panoramic landscape of Turkey in the 1980s, also including all the political parties, the leftist, the right-wingers. And in those years they were brutally fighting in the streets. [. . .]

DR: I want to go back for a moment to Fatma because she begins as a very sheltered middle-class fifteen-year-old girl. [. . .] And she marries a much, much older man who is very politically involved. He leaves her a lot. She's by herself a great deal.

OP: Her husband, Selahattin, has political ambitions and radical ideas that he wants his wife, Fatma, to acquire, while she's essentially conservative and doesn't even buy the feminist ideas her husband wants her to believe. This is a typical dilemma. There is in this book an influence of correspondence between my grandfather and my maternal grandmother. My grandfather went to Berlin to do a PhD. [. . .] They would marry boys before sending them to Europe so that they wouldn't be seduced by European girls. Anyway, and then [. . .] my aunt found these old letters in which he writes [. . .] to his woman back in Turkey saying, "Here, women believe in something called feminism. What do you think of it? Women promote that they should also vote—shouldn't we do this kind of thing in Turkey?" And giving a more enlightened—

DR: So he is much more progressive than she, in his thinking.

OP: Yes. This is unfortunately a typical situation in the non-Western world where men are educated. And then they not only bring Western ideas but also impose feminism on women, too.

DR: Well, but if you look at the other parts of the Middle East you have men imposing non-Western ideas on women. So Turkey—

OP: Turkey always aspires to be Westernized, part of Europe. And it's typical here, just like Russia, that the ruling elite is more pro-Western than the rest of the country. In fact, Turkey's Occidentalism is troubled by the fact that it's promoted by the upper classes.

DR: Now, one thing that her husband does—Selahattin is his name—he takes Fatma's jewels from her dowry and sells them. It breaks her heart.

OP: It breaks her heart, but then that's understandable because he is an ambitious man. He takes her jewels and sells them, not to misspend them. He publishes books, he writes encyclopedias. He wants to do some idealistic things for his country.

DR: So, he comes to the marriage expecting her dowry to help to finance his ambitions.

OP: Well, not exactly because they have some economic problems. This is at the beginning of the novel, because he's a political exile and he cannot practice. He cannot work as a doctor in Istanbul. And you cannot make money in a little fishermen's community at the beginning of the novel. [. . .] That's the first generation. Then the book chronicles three generations and in that sense, just like, say, Turgenev's *Fathers and Sons*, is questioning Turkey's history, problematizing, exploring the ambitions of the Republican secular Jacobean pro-Western first generation. And then what happened to them? And then we see the present situation as the novel unfolds.

DR: It's interesting because the eldest grandson Faruk is himself a historian, but he's questioning his own job. What is it he's questioning and do you see yourself in him?

OP: I have shared all my life in my character Faruk's desire for, or romantic involvement with, Ottoman history, a history that is not chronicled enough. A history, which even for the locals, is exotic, mysterious, rich, but is not cataloged. [. . .] So he's randomly working on some documents and trying to [. . .] come out with a story, trying to feel the clues for a story in an archive. While he's frustrated also by the country's present situation, where right-wing terror and left-wing terror bolt the country into a sort of deadlock or dead end. In *Silent House*, what I discovered were my youthful frustrations, angers related to Turkey's problems then. That in a democracy what you need is concession, understanding, identifying with Others. While here everyone in *Silent House* is shouting, expressing himself, herself, ideas about Turkey's anti-Western future, secular future—

DR: —without regard for Others.

OP: [. . .] I'd love to talk more about the grandmother, who is a central character. [. . .] She's conservative and her grandchildren who visit her with respect but with also a tender smile on their lips, looking at the strangeness of their grandmother. Her stories are so old-fashioned, her conservative behavior of trying to cover herself, on one hand, while also believing in Western ideas and she had a very Occidentalist husband, on the other hand, is a typically Turkish—or I would say a typically Middle Eastern—

DR: How long has she been a widow by the time the grandchildren come?

OP: Both my maternal grandfather and paternal grandfathers died young. And both my maternal grandmothers lived till their nineties. And I was always sitting on their laps and learning about the world from their point of view. I spent my childhood learning a lot from both grandmothers. Especially my paternal grandmother was sort of a school to me because she was educated to be a high school history teacher. She taught me how to read and write before even I went to school. She believed, not unlike my character here that is very conservative, in Western ideas.

Orhan Pamuk: "A Book Is a Promise"

Sameer Rahim / 2012

From *The Telegraph*, November 9, 2012, https://www.telegraph.co.uk/culture/books/book reviews/9663819/Orhan-Pamuk-A-book-is-a-promise.html.

In Orhan Pamuk's second novel, *Silent House*, published in Turkey in 1983 and newly translated into English, the lovelorn Hasan secretly looks through his beloved's handbag while she is out swimming. Among the suntan lotion, wallet, hair clips, and cigarettes, he spies a green comb. Before she returns, he swipes the comb, keeping it as a memento of his unrequited passion.

"Before I reread the novel, I had forgotten about this moment," Pamuk tells me when I meet him at his publisher's offices. Objects are incredibly important in the fiction of the Nobel Prize winner: in *My Name Is Red*, his murder mystery set among Ottoman miniaturist painters, one chapter is narrated by a coin. Pamuk's object obsession was brought to new heights in his wonderful 2009 novel, *The Museum of Innocence*, in which the narrator, Kemal, like Hasan, in unrequited love, collects dozens of things owned by his beautiful cousin Füsun and arranges them in a museum.

[. . .]

In other respects, Hasan in *Silent House* is a very different character from the upper-class dilettante Kemal from *The Museum of Innocence*. Hasan has dropped out of school, is hanging out with Turkish nationalists. He falls for an upper-class leftist with a taste for Turgenev. His story ends in violence.

I wonder where this pervasive longing comes from. "In classical Islamic literature, the desire for the beloved is a metaphor for the desire for God," says Pamuk. "But in my novel, Hasan's longing, in all its radicalism, reflects a desire for a better life. I like that idea; it's an artistic idea. But it's also a very realistic idea. We fall in love more deeply when we're unhappy." [. . .]

He is delighted the Turkish public took so warmly to *The Museum of Innocence*. "It was a sweet reception—not something, I confess, I was used to from the Turkish media. *The Museum of Innocence* is not about politics;

it's a love story, but I think it's political in the sense that it wants to capture how a man suppresses a woman. The more he is in love, the more he suppresses her—a typical non-Western, Middle Eastern situation."

Not that one should make easy assumptions about the place of women in Turkish society. "I have seen so many photos of women on the covers of English books about feminism and Islam," he says. "It's almost nearly always the same photo: two women wearing headscarves, driving around on a motorcycle, or using a computer, or doing something modern. These are naïve, almost uneducated Western responses in understanding what is happening. They seemingly imply that if you wear a headscarf you don't ever leave the house, whereas actually, you only wear the headscarf in order to leave the house."

In an unusual twist, *The Museum of Innocence* is not only a novel: It is also now an actual museum. In April this year Pamuk opened for real what his character Kemal created in his fiction: a collection of beloved Füsun's objects arranged according to his memories. It is an "uncanny" project, he admits, but one that has happily taken him back to his roots as an architecture student and an artist. [. . .]

Pamuk corrects me when I describe it as though it were, like a film, the museum version of the novel. "It's not that I wrote the novel first and it was successful, and I thought let's do an adaptation. I wrote the novel as I collected the objects that would end up in the museum." To help him describe them in the novel, the author bought his character's dress, earrings, and slippers, now displayed in the museum. "Postcards, photos, objects, not only Füsun's, but the whole epoch," he says, twitching with excitement. "It was a desire to grasp that period with objects."

He carries on: "When people read a novel six hundred-pages long, six months pass and all they will remember are five pages. They don't remember the text—instead they remember the sensations the text gives them. In the Museum of Innocence, we are trying to give illustrations to those emotions. The layout of the museum is based on the chapters of the novel: the novel has eighty-three chapters so the museum has eighty-three display cabinets, and each box corresponds to the emotion of that chapter."

One of the most extraordinary exhibits is the collection of Füsun's 4,213 cigarette stubs saved by Kemal. Each one is handcrafted to represent Füsun's emotional state on the day she smoked it: some are twisted from when she angrily crushed it on the ashtray, some only half-smoked from when she had to leave early; all have traces of red lipstick. If this were not detailed enough, Pamuk writes a sentence under each one adding up to a miniature history of their relationship: "You're very cautious," "Late-night shame," "There is no turning back."

"It didn't take too long—but it's fun," he says, bursting into laughter. "A lot of work—but all good fun!" He took six months off his forthcoming novel—also set in seventies' Istanbul, but this time from the point of view of a street vendor—to complete the project. Since the museum opened it has been well attended—about one-third are tourists and about two-thirds Turks.

Making a real museum memorial using a fictional person you have created might indicate that Pamuk has become as obsessed as his character. "I'm not an obsessive collector," he says. "I perhaps have sixteen thousand books and wouldn't mind if one was stolen. A collector is a person who has sixteen thousand books and he is proud to have not read any of them. I'm not like that—I use them and read them."

Pamuk has the habit of slipping a character called "Orhan Pamuk" into his novels: In *Silent House* he is "supposedly writing a novel"; in *The Museum of Innocence*, he is at Kemal's engagement party, chain-smoking with a "mocking smile." Why is he so interested in blurring the boundary between fiction and reality? "I appear in my novels not necessarily in a Hitchcock way," he says. "Not to make people wonder what is fiction and what is reality, nothing like that, but I appear to remind the reader that this is fiction."

Has he put his own picture in the museum? "I appear," he teases. "There are little hints to me and my family, private jokes, but you don't miss much if you don't get it."

He has lived with these objects for so long they are not mere fictional props but, like the books on his shelf, resonant with gathered meaning. "All art is about seeing other worlds through the details of this world. Holding a copy of a book is akin to holding optimism in your hand—that you will follow the story, you will learn about the human heart. A book is a promise."

Orhan Pamuk on Taksim Square, the Effects of *Breaking Bad*, and Why the Future of the Novel Is in the East

Pankaj Mishra / 2013

From the *New Republic*, July 29, 2013, https://newrepublic.com/article/113948/orhan-pamuk-interview-taksim-square-erdogan-literature.

Pankaj Mishra: There seem to be two common descriptions of your work in the English-speaking world. One is of you as a Turkish writer, addressing Turkey's history. The other is of you as an international writer, engaged in the project of creating a world literature. Neither of those descriptions seems to me to be quite right. Your work seems to belong to the tradition of people like Dostoevsky or Junichirō Tanizaki [1886–1965], who are writing about societies where the biggest preoccupation seems to be incomplete modernity, societies that have been prescribed the project of catching up with the West.

Orhan Pamuk: I agree with this description. One side of me is very busy paying attention to the details of life, the humanity of people, catching the street voices, the middle-class, upper middle-class secret lives of Turks. The other side is interested in history and class and gender, trying to get all of society in a very realistic way.

PM: What was the initial reaction in Turkey to a writer who belonged very much to the secular elite, drawing upon Ottoman history, Islamic history, in the Western art form of the novel?

OP: At first, some people were a bit upset and grumpy. I was not using the pure Turkish that the previous generation of writers had used. I used, not excessively, the language of my grandmother—including Ottoman, Persian, Arabic words, which Turks use daily. And so they were grumpy about that. I remember also when I was showing some of my early work, people would say, "Why are you interested in all this failed Ottoman history? Why won't you catch up with today's political problems?" I wanted to tell a romantic and dark side of Ottoman history that was also slightly political, saying to the previous generation of writers, "Look, I'm interested in Ottoman things, and I'm not afraid of it, and I'm doing something creative."

[...]

PM: I came across this line of yours about the period from 1975 to 1982, when murder and political violence and state oppression were at their heights: "To lock myself up in a room to write a new history, a new story with allegories, obscurities, silences, and never-heard sounds, is of course better than to write another history of defects that seeks to explain our defects by means of other defects."

OP: Around the age of thirty, I began to learn that complaint is the sweetest thing in the non-Western world. You're complaining about corruption, you're complaining about lack of this, lack of that. But in the end, that doesn't make good fiction. Good fiction is about asserting the beauties of the world, inventing a new, positive thing. Where am I going to get that? And it should be original; it should not be clichéd. So the way I looked at history was not to accuse it of failure. In a way, my generation was asking a naïve question: Where did we fail? Meaning Ottomans. Why didn't we come up with the bourgeoisie like Europe? They were always trying to answer this question.

PM: That question is now asked in different ways: Why has Turkey turned Islamist? There is the assumption that secularization leads to the development of progressive political forces and progressive art forms, but now Turkey seems to be going back and becoming more Muslim.

OP: I would say politically and also culturally, that this change is not that deep really. Perhaps the class that I belong to doesn't have political power anymore, but I feel that my generation has the cultural power. And yes, maybe Turkey has an Islamist conservative government, but on the other hand, they are not culturally that powerful. Culture is represented by—I wouldn't say the left, but definitely by the secularists. That's why, until recently, the minister of culture in Erdoğan's government was a secular, leftist guy, who was just fired some six months ago.

PM: But do you think the AK Party [Justice and Development Party] really feels its cultural powerlessness in that way?

OP: No, they feel powerful now. For quite a long time, the AK Party and all these conservatives always appropriated secular guys and—I don't want to say used them, which is a bad word—but encouraged them: Just write whatever you want, you can even express your secular ideas in our newspaper. Because at that time, they were insecure. They didn't know about modern culture.

They all felt provincial, backward. They felt they didn't even know how to run newspapers' art pages; they always borrowed. But they're not borrowing anymore.

PM: [. . .] I have come across a lot of praise for Erdoğan's toughness among leading politicians in Indonesia and Pakistan. They say, "We need a man like that to put the army and the crazies back in the barracks and to make the transition from decades of despotism or military rule."

OP: Yes, he is a brave guy in the sense that he can say no to the army. On the other hand, he was cleverly negotiating with Europe—saying, "Hey, you want to take Turkey in?" And also, "Help me, so the army won't throw me out." He also learned that hard-core Islamic policies would scare Turkish voters. Necmettin Erbakan, the previous Islamist, was more fundamentalist, but if he followed that ideology, he would lose votes. At the beginning, Erdoğan took a more modest approach—"I'll respect your culture, I'll respect your opera," or whatever. Now he trusts himself more, his party is more self-confident, and he doesn't need Europe, because the army is marginalized. It may be that he's feeling too arrogant.

PM: Let me take a leap here and go to *Snow*.

OP: Both *My Name Is Red* and *Snow* were written with the projection that political Islam may one day come into power.

PM: What was the reaction to *Snow* here?

OP: *Snow* is my most popular book in the United States. But in Turkey, it was not as popular as *My Name Is Red*, or even *The Museum of Innocence*, because the secular leaders didn't want this bourgeois Orhan trying to understand these headscarf girls.

PM: The review by Christopher Hitchens has the same expectation: Here is Orhan Pamuk trying to interpret the East for us. But why is he not interpreting in the way we want him to? Why is he soft on the Islamists?

OP: For me, the novelty is trying to identify with someone like Blue, who is much more of a hard-core fundamentalist than Erdoğan. Obviously, I'm also against his political program, and I wanted my readers to at least have a sense of a radical Islamist's point of view.

[. . .]

PM: There is also a character in the book who makes the journey from being a leftist to being a fundamentalist.

OP: That's someone who would probably be in Erdoğan's party today.

PM: This is a journey a lot of people in Muslim countries have made.

OP: Especially poets. So many poets who were very harsh Marxists in their youth, who were admirers of Western civilization, switched to Islam.

PM: The pattern seems to show that secular ideologies have been exhausted. And at some point, a lot of these people made the decision to embrace—

OP: The nation, the culture, history, the idea of belonging.

PM: What agitated a lot of the readers of the book at that time, including Hitchens, is that the book is portraying devout Muslims, or political Muslims, in a sympathetic light, when Turkey is already making the journey from religion to modernity. So why do we need a modern, Western writer talking about these people in a sympathetic way?

OP: The duty of the novelist, if he or she is going to be ethical, is to see the world through a character's point of view rather than obeying some theoretical inevitability. And believe me, those inevitabilities in history never work out. It's always something else.

[. . .]

PM: Is the economic success of countries like Turkey or India or China going to breathe new life into the novel?

OP: I think so. I strongly believe that. The novel is a middle-class art. And we see the proliferation of middle classes in India, China, definitely in Turkey, so everyone is writing novels. If you want to predict the future, I can predict that in Europe, in the West, the importance of literary novels will decrease, while in China, India, popular literature will continue. Innovation will come from there, because the populations are large, there will be a lot of production. I'm writing a novel now about immigration to Istanbul. Starting in the late 1950s, especially in the '60s, immigration to Istanbul from the poorest parts of Turkey began. And then Turkish shantytowns were beginning to be built in the mid-1950s, but in the '60s, they flourished. This is not a middle-class changing of cultures. This is the proletariat, the most dispossessed. I have assistants right now doing research, talking to people, reporting to me. How did street vendors or yogurt sellers in the 1970s behave? That kind of small detail. When I was collecting material, I said to myself, my God, I'm doing what Stendhal did, what Balzac did. All the experience from after Stendhal, from after Balzac, from Jorge Luis Borges to Thomas Pynchon, from surrealistic things to James Joyce or William Faulkner or Gabriel García Márquez—I can benefit from their experience. But essentially, I'm doing what Stendhal did in *The Red and the*

Black—a poor guy coming to town and striving—but in many different forms. Which proves that the art of the novel has immense continuity, because it has elasticity. It can use anthropology, it can use essays, New Journalism, blogs, the internet. You can make novels out of everything. Journalists call and say, "Mr. Pamuk, the art of the novel is dying." No, it's not. It's strong, everyone is writing them, everyone wants to read them. Maybe we're not so interested in what is happening in London, but we're interested in what's happening in Zadie Smith's new novel. I think the form has immense possibilities.

PM: In a place like America, the TV serial is now slowly replacing the novel—*The Wire* or *Breaking Bad*.

OP: I agree. Replacing Dickens. They're sophisticated. That really kills the novel—it takes away the regular pleasures of reading novels. The power of those sophisticated serials is that you watch it with your wife, your friends, and you can immediately chat about it. It's a great pleasure to enjoy a work of art and to be able to share it with someone you care about.

PM: Going back to recent events, do you think the conservative varieties of political Islam will only grow because of this process of millions of people coming into cities during a time of democratization, when people can express their political preferences?

OP: Partly, what you see with the Taksim and Gezi Park events is that, once the country is rich, the sense of individuality is stronger. You can't run it using the old authoritarian ways. Even if you control the media, as Erdoğan did, individuals go out and revolt in the park. And it was not organized. Political parties were not capable of managing it. Moderates and the modern individual can live together in a society if everyone knows their limits. The problem here was that Erdoğan was behaving like an old-fashioned, 1930s ruler. Doing everything, managing everything. Saying, "I have 50 percent, shut up." Well, yes, you have 50 percent, but we have seventy-two million people who are not completely like you. The Taksim events were a good way of saying to Erdoğan, or to any future leader of Turkey, or to anybody in this part of the world, that once a country gets too rich and complex, the leader may think himself to be too powerful. But individuals also feel powerful. And they just go out in parks and say no. They may not have a political program and a party, but they go out and say an impressive no. I was really happy about that.

[...]

PM: Do you find, as a writer, that you carry too much of the burden of explaining these very complex problems to the outside world?

OP: Yeah, the Taksim events happened, and my mail was full of letters saying, "Orhan, please explain them to us. . . ." I used to do this fifteen years ago, but I don't want to be a journalist. Maybe I'm old. I will try to write something poetic, more personal, than There is this party, and that party, and social democracy. The younger generation should do it. I don't want to explain Turkey in a journalistic way to anyone. Except you, Pankaj. [*Laughter*]

On Writing *A Strangeness in My Mind*

Erdağ Göknar / 2015

From Duke University, Nasher Museum, November 12, 2015, https://www.youtube.com/watch?v=6Fm-tIB8JHc.

Erdağ Göknar: The Nasher Museum is a perfect setting for tonight's event, as Pamuk's work embraces the idea of the novelist as archivist and curator. All of the facets of Pamuk's fiction are orchestrated through the city of Istanbul, a space that has become the memory of his fiction. It is perhaps not surprising, for someone who has a great love for walking through the deserted city streets at night, that the ideal protagonist would be one who does the same—a street vendor, Mevlut Karataş, a seller of the fermented wheat drink, boza. In *A Strangeness in My Mind*, Pamuk's version of the flaneur is an Anatolian migrant to the city whose strangeness is the alienation and displacement of a rural migrant who enters the city from the margins. *A Strangeness in My Mind* shifts Pamuk's narrative repertoire, as most of his novels do, this time into social history. The three-generational structure used here hasn't been used in a Pamuk novel since his first one, *Cevdet Bey and Sons*. *A Strangeness in My Mind* is not an ironic tale, but is a realist one, and even ethnographic. As with any ethnography, it is predicated on fieldwork. It is a class-conscious novel. It tells the rise not of the bourgeoisie, secular elite as in *Cevdet Bey*, but of a newly enfranchised Muslim middle class. These are the neighborhoods and characters who make up the base of Erdoğan's AK Party [Justice and Development Party], who has just won another parliamentary majority. That is, the novel offers both literary innovations as well as political revelations.

Orhan Pamuk: So how to go into a novel that took six years to write that covers a lot of social history? This one private individual's novel about a street yogurt vendor who loses his job. [. . .] This book is a sea of microhistories; it also wants to chronicle the change in Istanbul life seen through the point of view of people who migrated to the city from poor Anatolian villages. I was born in Istanbul in 1952; it was a city of a million. And this book opens in 1969; it was a city of two and a half million. Now, they say it's fifteen or sixteen million. This novel, in many ways, chronicles this development where the unregistered government land is appropriated by peasants who come from poor parts of Anatolia and do various jobs in connection with local gangs, mafia, and semipolitical organizations. [. . .]

All the yogurt sellers of Istanbul in the 1950s, '60s, '70s used to sell boza—a slightly fermented wheat alcoholic beverage. If you drink three glasses of boza, it is equal to one glass of beer. [. . .]

People who came to Istanbul penniless almost, but with some connections, built their own shanty houses—*gecekondu* in Turkish—with their own hands and tried to get government papers—*tapu* [deeds] in Turkish—so that it will legitimize their appropriating the land. There are now forty-floor, fifty-floor high rises in those places, and some of those people who came there in the 1960s, even '50s, now, just because they own this land, are rich. [. . .]

EG: I wanted to talk about something you alluded to, which was the process you go through when you're writing. And a novel like this requires a certain amount of fieldwork. And so, what is the process involved in preparing to write for you?

OP: So I decided to write a novel about a street vendor who loses his job. [. . .] The motivation, energy of the book is also related to my enchantment with, my encounter with, this person who seemed not only as if he's coming from the poorest of poorest of Anatolian villages but he seems to be also coming from Ottoman times. This is the romantic setting of buying boza, enjoying boza: Its ritual of inviting someone up to your apartment and buying something strange. [. . .] I'm not exaggerating, when you buy boza, you are also more interested in the ritual. And when I began to write this novel, [. . .] I talked to many, many, many not only street boza vendors, but street sellers. But 90 percent of the boza sellers knew that it's the ritual and romantic evocation of the Ottoman times, and perhaps the way middle classes, upper middle classes, pity the poor person, street vendor, who is working in a cold night under the snow to make ends meet—this is what's at stake in a boza encounter.

So, you may ask me, "How did you know that?" Well, that is because I had a chat with boza sellers, but not only chat, but also organized interviews. I not only did interviews with boza sellers and many, many street vendors or, say, retired policemen who were managing, overseeing Beyoğlu [an Istanbul neighborhood] streets in the 1970s and '80s, who would tell me [. . .] all the stories of the street life in Beyoğlu. The book is heavily based on what cultural studies professors would call oral history. But then I did oral history in my own way. I also had friends [. . .] and they also helped me in getting information, in getting details you would not find in books.

My novels are based, depending on the novel, on research. [. . .] I always enjoy this and my research never stops. [. . .] And the vanity of the author is not based on research but on the way my imagination converts this information into a novel, into a plot, into a story, into three-dimensional human beings. [. . .]

EG: I liked what you said about the boza seller coming out of the past in a sense—the Ottoman past and what that represents. That's interesting to think about if you think about the boza seller at night calling out, it's sort of a haunting call. But there's a way in which it also resonates as a metonym for the Ottoman past perhaps, the Islamic past perhaps. And there is this one very interesting scene early on where the boza seller is called up to the very, kind of, secular modern party and they want to have a discussion with this person. It's slightly demeaning. They're sort of talking down to him a little bit, and there's an interesting back-and-forth there that brings up the issue of politics. The question has to do with the position of the boza seller and politics in the present, based on what that boza seller represents in the past.

OP: Yes, there is a lot of politics in the book. But neither me nor [my protagonist] Mevlut is actually a political person. With that, I mean we are not initially motivated by politics. I have found myself in political situations because I just react to political developments in Turkey. Mevlut has many political friends but he is a street vendor who wants to survive, and he doesn't have strong political opinions. Mevlut has ultraright wing nationalist friends and also Alevi Turkish leftist/communist friends. And he also visits a sheikh in a [Sufi] dervish lodge, especially in the late 1990s, and it's sort of a modern dervish lodge. If he had strong political opinions and self-imposed moral constraints, he wouldn't be able to one day talk with a friend, leftist friends, even write slogans on the wall, and the next day be friendly with the sheikh of a dervish lodge. In fact, he is hiding these various activities from his connection with various groups in the city from each other. Characters with strong political and moral convictions in novels cannot navigate from one corner of that society to the other. That's why Mevlut doesn't have strong opinions. [. . .]

EG: The novel in a sense gives the background of the growth of Istanbul from a somewhat neglected city to really a global city, and from 1969 to 2012 you see an incredible amount of growth and change in the city. All of your novels deal with Istanbul in very particular ways. Could you talk a little bit about the importance of the city to your work, but also the way that different facets of Istanbul emerge out of different novels, so the Istanbul of *The Black Book* will be different from the Istanbul of *A Strangeness in My Mind*? What is the significance of the city?

OP: I lived all my life in Istanbul and I wanted to write about what I knew about humanity. And indirectly, since I came across humanity in Istanbul, and I was not aware of this at the beginning, my novels were all set, most of them, in Istanbul. [. . .] When I began writing my early books in the 1970s in Turkey, the main body of Turkish fiction was dominated by the so-called peasant novelists. [. . .] I had no connection to that kind of life. I was writing more about middle-class and upper middle-class secular, Westernized Istanbul bourgeois life in my novels. [. . .]

The book [*A Strangeness in My Mind*] also deals with that: What happens to us if the city we are living in grows from a million to fifteen million? [. . .] My autobiography *Istanbul* ends in 1973, which I published thirty years later in 2003, and a young generation of Turkish writers already told me that "Mr. Pamuk, your book and your sense of Istanbul as being black and white, poor and melancholy, is not the one we have. Our Istanbul is more colorful, more happy, more prosperous. And I agree with them." I argue that cities don't have essential attributes. [. . .] But I'm telling all this to say that there is not one Istanbul even in my novels. [. . .] When my autobiography *Istanbul* ends in 1973, more or less, my character Mevlut comes to Istanbul, and this novel covers the next forty years, and they are different in mood.

EG: You've been known for writing novels that change form. Each time that you're experimenting with a new type of form, each time a new novel comes out. Say a little bit about the trajectory of that change and form and how it reflects in this particular work.

OP: When I was writing this novel, I'm happy to say that I have also seen that the youthful, postmodernist in me is still alive and kicking. [*Laughter*] One of the self-imposed constraints, and I do that a lot when I write a novel, is for example, when I was writing *The Museum of Innocence*, the constraint was to pay attention to objects I should exhibit in the museum and never end the chapter without covering, in detail, a few objects, for example. [. . .]

I decided that I would write a novel like that in the manner of Zola, Dickens, and so forth and so on. But as I was writing the book [*A Strangeness in My Mind*], I was not satisfied with what I had, perhaps because of the strength and authenticity and sincerity of all the interviews that I did, and my friends did, and the texts I had, and my conversations with street vendors of Istanbul. Not only street vendors, but police, other guys, insurance people, electricity people, all sorts of mafia kind of people, taxi drivers. I felt that I wanted to represent the convincing power of these monologues I had, or interviews. So I began a little bit of an experiment. What if I insert, say, a third-person singular of a Dickensian or Balzac or Emile Zola novel, the first-person singular, which complements or sometimes argues or rejects or tells stories that refute what the main third-person singular narrative voice is saying. [. . .]

I decided to develop what I initially implemented in *My Name Is Red* in this novel, a novel that unfolds like a nineteenth-century Dickens novel, where suddenly characters that are mentioned begin to take the microphone and begin to talk and say, "It's not like that actually." They begin to negate each other, begin to be unreliable, and you begin to suspect the truth content of their monologues.

EG: Could you talk a little bit about the details that emerge in this novel, like youths going out and putting communist posters on mosque walls; the idea that there's a woman, Neriman, out there that the main character follows; the wonderful—you have this a lot in your work; there are usually a lot of archival scenes in way or another—the wonderful archive of the electric company, right, that tells its own history of the city. Are these things that you come across and they're gems that you find and you know immediately that this will be working very well in the plot of the novel? How does that unfold for you—the discovery of these details?

OP: [. . .] They all come in various different ways. I may have a chat with the guy, or it's just that they want to talk to me. Then I say, "Why don't you come in and tell me and drink coffee?" I like meeting people and talking and opening up. [. . .] Also, after a while I honestly tell them, "Actually, I'm not a journalist. I'm a novelist." [. . .] A novelist is a person whose tentacles should be open to all the wonders of life—paying attention to it, taking notes, then remembering them, then thinking how I would integrate this detail, this story. [. . .] I love this. I love the research part of writing novels.

"I Am an Accidental Politician"

Bruce Robbins / 2016

From *boundary 2* 43, no. 2 (2016), https://doi.org/10.1215/01903659-3469907.

Bruce Robbins: From the interviews I've seen, it seems that everyone wants you to talk about Gezi Park, the Arab Spring, and the political situation in the Middle East. If it's all right, can we talk a bit about literature?

Orhan Pamuk: I am an accidental politician. If you come from a troubled part of the world that is not well represented in the culturally dominant West, and if you're a bit successful, everyone asks you questions about politics. This was and still is my life's dilemma. I am essentially a literary person: an introvert who would be happy to stay in one room and write all the time. But of course I am also a person with a conscience. I have leftist ideas, whatever that means today. What I worry about is the sort of situation I will now describe. You give five years to a book, then you do an interview in Denmark or Spain. The interviewer realizes that you devoted five years to the book, that you are an introverted person, and he does the interview accordingly. But at the end he asks one final question: "I'm sorry, my editor pressured me to ask this. . . ." It's a silly, obvious question, but you want to be nice, so you answer. And the next day it's that answer to the final question, the political question, that is on the front page, and you are reduced once again to playing the public persona, the Jean-Paul Sartre scolding everyone. I am a bit averse to the Sartre/Zola attitude, though I have learned a good deal from it: that being a writer is not just a responsibility to write beautiful books, but also—unfortunately, it's rare that I say "fortunately"—a responsibility to the public. I am torn between being obliging and demanding that people recognize I gave five years to the book. Five years of solitude! [. . .]

BR: In *Silent House*, one thing you do to expand the form of the family novel is to begin with the point of view of the servant [Recep], who's also a dwarf, and then return to that point of view a lot.

OP: It was Trotsky who asked, "What about the servants? Why are they left out of bourgeois literature?" That remark stayed with me. I may not be a writer with a political agenda, but do we really need politics to understand what Trotsky means? The relationship between the old lady, the grandmother, and her servant/cook is based on the relationship between my paternal grandmother and her cook. She humiliated him, mocked him publicly to other members of the family. And he would make faces, trying to save face, so to speak. That book is quite autobiographical in that sense. The dwarf also serves to connect the story with the neighborhood.

BR: It's the connection with the neighborhood that I wanted to emphasize. That's harder for readers. They like the dining table but may not be ready for the point of view of a fascist thug, a poor boy who's in love with a rich girl. Some of the years of work you put into that novel went into making the plot function in a larger, more expansive, more ambitious way.

OP: Yes, of course. There is a strong demand for the representation of the whole nation through the aristocratic dining table, or now, the car and what you can see out of the car windows. The upper classes don't want to see themselves as alienated from the nation. We all want to see our problems as national problems, even if we think we as individuals are unique or unrepresentative. Proust didn't worry about representing the nation. Perhaps that's what gives him such purity. But even Proust was involved in the Dreyfus affair. We never want to say that our imagination is only about the upper classes. Tolstoy certainly didn't. He created characters like himself who were interested in mowing hay with the peasants. To be a writer, you have to have a crack in your head that stops you from identifying solely with your own class. Like Thomas Mann, you enjoy or hate or just observe your elite culture, but there's a crack in your mind that distances you from it. One has to be a bit of a Narodnik. For the Narodniks in Russia, it was the peasants; in Turkey in the 1950s and 1960s, it was the proletariat. Now it's the nation. In a troubled mind there is always a linkage to the nation. That's what the dining table and car conversation links you to.

BR: Tell me how you feel about the category of national allegory.

OP: You want me to punch Fredric Jameson? [*Laughter*] I'll ask you to delete that. [. . .] What I would say to Jameson's idea of national allegory is not so radically different from what I would say to Bertrand Russell's *A History of Western Philosophy*. That book has fifty pages in it on non-Western philosophy. That's not enough. If you don't know about non-Western philosophy, don't talk about it at all. Don't do it in fifty pages or ten pages. The same about non-Western literature. If you don't know about it, don't say anything about it. The example Jameson gave from Lu Xun was not even a good example. But of course there are many national allegories. The Turkish writer Tanpınar, for example, his *Time Regulation Institute* is a perfect national allegory. But Kafka is also a writer of national allegories! *Moby-Dick* is the biggest national allegory of all! All literature has an allegorical side. I'm a touchy non-Westerner. I'd prefer if we got off this topic. [. . .]

BR: Since you were just talking about postmodernism, and *boundary 2* has a certain historical connection to postmodernism, I thought I would ask you whether that category still means anything to you. Do you think it's worth talking about today?

OP: There's a famous story about a French lady who is asked, "Which French king do you prefer?" She says, "Louis XV." They say, "But there's nothing so special about him." And she replies, "I was young then." [*Laughter*] It's not just that in the period of postmodernism I was young; it's also the fact that I had just come to the United States for the first time—don't forget that I was a young Turkish boy who had never left Turkey. So I leave Turkey, I come to New York in 1985, where my wife was doing her PhD. I remember the bookshops. Postmodernism was everywhere, and I was eager for anything American. I don't regret it. Today I can say that there is conservative postmodernism, a highbrow postmodernism, a bourgeois postmodernism. There is also leftist postmodernism for the Third Worlders, and I care a great deal about that. It offers a gentle critique both of modernism and of development theory. It learns to pay attention to the culture of real people and not pigeonhole it, to recognize the genuine vitality of that culture rather than seeing it as doomed to vanish.

BR: I was also wondering whether, in the beginning, postmodernism served also to protect you against the demands people made on you to be a realistic, faithful representer of your culture.

OP: There were no such demands. In my youth—say, between the ages of twenty and thirty-five—there were no political demands made on me. The earlier generation was happy with its leftism, with socialism. Many of these people suffered a lot. They went to jail, their books were banned, they were afraid of the police. They were afraid of getting shot in the streets. I was not political. They pigeonholed me as a "bourgeois," writing about nothing. Even *Silent House* was taken like that. These days I tell them, "See, you were making fun of me for not being political. Now even *Silent House* has become political!" [*Laughter*]

BR: You could say this is evidence of how stupid the West is.

OP: I don't say that. [*Laughter*] I'm saying that unfortunately these well-meaning political guys were a bit vulgar, a bit unsophisticated. They thought too much in terms of black and white. Many of the things literature needs to care about didn't make it into their books.

BR: Many American readers will no doubt be curious about The Museum of Innocence, both the novel and the museum, whose catalog was recently published here as *The Innocence of Objects*. In a recent interview with you in the *Financial Times*, Simon Schama was extremely enthusiastic.

OP: This is what I call a good review. [*Laughter*]

BR: Is there a theory of love in the novel or in the museum? Or are you really more interested in time than in love?

OP: No, there's no theory of love. In Stendhal, yes, there's a theory of love. Maybe the nineteenth century was the right time for theories of love. Balzac also wrote a book about marriage. His book and Stendhal's are how-to books. Of course, they both needed the money. But Stendhal definitely believed in what he wrote. I didn't write *The Museum of Innocence* to develop a theory of love. But of course we all have a galaxy of little interesting points about love, and I put mine into the book. What happens to us when we fall in love, how we get jealous, how we get angry, how there's always an argument with the beloved—how much of all this is in our imagination, in our perpetually disappointed expectations. How you wait for the phone to ring. This is not a theory; it's a phenomenology. [. . .]

BR: And then everything is permitted. . . . Say something more about the word "innocence." Reading the museum catalog, I was a bit surprised to find that it offers a very strong experience which is a bit different from the experience of the museum itself. In this case, the text of the catalog is a strong text in its own right.

OP: The Turkish word is *masumiyet*. If we think of words as little handkerchiefs, their shapes are different even if they cover the same ground. The Turkish *masumiyet* is not Webster's "innocence." In Webster's, one of the word's connotations is "artlessness." We have this in Turkish as well, but it's less pronounced. The Turkish word also includes virginity, while virginity is not such a big component of innocence in English, though it used to be. There is also innocence of class distinctions. The greatest innocence is to live in a classless society. In *The Museum of Innocence* everyone is watching the same television shows. Kemal's upper-class mother and Füsun's petit bourgeois family, the doormen and drivers and other working-class people, they're all watching the same one channel of Turkish TV. There may be class distinctions, but in a sense, all these people are innocent, artless, naïve. My upper-class bourgeois character visits the family of the married cousin twice removed who was his lover and watches television with them for seven years. We are not sure whether he is innocently enjoying all this or just pretending he's innocent. Even the pretension to innocence is a kind of innocence. [. . .]

BR: Talk a little bit about the character of Celal from *The Black Book*. He's not a character in the sense that we live inside him. He's seen entirely from the outside, as the object of the protagonist's quest. It seems to me that through him, you imagine a particular relationship that a writer might have, not just with readers but with the nation.

OP: Celal is based on many, many Turkish newspaper columnists. I have also seen this phenomenon in Arab countries and other poor, non-Western countries where newspaper columnists write more frequently and have more visibility and power. They're not specialists; they're professors of everything. You will buy a newspaper to read a particular columnist. You believe in that guy. He has a sweet voice. You like his style. Like Balzac or Stendhal, these columnists might write one day about what love is and the next day on why the Pope and Gorbachev are quarreling. They write about the shape of the electrical poles in the streets of Istanbul. They review books. Some of them used to write six times a week. As a child, I used to read them a lot. I was addicted to some of them.

In my novel, I wanted to come to terms with that voice. As a novelist, I like the conceit of addressing the reader. A prominent columnist in Turkey in the 1950s, or 1960s, or 1970s picks up his pen and talks to the nation, and it's a joy, talking to the nation in a fatherly way. In coffeehouses in small towns and villages, they will buy one newspaper and somebody will read it. Some will get angry, some will write letters. The columnist will sometimes answer the letters. It's admirable. I suppose I'm a bit envious of the way they can engage in a conversation with the nation.

BR: I'm not surprised to hear you say that you're envious. As a novelist, how could you not feel in competition? These columnists have such an intimate relation with their readership. Not so many people read novels.

OP: I didn't win that competition. If I get into a taxi in Turkey, I'll be asked, "What do you do, sir?" "I'm a writer." "For which newspaper? I don't remember your face." [*Laughter*]

BR: You've never been tempted to serialize your novels?

OP: No one ever asked me. I would be happy to. It would be interesting. Constraints like that always make you creative. We're teaching *Anna Karenina* together right now [Robbins and Pamuk coteach a seminar at

Columbia]. It was, of course, serialized. I'm jealous of that period. Every six pages you would need some sort of cliffhanger. [*Laughter*] [. . .]

BR: One of the comments I was fascinated by in your interview with Pankaj Mishra was about TV serials like *The Wire* and *Breaking Bad* having taken over the role of the novel in places like the United States, though less so in other places, perhaps including Turkey.

OP: When the Turkish television boom started in the mid-1980s, every single novelist said, "My God! They're taking our jobs!" But it didn't work out as they had predicted. Don't forget that before the 1980s, television was not so big in Turkey. It started in the mid-1970s, but people didn't watch very much. Then suddenly there were more channels. Between 1985 and 1995 the complaint was that everyone was watching TV and no one was reading. That was the cliché. Fifteen years later, it was clear that it simply wasn't true. Since 2000, both the Turkish economy and the Turkish book industry have boomed unbelievably. When I said all this to Pankaj, I was thinking that, in the end, it's a great joy to revisit the texture of our lives through fiction. Fiction is a way of revisiting our lives ethically, aesthetically, nostalgically. When we read *Anna Karenina*, even our students, who see it as historical, are revisiting their lives. We reweigh the choices we've made. Good serials are doing that, too. They are hard to compete with. So we novelists have to be more literary, more original. We can't write like Balzac anymore. But there are no rules.

BR: It's interesting that these days the Turkish television industry is so successful internationally.

OP: In 1985, the first time I was in the United States, I was invited by the Iowa Writers' Workshop. There I chatted with a Mexican writer. I asked him what he did. He said, "In Mexico, we produce a lot of soap operas. I work for the soap operas." And I thought, "What a developed country Mexico is! They make soap operas and they export them!" Now Turkey is exporting even more television than Mexico.

BR: For the last four years, you and I have been teaching novels together. I wonder whether you have any comments on this experience.

OP: Before my Columbia job started in 2006, I never did university teaching. Everyone thought I was already teaching in Turkey, but no, I wasn't. In Germany and Holland, I participated in one-week seminars on my work, but that was the only previous experience. It was in English. Beginning in 2007, for the first time in my life, I began to teach students. I may have been a prominent international writer, but I was also extremely nervous. What was the source of the nervousness? Many things. I didn't know

American students well enough. I was also worried about my pedagogical limitations. I was afraid of asserting myself too much, being incapable of getting the students to open up, to make them talk. Slowly I've gotten to be more comfortable. With the help of friends like you. What did I learn? Even in the sleepiest class in the middle of the semester there's some brilliant student who says something you never thought of. Sometimes the novels that have become essential parts of my life, like a table or a window in my house, are new to the younger generation. They look at you with blank eyes and want to know what this is all about: "What's the point?" You have to make them feel the frame and enjoy the minor interesting clevernesses that you are manic about. The frame, the details—now I'm a bit more confident about managing all this in a class. About the novels we've been teaching together, *Anna Karenina* and *Demons*: I already knew these novels well. Recently I have been editing a series of classics for my Turkish publisher, and I included these novels. I'm happy to say that I'm teaching novels that are dear to me. I have reread them so many times. I can't say that I understand them definitively, but I've almost memorized these books, event by event, chapter by chapter, paragraph by paragraph. [. . .]

BR: You must be conscious of things that other people will not see in your work if what they are looking for (and looking in your work for) is a "bridge between East and West." What will Western readers miss not because they don't know enough about Turkey but because they want you to be a bridge?

OP: It's true that they won't understand a lot of things because they don't know enough about Turkey. But there's something else. Jumping from national to international readers, there will always be a slight distortion. I agree with David Damrosch that world literature is literature that gains in translation, gets new meanings in the second language. Yet there is also an inevitable distortion.

BR: Some writers, because they are a success at the international level and know they are going to be translated, will write in their original language in a style that will facilitate the task of the translator. As Rebecca Walkowitz [author of *Born Translated: The Contemporary Novel in an Age of World Literature*] has noted, they will choose not to use difficult words so as not to slow down the process of translation.

OP: I only worry about my English translator, with whom I work. I offer you a practical answer to this theoretical question. The translator and I work on the problems together. The other question I've been asked many, many times, always in a nice way, is, "Mr. Pamuk, you know that your books are translated into sixty-one languages. Perhaps you didn't know it before, but now it's a fact. How do you manage this?" The nasty way to put this is, "He's only writing for Americans." Years ago, *The Guardian* did a questionnaire among English writers. I never forgot the answer by A. S. Byatt, who said, "I only think of my English readers." Kazuo Ishiguro said the opposite: "I write for my international audience." I always get trashed on this subject: "He's writing for the foreigners." I always say, "I write for whoever reads me." Now, over the last ten years, the typical ratio is: if I sell ten books, one and a half books are sold in Turkey, and the rest are sold in the rest of the world. I try to be honest. I write knowing this ratio. I write for those who read me. It would be ethically problematic if 85 percent of my readers were outside Turkey, and I said I'm only writing for my Turkish readers.

BR: You may have been forced to speak on political subjects against your will, against your inclinations. But you've done so very bravely.

OP: I am trying to pull myself away from politics. It's not that I'm scared. Turkey has mellowed. Ten years ago, it was hard to talk about the Kurdish issue or other issues. Now I can talk about anything. The world has an abundance of things I want to attack and get angry about. One month after the Taksim events in Turkey, when I made international comments, there was the Egyptian military coup. The chief of staff of the Egyptian army said publicly to the Morsi [Mohamed Morsi, former Egyptian president] people two days before the coup, "Either you get out in two days or I'll handle this." He wasn't looking at the nation; he was looking at the international community, meaning America and Europe. And what did they do? They looked away. As if to say, "Don't say this publicly; just go ahead and do it." And he did. And he killed a lot of people. Generations of Turkish intellectuals were destroyed by military coups. The next generation of Egyptian liberals will hate this coup. I know it from my Turkish experience. Authoritarianism paves the way toward contempt for people's culture, religion, and so on. That's what the military coup is about. It shows an immense disrespect for the culture and the life of the people.

BR: *boundary 2* has recently published a number of essays in favor of secularism.

OP: Good.

BR: We were thinking first about an American context in particular, America not being an especially secular country—in some ways not at all. With your experience of Turkish secularism, what advice could you give to Americans who want to defend secularism but don't want to make certain familiar mistakes?

OP: Secularism is one thing. *Laïcité* is another thing. *Laïcité* holds that government decisions should not be involved in religion. Secularism wants the invisibility of religion. I am both a *laïc* and a secular person, secular in the sense that I don't want to see religion visible everywhere. But I am also a democrat. I want political change to come through democracy, and democracy demands that everyone's beliefs be acknowledged—not respected, but acknowledged. If you're an atheist, okay; if you're a believer, okay. You cannot allow religion to be curtailed by the army. That's not democracy. You don't have to believe in anything yourself, but you have to acknowledge other people's beliefs if you want to be a player in the game.

"I Don't Write My Books to Explain My Country to Others"

Isaac Chotiner / 2017

From slate.com, August 18, 2017, https://slate.com/news-and-politics/2017/08/orhan-pamuk-on-writing-about-turkey-his-work-process-and-his-daily-swim.html.

Isaac Chotiner: How is the process of writing your tenth novel [*The Red-Haired Woman*] different from when you started?

Orhan Pamuk: At the beginning, when I started almost forty years ago, I was more epic, more panoramic, and perhaps more experimental too. But this time, I wanted to write a short novel with metaphysics and philosophy in it. I almost wanted to tell a realistic story about a master well digger and his apprentice. These people I observed in the land next to where I lived in the summer of 1988. It was, again, on an island, and I was writing one of my books. They were the last old-fashioned well diggers, and they were still in business in the peripheries of Istanbul. Because there is not enough government water, especially in the 1970s and '80s, everyone dug a well and found his water in his own garden. I observed as they dug a well the father-and-son relationship between the old master well digger and his teenage disciple. The old master was both teaching and shouting at the boy and, very tenderly, protecting and caring about him. This I saw every day as I went at night downtown. Their relationship moved me, perhaps because I was raised by a father who was not around too much and who never tried to control me. In fact, that's how my father was—did not know much about me.

IC: Is your father still alive? Did he pass away?

OP: No, he passed away.

IC: When did he pass away?

OP: Twelve years ago.

IC: [. . .] Do you remember the feeling that you got when he [your father] read the first thing that you wrote?

OP: He was very kind, very respectful. I was moved by the fact that he didn't criticize me. He treated me, and my brother too, as if we were geniuses, and my relationship with my father set the tone of this book. Besides being—this novel, *The Red-Haired Woman*—as sentimental and [about] personal roots, it's also a fictional comparison of Sophocles's *Oedipus Rex*, which is about killing of the father by the son, as sort of a parricide, and the Persian poet Ferdowsi's classical tale *Shahnameh*, or *Book of Kings*, the story of Rostam and Sohrab, which is also a counterpart to *Oedipus* because this time the father kills the son. It's a filicide. These are canonical texts of Western and Islamic civilizations.

You know, each year, one semester, I teach at Columbia University, and at the top of Columbia University's Butler Library, in big capital letters, is Sophocles, Aristotle, Plato, Shakespeare. Columbia is good at teaching classics. I ask myself, "What about Eastern classics? What about something to compare *Oedipus Rex* with?" We tend to associate Oedipus with individualism because he kills his father, and they still respect him. We tend to associate Rostam, the father who kills his son, with authoritarianism. Why? Because the whole text in Ferdowsi's *Shahnameh* about Rostam and Sohrab is about legitimization of the father killing the son. I think, we moderns, the way we read it, Sophocles's *Oedipus Rex* is also a sort of legitimization of the son killing the father. We respect Oedipus, we understand his pain with our compassion. When we understand him, we also respect his transgression. So, I wanted to write about these things—fathers, sons, lack of fathers, individuality of the son.

IC: How much do you see your work as consciously, as, I don't want to say necessarily a bridging of East and West, but—

OP: When my books began to get translated internationally after mid-1990s, especially in early 2000s, everyone began to call me, "Oh, a bridge between East and West." I didn't like it. Why? Because I don't write my books to explain my country to others. I write—perhaps I'm deceiving myself as naïve—for deeper reasons. [. . .] I'm writing stories. In the end, when they are successful, it explains something, but that's not the motivation. My motivation is not to be a bridge.

IC: What was your first emotional reaction that there had been a coup [the failed coup of July 15, 2016], or that there was an ongoing coup against the current government?

OP: I did not learn about it. I watched it as it happened, really. At 9:20 when it started, I was already getting news from media, from internet, mostly from TV, and I watched it with amazement, horror. I continued to watch until three in the morning, realizing that the military coupists would not be successful, and I took a sleeping pill. I was so manic, so tense, that I realized that I cannot sleep. I was extremely happy that it failed, and I was also grateful for those brave people who went out to the streets and stopped the tanks. These people were not liberals like you and I in the Western European sense, but they were people who were defending Erdoğan, or their party or their democracy. They were not defending my liberal values, but in an indirect way, they defended Turkish democracy.

IC: Do you feel the same way now a year later?

OP: No, I don't feel the same way now. I'm grateful to those people, but the government used the military coup to purge most of the liberals. Most of the people who criticized the government are pushed out of the government offices. There are now forty thousand people in jail and one hundred forty journalists who are imprisoned. Writing fiction books is no problem in Turkey, but if you venture into politics, like journalists, political commentators, you are in trouble or—

IC: [. . .] Has your project, as a sort of writer, changed in some way as the country has changed through the time that you've been—

OP: Good question! [. . .] As a writer, I am definitely changing, but my determination to write—or my love of writing, or my infatuation with everything related to the art of fiction—is still around. In early years, I was writing fiction more like poetry, thinking that every line, every word, every sentence will be the final sentence. I was also trying to be very experimental, postmodern, modern, whatever, experimental. Also, in my early novels I was writing more about my culture, my people, middle-class, upper middle-class, secular, Westernized, European, Turks of Istanbul. This is where I was raised, and this is what I wrote about. Even this book, *The Red-Haired Woman*, is partly about them and partly not about them—the bigger circle, the whole Turkey. I began to write more and more about that second circle. Not only my secular and bourgeois Istanbul, but the bigger, popular, bigger Istanbul that I wrote in *A Strangeness in My Mind*, which is an epic about the forty years of development of Istanbul. This new one [is] a short novel, but again about a change, a poetic change and also about generations, fathers and sons. In fact, this book, in two hundred pages, comes to terms with three generations. [. . .]

IC: So then, just to end where we started, when you're working now in your office, or wherever it is in this beach house that you're in, are you not checking the internet? Are you surrounded by fiction? What's your process?

OP: I am in a summer house, where of course there is internet. I also came to this summer house with a lot of DVDs and books that I want to read. So, I am really very privileged and unique and happy with books, films, work all the time, and of course I'm doing this all the time. As I tell my girlfriend, all the time one feels guilty when one is just happy with books and films and when one's writing when so much horror is happening in one's country. So many guiltless people put into prison in an arbitrary way. It's impossible not to feel guilty, and my solution is to work all the time and try to help others. There's no way out.

IC: Tell our listeners what books and DVDs you've been consuming. I'm sure they'd be interested.

OP: [*Laughs*] Oh. You know, Mike Leigh's *Naked*. I haven't watched it for so many years. I went, "Oh, you haven't seen this? I want to see that." Also, many years ago, Luchino Visconti, this great Italian director, made a film called *Il Gattopardo* [*The Leopard*] based on—

IC: Lampedusa, right?

OP: Based on the novel of Lampedusa. Now, they are going to give me the Lampedusa Prize in a week in Sicily, and we are going to Palermo next week, so we are watching the film again. It's a great movie based on a great novel. Burt Lancaster, Claudia Cardinale, and Alain Delon also plays, but don't forget that novels are better than films. Just don't get me wrong.

Politics & Prose Presents Orhan Pamuk

Azar Nafisi / 2017

From politics-prose.com, October 19, 2017.

Azar Nafisi: The first question I had for you was that someone said this book [*The Red-Haired Woman*] is haunted by reality. And I wanted to ask you about this reality and the fact that this reality seems to be haunted by the myth. So perhaps you could talk about that?

Orhan Pamuk: Yes, this book has two sides. A sort of a fictional inquiry into the foundational stories, myths, of say European civilization—which is an abstraction, but I say it for the sake of simplicity—and the Islamic civilization of my part of the world, especially around the fifteenth, sixteenth, seventeenth centuries from Balkans to Calcutta. There was one unifying center: Persian culture. So, I wrote a book comparing *Oedipus Rex* of Sophocles with Ferdowsi's little two-page, three-page story, "Rostam and Sohrab," which is in the *Shahnameh*, or *Book of Kings*. [. . .]

In the summer of 1988, when I was finishing *The Black Book* [. . .], in the land next to my house, a well digger and his disciple began to dig a well. And this was well digging with old-fashioned methods that was being done for the last two thousand years in Istanbul, which is coming to an end because they invented new machines. [. . .] And I watched them, and watched them, and watched them. And one thing stayed with me, and that is why, perhaps, I wrote this novel.

In the morning heat, when they're working, the master, the old guy (or middle-aged guy . . . at that time I was much younger so everyone seemed old to me), was shouting a lot, and scolding the boy to make things work. But in a very authoritarian, powerful voice. And when they [. . .] had their dinner, my God, he was a completely different person. Now, this time, he was "Did you enjoy your food? Are you hungry?" Very tender, very compassionate, very friendly. This stayed with me because I had a father who was completely otherwise. That is, my father rarely scolded me, rarely shouted at me—treated me as his equal in a very respectful way. Also, on the other hand, never showed that compassion to me. Never paid attention to details of my happiness, whether I'm happy or whether I've had enough food, whether I'm listening to music. [. . .] He was an absent father. He was never around too much.

So, it stayed with me, their relationship, and I thought about this many, many years. And, in fact, when I decided to convert this story into a novel, and it took a lot of time, I decided to underline the authoritarian tendencies of the master well digger and also think of other myths, other stories. [. . .] When I began writing and reading for *My Name Is Red*, I came across the story of Rostam and Sohrab, which was almost a mirror reflection of Sophocles's *Oedipus Rex*. [. . .] I didn't immediately connect it with my master well digger and his disciple, but the symmetrical reflection of Sophocles's *Oedipus Rex* and Rostam and Sohrab stayed with me.

AN: [. . .] You talked about fathers, and it seems as if both from the myth that Sophocles brings about in *Oedipus Rex* and "Rostam and Sohrab," there are two kinds of father that we see in this book [*The Red-Haired Woman*]: one is the father who sort of is a shadow over his son. Who watches him but also has compassion. And the other is the absent father who also treats you as equal. Now how do these interact, and how do they interact with myths?

OP: OK, I was, of course, very happy about the fact that my father was not the Freudian father, or authoritarian father that we all know about. The authoritarian father, the suppressing father, is a cliché or doesn't fit my life. [. . .] But what was more interesting was the absent father—or, there is a father around but he's not compassionate, he's not following all the details, he's not there in a way. [. . .] But, the compassionate father, or the more authoritarian father, stayed with me. The black and white of the person. [. . .]

Let me clarify a difference between Persian culture and Turkish culture: we Turks, Westernized, intellectual Turks, when they go to Iran and come back [. . .] they all come back "My God, these Persians, they didn't forget their poetry! They know their classical literature!" [. . .] Turks in a way forget their stories, while Persians don't. And if you talk to a Persian, they immediately will say a few lines from Hafiz, while Turks are silent about that. [. . .]

When I saw my country getting increasingly authoritarian, I said to myself, "Why don't I write a story, a fast-moving story, that will underline, explore, make you begin to think about these relationships?" Why do people in my part of the world—although they know that their leader is authoritarian—vote for him? Because they choose to find water so to speak, they choose economic growth, while on the other hand, the father may be killing his son.

AN: Yes, and also it's the comfort that you get from the authoritarian father because he has all your problems solved, so you don't need to think about them. He has all the difficulties taken care of—

OP: Yeah, but he kills you! [. . .] Now we come to the interesting political part of my book. In the end, my book is not an allegory. [. . .] Allegory uses symbols, meanings and makes them come together and another meaning is produced but after the text ends, we deduce a final meaning and my book doesn't have that. And I'm not that kind of writer. On the other hand, my book makes you, provokes you, to think about the history and artificiality of the tropes and archetypes we take for granted without questioning, and puts them in the same level of the realistic story of how you dig a well. [. . .]

When I observed this master well digger and his disciple, after three weeks they were finishing, and I told them I'm a writer and asked them would you please talk to me, I will record it. And the guy was very nice, a dignified guy, "Sure," he said and we had a two-hour conversation. [. . .] And I had been thinking about Rostam and Sohrab and these two stories began to merge in my mind. [. . .]

AN: Now I want to come to the exciting part, for me at least, which goes back to the title, *The Red-Haired Woman*. She is not a natural redhead. She is a dyed redhead, and in the novel, when she meets a natural redhead she says, [. . .] "What was destiny for you was a conscious decision for me and I spent the rest of my days trying to stay true to my choice." [. . .] And she is the only one in this novel, as far as I can remember, who talks about choice and the fact that she made a choice and she stuck with it.

OP: [. . .] I did all my homework about this story, but something was missing, and that was seeing the story from a woman's eye. I'm telling this tongue in cheek, with irony: in my earlier novel, which took me six years to write, *A Strangeness in My Mind*, there is also a self-imposed, or enthusiastic desire to be a sort of "feminist" in Turkey. [*Laughter*] Of course, this is an oxymoron: a typical Turkish man wants to be feminist, and you're rightfully laughing. But, I also wanted to continue in that line and see this Oedipus story and Rostam and Sohrab story where women are continuously weeping and weeping . . . but simultaneously challenging, provoking the horrible events that will come. So, I wanted to see this story through her point of view, rewrote the story, wrote her version of the story, and pulled the story inside out: The book has three sections and the final section is the red-haired woman's story . . . and she's not passive. [. . .] Perhaps that's the only intellectual contribution that I brought to the story. [. . .]

If you see red hair in Turkey, the meaning of it is very well represented in Sylvia Plath's poem, I will not repeat it here, but from that [. . .] we understand that she is angry. She is different, she has some strong anger by which she can change the whole world. We are scared of her, we cannot control her, but she is different—we are aware of this. And also, all this enveloped [her] in some sort of mysteriousness around her. If you come to my part of the world, it's [. . .] obvious that the hair is dyed. [. . .] You might think that no one wants to be a red-haired woman in my part of the world because it's also related to "easy virtue." When you begin to think of this, you respect that woman, because they make a statement when they dye their hair red, that they're different. They're saying, "Well, I'm doing those things, but I'm different, I'm strong, I can do that." It's that quality of the red-haired woman which I liked, and I wanted to underline, she provokes—her strength is also part of the story or something I injected into these old stories.

AN: It is amazing how women in novels become so subversive, just their presence sort of disrupts everything. And I wondered if you thought of the women in *Shahnameh*, like for example, Tahmineh, who's Sohrab's mother, and she's the one who, she seduces—

OP: [. . .] It's also the strength of the women in the story. [. . .]

AN: I just wanted to say, when Tahmineh comes to Rostam, she says, "My name is Tahmineh, longing has torn my wretched life in two." And then talks about, "Desire destroys my mind."

OP: [. . .] A regular cliché we see a lot in European, Western, newspapers is that they are so crushed, that women don't fight back. My point in my last two books is they fight back. Not only that social structures, institutions, religion, tradition, men, yes, they suppress women, but they also fight back with their humor, with their anger, with their stories. They're not in power, yes, they don't control the property, but they have their humanity, they have their stories. Suppression of women can only be represented well if you represent and show their anger, their fury, their humanity, the way they play around and make fun of the men who suppress them. [. . .]

AN: Can I ask you one last short question? In this book, almost every major character talks about the stories as fate, almost. Would you say . . . well we know stories predict us, but has story replaced fate in this novel?

OP: The terrible thing about fate is that you have no will. And, in fact, in my teenage years I used to argue—or ironically argue, make fun of—my more seriously Muslim friends in issues like *irade-i cüziyye* [free will of a person] and *irade-i külliye* [the absolute will of God]. That if all is decided by God, then we have no will because even our crimes are decided by God. To say this is agreeing with the devil. But, if all is not decided by God, or if we are free to make our choices, then all is not decided by God. [. . .] *İrade-i cüziyye*, the will of one person, and God's will contradict. If God's will is total, how do we underline the will of a single person? All modernity is based on underlining Oedipus's will, right, it's not given by fate. Or, it's given by fate. These are the issues—whether it's a story, a myth, or out of the Bible or Qur'an. In the end, the father of all stories about killing the father, killing the son, is Abraham and Isaac.

On the Photographs in *Balkon*

Gerhard Steidl / 2019

From the Strand Bookstore interview, January 30, 2019, https://www.youtube.com/watch?v=vTlzzkH9Wvs&t=39s.

Gerhard Steidl: Thank you for coming. I am giving you a short introduction. I have been working for an art collector in Istanbul together with Orhan Pamuk. I already knew that he was working as a photographer when he was young, and then he found his passion for literature, but I had no idea that he was photographing all his lifetime. And I was very thrilled about what he was introducing me to, and the result is the book that we are launching today titled *Balkon*.

Orhan Pamuk: Gerhard came to my house in Istanbul a few years ago for another project, and then I explained to him that in the winter of 2012 and '13 I was a bit depressed, and I had a new camera and I was continuously taking photos and then this was related to my mood, to my depression, to the fact that I was not happy with the novel that I was writing then [*A Strangeness in My Mind*]. [. . .] Then Gerhard said, "You have eighty-five hundred of them here, please reduce them to six hundred." [*Laughter*] [. . .]

GS: Out of the six hundred photos we could have made, of course, a huge coffee table book, but that was not our intention. For me the photos were something to "read." They are organized on the pages like comic photos. So all photos are landscape or horizontal, and there is a reading direction. And there are no words, no captions, but if you concentrate, you can read the story . . . in the photos. [. . .]

OP: I chose this form, a perpendicular book, perhaps because I am a literary writer, not honoring one single moment but a sense of continuity of time, continuation of time. [. . .] I took these photos in four months and they are landscape photos. My balcony—the word *balkon* in Turkish—looks at the entrance of the Bosphorus. I have a very beautiful landscape, but I was not after beautiful landscape photos. I was after something that would represent my mood. I wrote a little essay in the introduction about photography and mood.

I would follow a chronological order; that is, I started taking these photographs continuously, intensely. Then I wanted to group them both chronologically and then also by colors, by the things that the photographs show us, by the subject matter. [. . .]

All day I am sitting at my table writing my novel. Then I see something is approaching [on the Bosphorus]. And I leave my table, go out to the balcony, and "click." [. . .] At the beginning I was after light, after the mood, after giving the sense of an atmosphere. Then, I developed a sort of series: All the ferries of the city lines, for example, or all the international boats. [. . .] Although there is not much writing inside the book associated with the photos, there is a sense of storytelling. Because if we see a boat here it gets bigger and then it disappears. There is a continuity of space. Once there is a continuity of the space, the human mind automatically adds story to it because things are changing. [. . .] Literature works in time while art works in space.

GS: There's a new freedom for storytelling with a series of [digital] photos which Orhan picked up on. [. . .] So the book *Balkon* and the photos educated me in a certain way to look differently at photos. [. . .] I am not getting tired by looking at the six hundred pages and to discover the sensations [. . .], it is an extremely exciting education for the eye and for the brain. [. . .] By reading this book comes to my mind the famous words of Walker Evans, "For the thousandth time, it must be said that pictures speak for themselves, wordlessly, visually, or they fail."

OP: The most popular question that I have been asked all my life is "Why did you write this novel?" And my answer is that there is not one single reason. The same about photography. [. . .] I was not taking these photographs to represent the outside world. I was in a mood, and I felt like the photograph that I was taking corresponded to that mood.

"I Am Content with My Novel"

Erkan Irmak / 2019

From *Benim Adım Kırmızı Üzerine Yazılar*, Istanbul: Yapı Kredi, 2019.

Erkan Irmak: I'd like to start with a general assessment in the first question: How would you evaluate *My Name Is Red* after twenty years?

Orhan Pamuk: I am content with my novel. Good thing that I felt that way and wrote it that way. Do I have any regrets? A lot! There is not one novel that I leave behind without regrets. Whenever I write a novel, my mind grapples with all sorts of knots, scenes, over and over and I wonder whether I could write it better. When I was close to completing the novel, as I finished writing it, I said to myself that I wished I had time to finish it better. Therefore, none of my books give me complete satisfaction. I always feel guilty in the face of praise; because I know that it has flaws, missing parts or parts that could be much better. In the context of such regrets, *My Name Is Red* is one of my novels that I cherish. It doesn't make me unhappy or restless. It doesn't keep me awake at night because it didn't turn out well. Sometimes I think that it's perhaps my best novel.

EI: You told me once that this book was your happiest novel.

OP: Yes, we do not remember our books only to evaluate them. The beauty of that book, its success, and the fact that it satisfies us are all important things; but the more important feeling when remembering a book is attached to the process of writing that book. Just like some people say, "I was in my third year of middle school back then," "I was working in that company during those years," "it was the year of the military coup," or "Demirel was the prime minister." I also remember my life by saying, "I was writing *The White Castle* at that time," "I was writing *My Name Is Red*," "I was writing *Cevdet Bey* that year." These are activities that are instrumental in making a calendar of my life, such as school years or important family events, but it is also very important for me to remember the happiness of those writing days. I remember both my happiness and unhappiness during the years when I wrote *My Name Is Red*. In my private life, I was partly unhappy and partly happy. My daughter [Rüya] was born while I was writing this book.

I used to put her on a swing in the garden in the summer and swing her, then I would go inside and write a few more sentences while she was swinging. After a while she would say, "Push me, Daddy; where are you, push me." I would go and push her again and go back inside and write. Yes, that was nice. The flowers outside, the spring, the summer, and the family. I would work for twelve hours without stopping, then I would go for a swim. During that period, during the years when I was writing *My Name Is Red*, I used to write for *Öküz* magazine and talk about Rüya, how we used to go to the sea, and our daily life.

EI: Yes, I remember those articles.

OP: Also, if we're happy in life while writing a book, we will remember it happily too. This feeling is not necessarily related to how good the book is. Because I rely on research in my books, and this is relatively a research-based book, I remember the days of doing research while writing *My Name Is Red* happily. Because I was doing the research I did for this novel with pleasure. It can even be said that this book has finally turned into a historical novel, because I wanted to learn those subjects better, see more, take that responsibility. Secondhand book shopping on the internet, shopping for digital paintings . . . there was none of those things at the time. I am very glad that I gave this answer, Erkan, because it was a long answer.

EI: It was long and beautiful, yes. Now we can address "the novel about painting" issue a little, I think.

OP: Sure. The novel I dreamed of was based on the following situation: In the mid-1990s, I was talking left and right about how I actually wanted to be a painter. Everyone was asking me, "Why didn't you become an artist?" "Why did you quit painting?" I explained this in my own ways in my book *Istanbul*, but the subject that I thought compelled me more was the question of what the painter felt while painting. I recognized that feeling from experience. While painting, I felt that I was doing something more about the body, about the hand, about the craft. When I write novels, I feel that I am doing something more about the mind, the concept, the word. Actually, while thinking about writing a novel about painters, I dreamed of the story of a contemporary Turkish painter who would talk about the happiness and unhappiness, satisfaction and dissatisfaction that I felt while painting between the ages of seven and twenty-two, and this was how I imagined the book at first. I wanted to convey what I felt while painting. When I was painting, what I always felt in my childhood was that my hand, not my mind, was painting. As a matter of fact, I paint more comfortably when I'm drunk. In the last ten years, I started painting again. I'm much more comfortable with painting after drinking. In the evenings, I sometimes even drink just to paint, or I say, "I drank a little tonight, at least I'll paint so that it doesn't go to waste."

The reason I'm saying this is because there's no such thing as writing after drinking, because I don't trust my mind. But I don't paint with my mind. I feel it; I do it with my hand or something else. I don't know exactly what it is. I tried to express that feeling with the descriptions of how the miniaturists drew horses in *My Name Is Red*. The miniaturist paints, but he tells it as if it was someone else's hand in those chapters. In addition to describing what his hand draws, he also shares his feelings about the thing that he draws. Perhaps the most genuine feeling of this book is in those chapters, in the pages describing the competition to see who will draw the best horse.

I didn't begin this book as a historical novel. I was going to write about the problems of a contemporary painter's world. But after a while, I realized how this world would lead us to a limited view of the topics about originality, imitation, the efforts for finding something new, modern painting in a country without a painting tradition, or else collapse into discussions of authenticity or the anxiety of influence. However, our twentieth-century modern painters, unfortunately, were destined to be overinfluenced by Western painting. Even if they were not influenced, critics would still write that they were because we had a very limited tradition of modern painting. But I no longer wanted to deal with issues such as the psychology, tragedy, emptiness, moral aspects, or the aesthetic criticisms of being influenced by the West. These problems seem to have remained in the 1950s, '60s, and '70s. I wanted to advance to the genuine pleasure of painting; it was unattractive to explore the negative psychology of imitating Western painting.

So, I decided to write a historical novel, to make my novel historical. This was a very important change of mind. I had finished the novel that I wrote before *My Name Is Red*—*The New Life*—and sat at my desk for this one. And I sat down at the table to write a novel that would take place today, but I left the table with the decision to write a historical novel. After this decision, I studied for a year to learn about the subject.

EI: How did the research process begin and how did it progress? Was there anything that surprised you during that time?

OP: Ottoman miniatures is a subject that I've loved since my childhood. For a very simple reason: I wanted to be a painter in my youth. In the 1960s, when one mentioned Turkish painting, the Ottoman miniature came to mind, and there was no other subject—if we put aside the imitators of the Impressionists and Orientalists. I had read two or three books on this subject in Turkish. But when I decided to write this novel—or rather to base it on miniatures—I read old books, introductory books, taking everything seriously and taking notes. You have seen the notebooks I kept while writing this novel. You may have seen that I started with Metin And's introductory books. I had the determination to be a passionate, hardworking writer who wanted to start everything from scratch! A book that shocked me, affected me, and stunned me was the great book written by Martin Bernard Dickson and Stuart Cary Welch about the copy then known as the "Houghton *Shahnameh*."

Shah Ismail and his son Shah Tahmasp had a very special, rich, and large illustrated copy of Ferdowsi's *Shahnameh* prepared in the 1520s. For this, they appointed the greatest and most famous painters and *nakkaş* of their day. The project took more than ten years. Some painters died; some left the job. There were some other new *nakkaş*; they joined the book illustrators—that is, the workshop. There are 258 great miniatures in the book, which are very beautiful. (I've looked at them so much that I recognize them as soon as I see them.) Whereas, in an ordinary, average Islamic book manuscript, there are only twelve to sixteen pictures/miniatures. Commissioned by Shah Tahmasp, this great book was given to [Ottoman sultan] Selim III as a gift. It was probably stolen from Topkapı Palace at the end of the nineteenth century and first passed into the hands of Rothschild and then an American oil tycoon named Houghton. While Tahmasp's *Shahnameh* was in Houghton's hands, it was named after him. Dickson and Welch, one a historian and the other an art historian, tried to identify the miniaturists who made the paintings from their styles, one by one, by looking at the miniatures in this book. While doing this, they discussed hundreds of topics, from style to story, from color to copy, in a very interesting and profound way.

I was surprised when they brought me this famous book on a wheeled cart to the reading room at the public library on 42nd Street in New York, because even a single volume of the two-volume book was too big and heavy to carry. And all the pictures were in black and white. As narrated and discussed in the book [by Dickson and Welch] published in 1980, this volume of the Shah Tahmasp *Shahnameh* was cut into pieces by its then owner, Houghton, and sold page by page to museums around the world. He later donated what was left to the Metropolitan Museum with feelings of guilt. Today, the Iranian government is trying to buy back the pages sold individually from their owners and museums. The fact that the pictures of the book are scattered page by page in museums and collections all over the world recalls the story of the painting in my novel that has been torn from its context, or rather its volume.

EI: When the focus of the book changed from a novel about a modern painter to a historical novel about a miniature painter did you revise your purpose?

OP: While reading Bahadır Sürelli's writings, I enjoyed remembering that I was influenced by all those texts whose names he listed. He talks about the effect of written sources ranging from *Kelile and Dimna* to *Kitabu'r-Ruh*, from *Acaibü'l-Mahlukat* to the *Holy Qur'an*. The forms of these influences can also be discussed. But the novel touches this whole literary geography and uses it as material. The literary and historical texts that the article draws attention to can be considered as a kind of encyclopedia of a wide world between 1350 and 1850—what we can call classical Islamic culture. All people live in this encyclopedia. Therefore, after a while, representing, using, and being influenced by this whole culture became a new goal. The most enjoyable aspect of my novel is that it speaks in the first person while representing the main elements of this vast culture. Thus, we see that world, that vast culture as an extension of the imagination and as a living thing and as part of a story. But I had not intended all this when I started writing the novel. I discovered these pleasures while writing: Just as I was reading things like old histories, lists, estate and *narh* [fixed price indexes] books, like discovering the poetry of things in the novel.

EI: Let's talk a little more about these forms of influence.

OP: The way the author approaches the material he will use and touch, whether it is a text, an object—as in *The Museum of Innocence*—or a painting, is meaningful. Let me remind you how I wrote my novel *The Museum of Innocence* after *My Name Is Red*: I had the story of that novel very roughly in my mind. Finally, the protagonist who is deeply in love creates a museum of items that reminded him of his lover! I was going to both write the novel and create the museum. Then I had to collect the items from scratch. First, I collected the objects, then I wrote the novel by looking at them. I was picking things up intuitively because they were filled with memories or because they were beautiful, interesting, pleasant. Like a thermometer in the shape of a mosque, an old taximeter, a dog figurine, or the lantern of a phaeton from old Istanbul. I was bringing the story I was writing closer to these items. But sometimes the story just couldn't touch the item, couldn't swallow it. So, I couldn't get my characters on a phaeton, and I couldn't put the lantern in the museum. I would like to say that I used the method of writing a novel based on things for the first time in *My Name Is Red*. There, there are old literary texts and pictures made of them instead of objects.

EI: How would you describe the influence of a painting or an object on you?

OP: Yes, "influence"; it summarizes many of the relationships we describe with words such as imitating, representing, mirroring, mentioning, implying. The ways we can be "influenced" by another image, text, or item are endless. But in *My Name Is Red*, there are three main ways in which I am influenced by old texts and pictures.

First of all, I wanted to depict a love scene like Hüsrev looking up from his horse at Shirin in the palace window. At the beginning of the novel, the scene in which Black on his horse sees Shekure in the window that suddenly opens is such a scene. Moreover, as the protagonist of a postmodern novel, Black helps the reader with good intentions and tells the reader in his own words and in the first person how this encounter resembles the pictures of Hüsrev and Shirin, "that have been painted thousands of times." Thus, Black becomes one of the first critics of the novel. He makes art-historical observations. The point I want to draw attention to in this relationship is that the novel is influenced by Hüsrev and Shirin as a picture, not as a literary text. In other words, the thing that impresses me in the painting is the poetry of the encounter; I don't think this is in the literary text. Or I felt that poetry in the picture, not in the text, and wanted to rewrite it. In other words, while I was writing this novel, I was more impressed by the pictures based on them than by the old literary texts. I "imitated" the mood of those paintings. This means that I was more impressed by the mood, the aura and the emotion of the paintings than the story. This intention to be influenced means the intention to write a novel that captures the poetry of the pictures. But I am not imitating the story of Hüsrev and Shirin.

EI: What were the other "influences" about?

OP: The second effect is more of an ekphrasis-like effect. Ekphrasis is the name given to expressing the works of visual art (sculpture, architecture, painting) in words in a dramatic and pleasant way in Ancient Greece. This was before the art of photography. The poet describes a sculpture with words to those who have not seen it. But he tells it in such a way that his narrative becomes a story, a drama, an aesthetic. Scholars, art and literary historians call such depictions and dramatic expressions "ekphrastic" today. In my own words, I am describing the sixteenth-century Herat miniature, which "represents" the meeting of Hüsrev and Shirin. In the novel, I explain the picture to those who can't see it. But I tell it poetically and dramatically, trying to identify with the scene. "There is a 12-by-6-centimeter painting, in such and such a book," write art historians and librarians, who publish these miniatures in catalogs. They do not deal with the feelings of the painter, the new emotion and drama created by the painting, nor the emotions and conflicts that people of the past and modern times can feel when looking at the painting. The biggest shortcoming of Islamic art history and cataloging is that they cannot depict the emotions, conflicts, larger culture, and ironies in the miniature paintings. In this book, while I describe the pictures with an ekphrasis-style description, I try to make some sense of the feeling that miniature created in me. The second style of painting can address the poetry of the painting, or it can turn into a kind of museum visit and allow the most important paintings to be overhauled, as in the [Topkapı] Palace Library scene between the chief miniature painter Master Osman and Black.

EI: I know that you have been planning an illustrated edition of *My Name Is Red* for years, just like the edition of *Istanbul* with pictures.

OP: Most of the miniatures I describe in the novel are not imaginary; they are real. It has been my biggest dream for years to publish them together with the novel, where they are mentioned and described in the text. So, to prepare an illustrated *My Name Is Red*. Let's see if I can achieve it.

[. . .]

EI: There is also the literary aspect of influence.

OP: For example, [there is] Umberto Eco's merging of a historical subject with a detective novel. There were others who had done this before. The main influence of *The Name of the Rose* is not the detective novel, but a context that I can call "postmodernism and the historical novel." While reading *The Name of the Rose*, we encounter a hero like Borges. The novel, yes, plays a little trick with us, pays a lot of attention to historical facts, but sometimes says, "I don't care and I show it." Without *The Name of the Rose*, it might have been more difficult for me to capture the "playful" atmosphere in my novel. Or maybe I wouldn't have thought of basing the relationship between the three protagonists, Shekure, Orhan, and Shevket, in the novel on the many authentic details of my mother, brother, and my childhood— when our father was not around—and to show them to the reader. But with the historical novel, Calvino was the first to reveal details from other periods and environments. By doing this in a fun and creative way, he freed the historical novel from an impossible "realism." As we speak, I am writing a new historical novel, *Nights of Plague*, and doing what I did in *My Name Is Red* again: On the one hand, authentic knowledge found in books, documents, the fine details in memoirs, and on the other hand, fantastic situations incompatible with the reality of history. . . . Of course, there are also nonfictional literary influences. . . . For example, Derrida's writings in *Memoirs of the Blind*. There are no critics yet who speak of this influence, or the influence of the Japanese writer Tanizaki. Yourcenar's influence is more poetic. As in Hadrian's *Memoirs* . . . Yourcenar used first-person narration creatively and poetically in a historical novel. I also like the simplicity of [Byron's] *Eastern Tales*.

EI: Let's continue from the first-person narration and move the discussion to perspective in painting.

OP: In my novels, I like that a subject, a main element functions at more than one level and the reader senses and sees this. I try to bring out two such trivial focal points. Such are the subjects of portrait, perspective, and personal style in this novel. The "history of the Renaissance" in the West shows us that this great change was possible with the discovery of perspective in the art of painting. The Ottomans were incompetent in painting, not in miniature, and they did not, or could not, learn perspective. Maybe that's why today it has become an even more important "factor of difference."

Perspective in painting was made possible by respecting the humble point of view of someone in that world, an individual, a single eye, a person. A picture with perspective is made possible by a humanistic eye. We say, "Everyone sees things from their own 'perspective.'" This point of view is particularly emphasized in the novel *My Name Is Red*. Everyone tells the story the way it appears to them. We watch reality not from the point of view of the all-knowing "omniscient narrator" but from the point of view of everyone, just like post-Renaissance painting, and I emphasize this in the novel. Since everyone sees reality from their own point of view, they interpret it imperfectly, incompletely, or differently. This leads to the emergence of what is called "personal style" in painters. Personal style, on the other hand, emerges with the understanding and the acceptance of individuality and the fact that each individual can be different. Thus, at the deepest point of the novel, we see that these two significant focal points are in dialogue. This dialogue deals deeply with particular concepts: Focal points such as seeing, thinking, identity, style, individuality, guilt, death, life, and happiness are intertwined at the conceptual level. It is difficult to establish this "idealistic thinking model" in a "realist" naturalist novel where everything is realistic.

"*Nights of Plague*, the Novel I Am Currently Writing, Is Also Something of an East-West Novel"

Ramil Ahmedov / 2021

From *Kitap-lık*, "Interview with Orhan Pamuk," September–October 2018, vol. 199.

Ramil Ahmedov: I recently heard that you had an interesting project: Views from Orhan Pamuk's balcony [*Balkon*] . . .

Orhan Pamuk: Yes, such a book is coming out. It'll be published at the end of August. I have a camera as you can see here. I take pictures with it everywhere, but especially on that balcony (pointing to the balcony). I took a lot of pictures in 2012, maybe because I had just bought this camera. Some might call it a depression, but I had a lot of unresolved problems in my head. I couldn't write my novel the way I wanted. Instead, I went to the balcony and constantly took pictures of everything that passed. Years later, I met a photography book publisher and thought more reflectively about this period of my life, and the publisher said, "I would like to make a book with your photos; can I see them?" He liked them, and said, "Let's make a book." The project progressed slowly but eventually became a book. I wrote an eight-page preface. Photography books are not popular bestsellers in the world or in Turkey, but I am glad that I prepared such a book. [. . .]

RA: You said that *The Red-Haired Woman* was your "most feminist novel." In *Silent House*, Hasan kills his beloved Nilgün; in *A Strangeness in My Mind*, we see women being excluded from society. You claim that Füsun's tragic story is "the story of women in Turkey." . . . How do you evaluate the way men oppress the women they love in societies like ours?

OP: This is an important issue for me. "How do you evaluate it?" is a question whose answer varies. Let me try to talk about myself by making a little self-criticism. I couldn't identify enough with my heroines in my first books, but back then my outlook on life was not that mature and rich. I also knew less about life. I felt this lack, I was criticized, and the critiques were right. After my forties, maybe after getting to know life and women more, I became tired of describing my own life, my social milieu, the secular middle-class, Westernized bourgeois environment in Nişantaşı. I said to myself that I should step out of my comfort zone, not only socially but in terms of gender too, to talk about the world from the eyes of women.

RA: In fact, you wrote with a female voice for the first time in *Silent House*...

OP: Yes, I think I told you about Fatma in *Silent House*. Fatma is a mix of my maternal and paternal grandmothers. Both of my grandmothers were women whose husbands had died and who lived long lives on their own. My paternal grandmother lived in a crowded house; my maternal grandmother lived alone in a big house, almost like in those haunted house tales. But they had something in common. They lived in their dreams. They both had big mirrors. They would sit on their beds and watch the entire house through those mirrors. They would look at things. The sugar bowls, tablecloths, curtains, the newspapers they read, and the way they spoke were all very similar to each other. I depicted such a woman in *Silent House*. I was able to identify with them a little bit there. At least Fatma's voice has something of my grandmothers'. But I always thought that I couldn't explain women enough. We could not fully see Füsun's anger in *The Museum of Innocence* either. Why didn't we hear Nilgün's voice, why didn't Füsun appear more? I realized and heard these shortcomings.

I think I got over this for the first time in *A Strangeness in My Mind* through a project with a determined systematic intent. I highlighted the women characters there. I had two goals: first, all my books are now published around the world, and there are some stereotypes about Islamic women circulating in the world: that they are oppressed, they cannot go out on the street, they cannot travel alone, they cannot go to the cinema, et cetera. These are true, and I have tried to show that they are. To give an example, 65 percent of the wealth in Turkey is registered to men. This figure rises in the East and decreases in the West. Or, the vast majority of marriages in Turkey are arranged. And this is something that oppresses women. These are things we all know. Despite all my good intentions, I am a Turkish man in the end—when I say "feminist," I do it with a slight irony. Secondly, people in the West talk about these issues as if women who are oppressed are crushed under their oppressors. No! Women also protest, respond, impose their personalities, joke about things, mock other people. Yes, you oppress women, you suppress them, but they do not get crushed easily. As in *A Strangeness in My Mind*, they run away, they don't marry the man that you want them to marry, they run away with someone else, they make fun of them, they mock them. These are very precious moments and that mockery, that sarcasm, that escapism also shows a lot about society.

[...]

RA: Your first novel, *Cevdet Bey and Sons*, and your last novel, *The Red-Haired Woman*, come to terms with three generations. There are forty years between these two novels. What is the difference between the Orhan Pamuk who wrote *Cevdet Bey and Sons* and the Orhan Pamuk who wrote *The Red-Haired Woman*? [...]

OP: I've been doing the same thing for forty years; I think I can do it for another four hundred years. But on the other hand, I know with part of my mind that unfortunately my health will not stay like this, and the time is approaching to cross over to the other side. However, it seems like I'll be writing a novel every two or three years for another four hundred years. That's the sad thing. [...] I have the same feelings of despair and joy. I am the same person. As a novelist, yes, I have more experience, I waste less time, I no longer say, "Look, Orhan, you can do it if you force yourself." Instead I say, "Put it on hold for a while; go to the next part." I can sense it when failure and difficulty approach. Or I sense it when I should focus on a scene more. On the one hand, [there are] awards, and the fact that my books have been translated into sixty languages.... Success does not make me more humble, it makes me more ambitious. Rather, I am humbled in my own mind. I may have had confidence in myself as a novelist. I might think that if I do it like this, I can write this scene well, but this was also in my youth. The best thing about writing a novel is to think about it scene by scene, chapter by chapter, before starting it. I still think so. As a result, there is no big difference. In the same way, I get discouraged from time to time. I sometimes say that it didn't turn out well. Such things still happen like they did forty years ago.

RA: For the last twenty to twenty-five years, critics have been evaluating your novels on an East-West axis. Do you find such readings accurate?

OP: I have written novels like *The White Castle* and *The Black Book*, but that's not all I do. I'd also like to talk about the cultural history and foundations of my interest in this subject. History progressed in such a way that after the Enlightenment, modernization and the Industrial Revolution, the difference between the West and the East expanded. The production, wealth, and military power of the West suddenly increased twenty or thirty times.

Imperialism emerged, there were colonies, and they got humiliated. This time, people outside of Europe began to feel inferior to and humiliated by those in the West. Especially the intellectuals. Because they see what is going on in the world, and when they look at their own countries, they see that there is nothing of that kind. Thus, there were both imitation and admiration. Along with admiration, imitation, there also began to be hatred and disgust. This is called the East-West problem. This way of thinking has inevitably shaped my generation. Now Turkey has become relatively rich, a pride of success has come, especially due to the economic successes in the last twenty-five years. Now we have moved away from the state of anger and hatred toward the West, from the excitement of imitation. Maybe my novels got a little further away too. *A Strangeness in My Mind* is no longer an East-West novel, but *The Red-Haired Woman* is.

RA: In one of your last interviews, you announced that you would write a historical novel called *Nights of Plague*. Faruk, who was looking for the traces of the history of a plague in *Silent House*, came to my mind. Plague also has an important place in *The White Castle*. Is there a connection between this novel and *Silent House* and *The White Castle*? Can you share some details?

OP: *Nights of Plague*, the novel I am currently writing, is also something of an East-West novel. I've been thinking about this novel for thirty-five years. It is a historical novel set in 1900. In fact, Faruk was indeed doing research for this novel in *Silent House*. Or I took a few scenes from the novel I was going to write in *The White Castle* for this book. There was also a similar situation in *Snow*, I detached Kars from its surroundings, not with the plague but with heavy snow. In short, I can say that I am writing a novel that I have been thinking about for thirty-five years.

RA: The impact of cultural and technological changes on our identities has an important place in your novels. You look at these changes through the eyes of the characters. One of the important points in *A Strangeness in My Mind* and *The Red-Haired Woman* is how Istanbul's urban, cultural, and social fabric has changed in the last thirty years. How does the rapid change of the city influence you and your writing as an Istanbulite?

OP: When I finished *A Strangeness in My Mind*, I said, "Let me see what happens to Istanbul's skyscrapers." (*Pointing to the places seen from the balcony.*) Five years ago, none of these buildings existed. The city I live in is changing in an incredible way. The population of Istanbul was two and a half million when I was born, now it is seventeen million. During this whole process, I was here, I was in it, and I witnessed everything. Let me first say that there are very few writers who have seen such a change in the history of humanity. I was there the whole time. In my first four novels and in *The Museum of Innocence*, I described middle-class Westernized, well-to-do bourgeois people of Istanbul. Then everyone started calling me an Istanbul writer. I thought that I'd tell you about the other parts of the city, the newly added neighborhoods, the poor classes, the dispossessed classes. I continued to be an Istanbul writer with a planned agenda to explore not only the environment I lived in but the whole city. What can I say? I am not saying that the city has changed a lot and they killed my old, beautiful Istanbul. There is a grain of truth in this. I'm not nostalgic. On the other hand, everything is not great. I see concrete everywhere. I do not have a single systematic philosophy. That's what life is like. Your generation comes, does something, then their buildings, their poetry, their music, their bodies, all of them, a great wave called history comes and takes them, bringing new things to take their places. Accepting this is like accepting aging and death.

RA: There are [some who think] that *The Museum of Innocence* alludes to the avant-gardes of the early twentieth century, particularly Walter Benjamin. What are your thoughts?

OP: Especially in the US, I get a question about Benjamin on every college campus. Benjamin has become a cliché. Once it was Foucault, Edward Said, Karl Marx; now it's Benjamin. He's a great writer, but one does not need Benjamin to do what I did with the Museum of Innocence. Others are also writing about these issues. I didn't build the Museum of Innocence with Benjamin in mind. I value Benjamin a lot, don't get me wrong, but not everything can be associated with Benjamin.

Turkish Interview Excerpts on *Nights of Plague*

Various / 2021–2022

"My World, Which I Thought Wouldn't Interest Anyone, Was Suddenly on Everyone's Lips"

İhsan Yılmaz / 2021

From *Hürriyet Pazar*, "Kimsenin ilgilenmeyeceğini düşündüğüm dünyam birdenbire herkesin ağzındaydı," March 29, 2021.

İhsan Yılmaz: What did you feel when the plague novel that you've been thinking about for forty years and working on for the last five coincided with the COVID-19 pandemic?

Orhan Pamuk: At first, I felt astonished. My world, which I'd created for years by digging a well with a needle, which I sometimes thought was too bookish and that wouldn't interest anyone, was suddenly on everyone's lips. Everyone was talking about quarantine, about the death toll. While I was creating that world, thinking that I was doing something very special, that I was going to surprise people with the subject, everything suddenly spilled out into the open. It was like watching something you do in secret being exposed. In this regard, I felt jealous at first. It was as if a world that I'd created on my own had passed into the hands of everyone in a way that I did not want. I got used to it, but then I began thinking that people would say, "Oh look, there was a pandemic and he immediately used it for a new novel."

I was in America last year because I was teaching when the pandemic started on March 15. I immediately returned to Turkey. I learned in Istanbul that they had quarantined those returning from the Hajj. They handled the situation badly out of incompetence and the pilgrims rebelled against them. . . . This was so similar to the story I told in *Nights of Plague* that I immediately published that part in Turkey, the part about the rebellion in the pilgrim ship. The story I wrote was harsher, more brutal, deadlier than what really happened. Then, I wrote an article for the *New York Times*, which was also published on *T24* [online Turkish newspaper], so that it would be known that I'd been writing this book for four years. In this article, I explained how human psychology was affected by ancient plague and cholera epidemics. And I talked about the novel I'd been writing for four years and I'd thought about for forty years. When this article was published in many parts of the world, my publishers from more than fifty countries started to put pressure on me to finish the novel. I thought that I'd finish it very quickly and started working hard, but as you can see, it took me another year.

İY: We see how important people's religious beliefs, traditions, and educational status are in the fight against pandemics. Their jobs were more difficult back in the day, but I guess not much has changed in one hundred twenty years. What do you think?

OP: There are things that haven't changed from the old epidemics to the present, and things that have changed a lot. First let me tell you about the things that haven't changed: Our basic instincts do not change. Whether it's cholera or the plague, people deny their symptoms and insist that they don't feel sick. The state denies it, even the doctors. There is denial at first everywhere all the time. It's not the denial that I'm criticizing; it's the long denial, the inability to accept it. Because it leads to deaths. Then gossip and rumors begin. Because of all this, when the pandemic spreads rapidly, people start to blame the state for not preventing it, and they don't comply with the quarantine bans. As the epidemic progresses and deaths increase, this time the state becomes more aggressive and authoritarian by taking advantage of this opportunity. This happens in every country.

But the world has changed a lot compared to the period I describe in the novel, the situation on the island of Mingheria in 1901. At that time, 5 to 10 percent of the population could read and write. Today, this rate is 95 percent in Turkey. Seventy-five percent of the population uses the internet. This cannot be compared to the past. Today we have a lot of information. You turn on the television and see what is happening in which country. You see what the situation is in your neighborhood, in your apartment. This makes a big difference compared to the period in the novel. The death toll of the plague is very high. One would say people should be more afraid in this situation, but no, they aren't. Because they don't know what will happen to them. But now we know what will happen. That's why we're scared, even though the death toll was very low compared to the times of the plague. But my novel is still scarier than today's reality.

İY: Did this overlap between fiction and reality cause any complications in the world you created?

OP: Yes, it did. Even when I was writing my novel, in the first three years, I thought about how my reader would understand the story. I was thinking how to explain the plague, how to convince people that this had happened. Suddenly, an epidemic started, and everyone understood what quarantine was. I felt that I didn't have to struggle so much. When we say quarantine, when we say bans, when we say stay at home, everything was clear. I just paid attention to not using contemporary concepts and terminology. As such, I shortened the parts where I described the quarantine and the history of pandemics. Most importantly, I was afraid to catch the coronavirus myself.

We all remember how it was at first. Leaving our shopping bags outside for a day, washing everything. . . . That fear also reminded me of this: At first, I felt that I hadn't adequately described this fear in my book. I realized that my characters weren't frightened enough. So, the coronavirus pandemic made it easier to write the novel I'd been writing for three and a half years. But I think it made it more difficult to put the reader in an atmosphere of fear. Because after a while, people learned not to be afraid. The disease is still around, the numbers have dropped a bit, gone up a bit, we're spending time in more or less the same places, but we're less afraid now. Because we know a lot now; we have experience. People are afraid of what they don't know. In the old plagues, people were afraid because they didn't have any information. . . . However, their fear was not directly proportional to the damage the disease would cause. Now we have so much information that you can almost watch a live broadcast from the hospital of a man dying. How is it possible not to be afraid?

İY: Which island inspired you the most for Mingheria?

OP: First of all, Büyükada [near Istanbul in the Sea of Marmara]. I borrowed many things from Büyükada, such as horse carriages, ferry schedules, the Splendid Palace Hotel. . . . When I was a child, there used to be *lodos*, or southwesterlies, on Heybeliada, and ferries couldn't run. I loved the sense of detachment there. The days of the blockade in the novel, the romance of being disconnected from the world are from there. Or running to the pier when a new ship arrives. These feelings I get from the Istanbul islands are also present in *Nights of Plague*. Of course, I also had trips to the Greek islands. . . . I love going to the Greek islands and especially Crete. I borrowed the dervish lodges, mystical buildings, and the wealth that I described in Mingheria from Crete. I've been to Rhodes quite a few times in the last six years. The smallness of Kastellorizo [Megisti] opposite

Rhodes also influenced me. These three are the main influences. Of course, my imaginary island hosts a variety of things from Istanbul's slopes to the Maiden's Tower.

İY: You've fictionalized Mingheria, an imaginary island, like a movie set. You've sketched the novel plan. Not just by telling but by illustrating and mapping. Did this make it easier for you to write the novel, or did you do those things so that the reader could visualize it better?

OP: I started to plan and map my imaginary places, whether an island or a house, with *My Name Is Red*. There, more than half of the events take place inside a house, and I'd made an architectural plan of the house. Now I was going to create an imaginary island. I didn't know how the whole island would look, but I had a rough idea. I drew a map of the island, looking at it, I first thought about what would happen in a typical Aegean island, under Ottoman rule, for example. It becomes a province, as in Crete. The Crete Governor's Hall was built in the 1890s. There is a telegraph office and a post office. They are on Hamidiye Street [in *Nights of Plague*]. There is a bridge, maybe a stream. Then there are ports, piers, hotels on the beach. Taverns, restaurants, drinking places look over them. Then comes a Muslim quarter, a Greek quarter. . . . I marked them on the map as I wrote them. Mosques, churches, various Sufi lodges, monasteries. . . . I mean, I didn't make the map you call the "novel plan" from the beginning and place the novel there; or I didn't finish the novel and make a map of it. As I wrote the novel, I made the map, marked the houses; a new character emerged, it went like this, amusing myself to see where this person would live. That's why it was first a map, and then two years later, I revised it. I embellished the last version and put it into the book. Now this map is an integral part of the book. You can look at it while reading.

İY: The book has been published and you have it in your hands. Do you feel great relief or have you started writing a new one right away?

OP: Toward the end of the book, it's been like this with all my books, I start to think about the next novel I'm going to write. I wake up at night, for example, to write my current novel, but scenes from my new novel come to my mind. One starts to get tired of his own novel after a while. He wants it finished. He wants to give himself an award. Starting a new novel is happiness. On the other hand, I thought about the new novel for years. Now I'm eager to start writing it.

In this book, I initially thought that Doctor Nuri would be someone like me, but he didn't turn out like me. I couldn't do what Doctor Nuri did to tolerate his wife Pakize Sultan, the sultan's daughter. Since there's no character like me in this novel, perhaps next I'll imagine a character, just like I did in *The Black Book*, to whom I feel close, with whom I can share my past, and who is a painter but a failed one. I develop topics such as the strange visual world of my character, his spiritual world, the metaphysics in his head. So, I am beginning a novel about seeing and painting, the loneliness and strangeness of the artist. The protagonist of my new novel will be from Istanbul, look like me, maybe not from Nişantaşı, but from Cihangir. This will be the only change.

"Mingheria Is Not the Starting Point for an Allegory about Turkey"
Şeyda Öztürk / 2021
From *Gazete Duvar*, "Minger Adası Türkiye'yi gösteren bir alegorinin çıkış noktası değildir," April 8, 2021.

Şeyda Öztürk: It is clear that *Nights of Plague* started to emerge as an idea in the 1980s, when you were writing *Silent House*. How has the initial idea changed in these forty years?

Orhan Pamuk: While the encyclopedist hero of *Silent House*, Selahattin Darvınoğlu, overwhelms his wife Fatma with his thoughts on the Enlightenment, dreams, and long speeches, he constantly reminds her of two important issues: being an individual and death. According to Selahattin Darvınoğlu, Westerners discovered being an individual because they were afraid of death. At first, I dreamed of writing a plague novel about the fear of death, which I would consider from an existential perspective. But this impulse was soon replaced by another. After 1985 with *The White Castle*, the topic of "Westerners dreaming of the East," the subject Edward Said discussed in *Orientalism*, came to the fore.

Many Western observers—primarily Busbecq [1522–1592]—said that Turks did not flee from the plague because they were fatalistic. Busbecq and others—Daniel Defoe [1660–1731] as well—repeated this stereotype. But were they right when they said Turks/Muslims were fatalistic and that they did not take any precautions? Yes, they were partially right. But they weren't exactly right. But, more importantly, they weren't correct in the force with which they said they were. This complex, difficult, but viable subject attracted me. After pondering this subject until 2000 and reading books about it, I had another idea. The technical, medical, military, and, of course, social dimensions of quarantine. . . . When quarantine is mentioned, revolts come to mind in many places. This time, opposition to quarantine, the authoritarianism of the state, quarantine, the reaction against it, and anarchy started to attract me.

ŞÖ: In other words, to draw a mental map of the development of the novel, we can say the following: Your attention turns to the different perceptions of death in the West and the East, more precisely, the complex perception of the East's attitude toward death and illness by the West. Ultimately, the ways in which the state manages the life and death of its citizens and their political consequences came to the fore. *Nights of Plague* contains all of this and more in its final form. It would be interesting to consider the relationship of the novel, which will be perceived as a novel about the pandemic because of its name, with similar novels that came before it. Can you evaluate the novels written before yours that also talked about epidemics? Which ones impressed you?

OP: Let's divide these novels into two categories. Plague novels and novels about other diseases.... I have carefully read all the novels about plague. I was not interested in novels about other epidemics. First of all, let's remind ourselves: If we consider that the art of the novel as it is today has been shaped during the time of Balzac and Dickens in the 1850s, the main epidemic after the emergence of the novel was cholera for fifty years. But it is always in the background in other novels. As in García Márquez's novel *Love in the Time of Cholera*.... The subject in that novel is not cholera but love and the lover's patience. Cholera is just one of the many occupations of one of the important heroes, the cultured Doctor Urbino. It is a historical novel.... In other words, the novelist did not experience the panic and the fear of death by cholera. Cholera is in the title because it situated us into a historical period.

ŞÖ: What do you think are the most important novels about the plague?

OP: The oldest and most famous text is Daniel Defoe's *The Journal of the Plague Year*. Actually, that book is not exactly a novel.... Albert Camus was very impressed by Defoe's book. In *The Plague*, Camus talks about ordinary things in an airy and slightly sarcastic—ironic—style that he borrows from Defoe. The novelist J. M. Coetzee drew attention to the Defoe-Camus relationship years ago in a favorable article on Philip Roth's failed novel *Nemesis* [the subject of the novel is a polio epidemic in a small American city]. But Camus is not concerned with what Defoe is interested in, with the social impact of the plague. He talks about what happens in the city, but his main interest is morality: The most important issue for him is whether his heroes are egoistic, self-sacrificing, cowardly, heroic, socialist, or individualistic. Camus's *The Plague* is a moral novel in the Diderot tradition. Despite this moralistic interest, Camus successfully establishes the atmosphere of a plague-stricken city. After Camus's *The Plague*, one can no longer write a plague novel that begins with the death of rats bleeding from their noses.

ŞÖ: How did you relate to these novels while writing *Nights of Plague*?

OP: I was not influenced by Camus, as I tried to delay the moral judgment of my characters. But in my early youth, I eagerly read this novel's Turkish translation by Oktay Akbal. The book has an allegorical structure: The plague is equivalent to Nazis. . . . To be taken to the hospital by cars in the middle of the night is equated to being taken to a concentration camp like Jews and resistance fighters. On the other hand, perhaps because of this allegorical/political structure, the book does not deal with the material details of the quarantine, the disobedience of people, the distribution of food in the city. It depicts the plague as something frightening descended from the sky!

ŞÖ: However, you are more preoccupied with the details of daily life such as quarantine issues, restrictions, food, and marketplaces.

OP: I took your saying "more preoccupied" negatively. . . .

ŞÖ: No, I didn't mean it in a negative way. I think that the details, imagery, and descriptions of daily life deepen the narrative by conveying the transformation of both social life and the moods of the characters observing that life.

OP: Yes, especially when describing quarantine decisions, I wondered if *Nights of Plague* was turning into a government and bureaucracy novel. But I also wanted to write about the daily life of the city. My purpose was not only to show cowards and heroes. I had in mind the transformations of ordinary life, eating habits, and social life. I always would like to see what is going on mostly through the eyes of ordinary "citizens," the underprivileged. . . . But I was setting up and describing a world where the literacy rate among Muslims was very low. I could only write a few pages of my story through the eyes of a person who did not believe in microbes. Writing a novel is always like this. . . . It is a matter of making tactical decisions such as who should tell the story and where, and how, and for how long to reach the deepest and the most interesting parts of the events.

ŞÖ: These are tactical decisions. How do you make the main decisions in general? Or specifically in *Nights of Plague*?

OP: Main decisions are made at the very beginning. I first wanted to write a novel that would take place on an imaginary Ottoman island in 1901, during the third plague pandemic. Then the main decision is to identify the protagonists, to determine who will "see" the story (as Henry James puts it) or tell it. I made all these decisions over the course of thirty-five years. Changing his mind exhausts a writer; it upsets him. . . .

ŞÖ: How so?

OP: If I've been thinking about this novel for forty years, I've planned for the last ten years that one of the narrators would be blind. But in the first year, I could not write my blind hero in the first-person singular in a convincing way. Even though I tried very hard. . . . So that means that I have wasted weeks and months of work. That's why the novel couldn't progress. Then I gave up on these literary acrobatics. Being a novelist also requires the maturity to let go of an idea that doesn't work. . . .

ŞÖ: Let's talk a little bit about Manzoni, whom you mentioned in the epigraph of *Nights of Plague* and *The Betrothed*.

OP: *The Betrothed* [1827] by Alessandro Manzoni [1785–1873] is one of the three most important literary books in history that talks about the plague, in my opinion. But unlike in Defoe and Camus, the plague is not the only issue in *The Betrothed*. A complete Italian aristocrat, Alessandro Manzoni, like Count Tolstoy, wanted to write the national epic novel of his country—Italy—forty years before him, and he succeeded. Today, all Italians know the name of Manzoni. Let me remind you that the Grand Hotel, where Kemal Basmacı, the hero of *The Museum of Innocence*, died in Milan, is in the center of the city, on Manzoni Street. Since the novel is compulsory in high schools and schools in Italy, I have known many Italians who do not like Manzoni, like the Russians who hate Dostoevsky. But even they must have read parts of the novel about the plague epidemic (thirty to forty pages of the novel). What excites me in Manzoni is that he talks about subjects that Camus is not interested in—but Defoe is interested in—such as quarantine, isolation, the state, politicians. More importantly, he reads old documents, historical documents.

ŞÖ: Yes, I was going to ask that too. What have you read in this genre?

OP: Like Manzoni, like historians, I also read from primary sources, for example, the reports of British health inspectors. . . . When a plague epidemic started around Bombay in their colonial India, many British doctors went there. Health inspectors went there later and wrote reports. To understand why the quarantine succeeded, why it failed, and to report to London. . . . These annual reports are available online. It is even possible to get them cheaply in India and send them to Turkey. I read them extensively. To see how the plague spreads in the field, both in the city and in the countryside, from house to house, from village to village, to sense the effects of the measures and people's reactions to them. These books describe the measures, the details of government decisions, the behavior of the people, the behavior of local women, the behavior of the religious, the establishment, and various committees and commissions. I thought it would be best to read the medical inspector's reports to feel how it would be to live through a plague epidemic. I would open the volumes of the reports titled *Plague in India 1896–1897–1898*, written by the British bureaucracy in India called the "Indian Civil Service," and take notes of all kinds of events, stories, and most importantly, medical details in the back of my head and in my notebook. [. . .] The point was to imagine how these medical and social events would unfold in the Eastern Mediterranean. Reading these reports by the British, I actually thought I had more material and resources in front of me than what Daniel Defoe had (who had only his uncle's diary). My main criticism of Camus's *The Plague* is that it is not at all preoccupied with such medical reports and quarantine details. In my opinion, the real political development comes out of quarantine. But what is political in Camus is the replacement of the plague by the Nazis and the German occupation.

"I Thought I Should Also Show the Strangeness in My Mind as a Historian Would"
Dündar Hızal / 2021
From *Ot Dergi*, "Bir tarihçi olarak da kafamdaki tuhaflığı göstereyim dedim," April 1, 2021.

Dündar Hızal: If you were a historian, what would you be interested in?
Orhan Pamuk: If I were a historian, I would like to tell history through things. I would like to tell history from inside the women's kitchen. I tried to do that in *My Name Is Red*. There are two centers in *My Name Is Red*: The first is the room where the miniaturists paint, the second is the kitchen of Shekure, the woman in charge of the kitchen. While writing that novel, Mübahat Kütükoğlu's work on Ottoman *narh* [fixed price index] registers was very useful. All the prices are listed, how many piers you stop at when you get on the boat from Eyüp and travel to the place we know as Karaköy today, how much it costs to go from here or there, or when you go to a barbershop for a haircut. . . . Then you understand: The Ottomans were a civilization, a bureaucracy, everything had a price. One could see all the services, goods, even the types of baked goods you would buy in Istanbul. All of them are written in the *narh* book so that they were not overpriced. A hardworking professor took these reports and put them in a book. For my novel, I first put those items on my desk as ideas. They talk about a kind of mullet there, I try to understand what it is and feed it to my heroes. Sometimes I build my novels by looking at the things that I am not familiar

with from such archives, and then a few years later, a translator calls from Croatia to ask: "What is this?" But if I were a historian, I would have liked to do as I did in this book. First, I would put an item in front of me and try to extract history from it. I would rather pretend to be an archaeologist with little material and dream of history.

DH: Female characters are prominent in the novel: the narrator Mîna, Pakize Sultan who wrote the letters, Marika who conveyed the rumors to the Governor, Zeynep, the commander's lover. . . . In a sense, was it a choice or a coincidence that the narrators were all women?

OP: This might be a coincidence. But there is also this: We are in the Ottoman Empire in 1901, and there are plagues or disasters. Women are not at the center of those events. Women do not make diplomatic history in capital letters. They are at home, their contribution to history is perhaps limited. But they see everything; they watch everything silently—or some speak, too—they detect, they pay attention. They are not impatient and careless like men trying to achieve things.

An Interview about Interviews

Pelin Kıvrak and Erdağ Göknar / 2022

Erdağ Göknar: In framing this volume, Pelin and I have articulated the idea of the interview as an alternative literary history. As a novelist, how would you characterize the art of the interview as a genre?

Orhan Pamuk: Doing interviews was an important part of my literary life and I think it is a literary activity. Some authors look down on it perhaps because most of the time it is unfortunately imposed on the author for commercial reasons by the publishers. Yes, it is. I have done more than a thousand interviews in my life, and I'd say 80 to 90 percent of them were imposed on me by the urgency of the publishers' demands to advertise the book, to make people know that this book has been published by this author, its themes and relevancies, that it has something to do with some event. There is always that urgency that I felt, which of course blurred "the pure interview." It is something imposed on you although you pretend or frankly partly believe or hope that the interview is about the content and literary aspects of your book.

Pelin Kıvrak: Do interviews connect you and your work to new readers?

OP: I think that it's my success or luck that I never looked down on interviews as only commercial things. I sincerely enjoyed answering interview questions. One of the most popular questions that I have been asked by publishers, by editors, by people who are around or journalists themselves: "Well, I have seen you answer this question many times and now you are answering it with the same enthusiasm. How does that work?" It happens because I enjoy talking about my literary activities, especially when I see in the listener's or the journalist's face that they understand me. As a professor, I also sometimes teach the same course for two years, three years and never get bored, because I enjoy the happiness of sharing the enjoyment of the students. The interview has commercial sides, yes, your publisher wants to sell more books, this is bad. It's not that bad, by the way, but it has the joy of communicating your inner thoughts about a novel. How you start at one place, how a coincidence takes place, how this page is extremely autobiographical, that page is purely fantasy.... I love to talk about my novels. I am alone with my novel except when I read it to my wife. Then I am all alone. Doing interviews is a sort of a public introduction to the reception of the book and also the possibility of manipulating it.

EG: What do you mean by manipulating?

OP: Maybe I'll tell you a joke about this. I wrote *Snow*. It was a political novel. I called my publisher saying I finished a political novel in 2001. And I said to them, "Would you please read it and send it to a lawyer for them to read it as well before we publish it?" My publisher said, "No, we are in Turkey. We are close to joining [the] European Union. Turkey is a free country. We're not going to show it to a lawyer." And I said, "OK then, here is the book." I sent them the book, and two weeks later they called me and said, "Oh, we read your book and it is very political. We want to show it to a lawyer." Then the lawyer read it and gave us one or two suggestions. In fact, I listened to them.

PK: What was their advice? What did you change?

OP: Just a minor change that I forgot to undo when it became possible. There was a corpse of a fundamentalist which was dropped into the sea from a Turkish military airplane just like what happened to Osama bin Laden. Sort of a prophetic thing. My lawyer said: "Please make this just an airplane, not a military airplane." So that I wouldn't have problems with the Turkish military. So I deleted it. When it was possible to change this, I had forgotten about it. But, having said all these jokes, it was obvious that my novel was a bit political, and the atmosphere in Turkey was relatively tolerant but it could always be explosive. And the sales of any book of mine in Turkey happen in the first month and a half and none of the aggressive pundits, columnists, people would read my book. So, we decided that if I talked about the book as a love story, which is partly so, we would hide the fact that it was extremely political. So, when I was doing my first *Snow* interviews, I avoided the political parts.

Of course, if they had read the book they were interested in the political questions, but they were also afraid to ask political questions. Because lots of taboos were not destroyed but mentioned. The book was not as brave as they thought it was, but at least it was mentioning the problems they also didn't want mentioned. Or if they mentioned [them], I avoided them. Why? Because I did not want any problems and the publisher in particular didn't want any problems.

PK: What can a writer convey to their audience in an interview that can't be conveyed through fiction?

OP: Of course, in the interviews you talk about your book. But in the end the motivation for the interview is to make the book reach Turkish readers or readers wherever you are. It is also the case, for example, that you can control how the reader will read the book. In that sense, for me, the interview can definitely be categorized as what Gérard Genette calls the paratext. Paratext is all the other texts that prepare the reader for the novel—the cover, the cover picture, back cover, flaps, advertisements, interviews, the publisher's statement. . . . They prepare the reader for the novel. The title is obviously one of these. The back cover summary is also a paratext.

If you have a book called *Nights of Plague*, the reader understands that it is a novel about a plague. But if you don't call it that, then the back cover says there is a plague, in 1901 in the Ottoman Empire. Then I know Genette is right. I know that my readers would at least enjoy some of the paratext before reading the book. Or they would have access to what the paratext includes through a conversation with their friends. A reader might skip the Penguin Classics "Introduction" to *Dante*, but it is impossible to avoid paratexts because you are curious and you prepare yourself to read. For me, an interview is at least a paratext. But then I do my best to make it more than a paratext, to make it not only a preparation or manipulation but also a discussion of the book.

EG: How do you reconcile your roles as the author of the novel and the creator of the paratext when you give interviews?

OP: An interview gives me a space to situate myself and the text, so that it is contextualizing the first reception. I prepare the audience in the manner of Genette and provide the paratext. But on the other hand, I am not a utopian, idealist, foolish writer. I know that there are no perfect conditions. This is the world given to you. While you situate yourself, you can also be inventive and say new things. The interview is also an opportunity given to you not only to advertise, announce your book but also, in a popular way, in a very brief period of time, in a three-minute prime time news interview, to say something that is inventive. Both can work as situating, advertising, but also a spoonful of deep thinking about your book. The interview makes this possible. That is why I disagree with writers who look down on writers who do interviews for commercial reasons. People who say, "Oh Samuel Beckett never did an interview. James Joyce declined so and so." Yes, they were lucky, for this or that reason. But I couldn't have survived as a writer without doing interviews. But also, don't forget that I could have been killed because of interviews too.

EG: Can you remind us of what happened back then?

OP: That was the famous interview. When we were talking about this book, we discussed whether we should republish it. In the beginning, I did not want that interview to be seen again. Because that interview put me in a courtroom. I made the Turkish nationalists eternally angry at me. In the interview I made an off-the-cuff remark about the Armenian genocide, and the Turkish press made it into something big. That taught me to be careful when talking to the interviewers. And I have never, even before that, given an interview with only literary considerations, unless, for example, the *Paris Review* interview or other major interviews when you know it's only for literary interest. But any interview from the most popular newspapers to the highbrow literary magazines is never only a literary interview.

PK: You were studying journalism at Istanbul University when you decided to become a novelist. Of course, there are visible traces of your training in journalism in *Snow* and *The Black Book*. But you also mentioned that you spoke with many street vendors and interviewed people living in the slums of Istanbul to create the characters of *A Strangeness in My Mind*. Would you say that journalism, similar to your perspective as a painter, has bled into your writing since the beginning of your career?

OP: First of all, yes, in the 1930s, '40s, '50s, in the first decades of the twentieth century, more journalists were writers. Or more writers were journalists. And the distance between journalism and writing as creative activities was not that great. There were so many writers like that. I think that the greatest example is Graham Greene. For a while, he was the most popular and most respected British writer. He would go to Cuba for an assignment or Africa for another assignment and not only stay in those places for a few weeks as a journalist reporting the latest revolution or uprising, but he would return and in six months write a novel about the place. Those novels are about things that should be mentioned in the newspapers. Those novels have qualities of the news. This idea is still around. We now have what we call the immigration novel. I sometimes think that I should teach a seminar on the immigration novel partly because I am also planning to write one. So there is a difference between being a journalist. . . . On the other hand, there is the fact that fiction, literature, has always had journalistic, news-like qualities, alarming you. . . .

PK: If you were given a chance to interview a novelist who is no longer with us, who would you interview? What would you ask them?

OP: Tolstoy and Virginia Woolf. I have read Tolstoy very carefully, and I have so many questions to ask him as a craftsman.

EG: What insights did you gain from reading the literary interviews of established writers when you were a young writer? What is the significance of the *Writers at Work* interview series for you as a world literature forum?

OP: I have read all the volumes of the *Writers at Work* series from A to Z. They are unpretentious, great interviews about the craft of writing in which George Plimpton always asks the right questions. I have learnt a lot from them, from other writers. For example, how Hemingway said he always worked until he had something done and only stopped when he knew what was going to happen next. That way he could be sure of continuing on the next day. I learned about craft through those interviews.

PK: What ingredients make an interview successful: discussion of novels, comparison with other novels or novelists, writing practice, personal life, historical contexts, or politics, et cetera?

OP: I can give you a list of four things. First, an interview allows the novelist to frankly talk about their intentions. Not the intentions of the text, that is a different thing, but the intentions of the novelist. Second, you can pass some of your hidden thoughts about the novel to frame it better for the audience, situating the book. Third, sharing details from the daily life and writing habits of the novelist is important. It provides clues to the ocean of words that is the novel. Finally, the novelist can discuss the characters in the book, and share how they came to life.

Index

Abasıyanık, Sait Faik, 5
Abdülhamid II (sultan), 4
Acaibü'l-Mahlukat, 155
Ahmedov, Ramil, 159–63
AK Party (Justice and Development Party), xx, 121, 126
allegory, xii, 18, 132–33, 146, 168
allusion, xiv–xv, 26
Anatolia: labor migration from, xiii, xxiv, 126–27; as literary setting, 17, 18, 45, 49
And, Metin, 154
Anna Karenina (Tolstoy), 107–8, 135–36, 137
Arab Spring, 131
Arabian Nights, The/The Thousand and One Nights, 15, 26, 28, 57, 75–76
Arabic language: alphabet, 14; literature, 76, 135; words in Turkish, 20–21, 120–21
Aristotle, 141
Armenians, xx, 51, 63, 64, 68–69, 70, 80–81, 92, 177
Atatürk, Mustafa Kemal, 14, 18, 20, 49
Atikoğlu, Ayça, 25, 33–34
Atwood, Margaret, 45
Ayatollah Khomeini, 14, 92
Azerbaijan, 62

Baker, Nicholson, 20
Balabanlılar, Mürşit, 30–31

Balkon, xxiv, 149–50
Balzac, Honoré de, 4, 39, 96, 107, 123, 130, 134, 135, 136, 169
BBC, 39, 49
Beauty and Love (*Hüsn-ü Aşk*) (Sheikh Galip), 28
Becker, Carol, 84–91
Beckett, Samuel, 109, 176
Bengisu, Nihal, 35–36
Benjamin, Walter, 163
Betrothed, The (Manzoni), 171
Black Book, The (*Kara Kitap*), xi, xii, xv, xxiii, 13–14, 16, 23, 27, 28–29, 56, 57–58, 65, 73, 75–76, 84, 92, 93, 105, 129, 135, 144, 161, 168, 177
Bloom, Harold, 65
Bombay. *See* Mumbai
Borges, Jorge Luis, xii, xvi, xxiii, 17, 57–58, 75, 88, 97, 123, 157
Bosphorus Strait, xxv, 23, 40, 45, 53, 66, 149–50
Brod, Max, 99
Brodkey, Harold, 20
Buddenbrooks (Mann), 10, 23, 55, 81
Busbecq, Ogier Ghiselin de, 168
Bush, George W., 43
Büyükada. *See* Princes' Islands
Byron, George Gordon (Lord), 158

Çağdaş, Hami, 29
Çağman, Filiz, 33

179

INDEX

Çalışlar, Oral, 36–38
Calvino, Italo, xvi, 57–58, 75, 157
Camus, Albert, 169–70, 171, 172
Canetti, Elias, 19
Carroll, Lewis, 13
censorship, 68, 83, 106
Cevdet Bey ve Oğulları ("Cevdet Bey and Sons"), xi, xviii, xxiii, 3–5, 6–7, 10, 11, 18, 23, 25, 27, 55, 56, 113–14, 126, 151, 161
Chaplin, Charlie, 96
Charterhouse of Parma, The (Stendhal), 85
Chekhov, Anton, 48, 114
China, 43–44, 58, 61, 123
Chomsky, Noam, 106
Chotiner, Isaac, 140–43
clash of civilizations, 72, 78
Coetzee, J. M., 89, 169
colonization, xvi, xvii, 60–61, 97, 162, 171
Conrad, Joseph, xvi, 18, 85
Çubukçu, Mete, 27
Cumhuriyet (newspaper), 3, 11, 25, 31, 34, 36

Dadaism, 58
Damrosch, David, 137
Dante, 14
Defoe, Daniel, 168–69, 171–72
Demirtepe, Ülkü, 24–25
Der Spiegel, 66, 80
Derrida, Jacques, 158
Dickens, Charles, 39, 100, 107, 124, 129
Dickson, Martin Bernard, 154
Diderot, Denis, 85, 169
Dinesen, Isak, 13
Dink, Hrant, 80
Disgrace (Coetzee), 89
Don Quixote (Cervantes), 107
Dostoevsky, Fyodor, 5, 40, 55, 68, 79, 84–87, 106, 120, 171
Duruel, Nursel, 3–5

East-West conflict, 7, 19, 21, 26–27, 44, 161–62. *See also* Orientalism
Eberstadt, Fernanda, 17–21
Eco, Umberto, xvi, 157
Egypt, 138
Elementary Principles of Philosophy (Politzer), 31
Engdahl, Horace, 75–89
England, 92, 100, 107
Erbakan, Necmettin, xiii, 122
Ercan, Enver, 35
Erdoğan, Recep Tayyip, 69–70, 121–24, 126, 142
Ertop, Konur, 6–8
Eryılmaz, Serpil, 22–23, 27–28
European Union, xx, 45, 47, 59, 60, 67, 70, 82–83, 110, 175

Fathers and Sons (Turgenev), 115
Faulkner, William, xviii, 18, 21, 31, 52, 55, 97, 114, 123
Fay, Sarah, xvii–xviii
feminism, 114–15, 118. *See also* women
Ferdowsi, 141, 154
Fitzgerald, F. Scott, 94
Flaubert, Gustave, 19–20, 65, 107–8
Forsyte Saga, The (Galsworthy), 55
Foucault, Michel, 163
Freud, Sigmund, 16, 58, 76, 145
Fuentes, Carlos, 4

García Márquez, Gabriel, 88, 113, 123, 169
gecekondu (shanties), xiii, xxiv, 127
gender. *See* women
Genette, Gérard, xxi–xxii, 176
German Book Trade's Peace Prize, 66, 70
Germany, 14, 26, 62, 66, 80, 82, 110, 136, 172
Gogol, Nikolai, 5
Göknar, Erdağ, xi–xxii, 126–30, 175–78

Greece: islands, 167–68; visual arts, 156
Greek minority in Turkey, xiv, 81
Greene, Graham, 177
Gün, Güneli, 16
Gurría-Quintana, Ángel, 52–65

Hafiz, 145
Hazlitt, William, xviii
Hegel, 9, 21
Hemingway, Ernest, 94, 97, 108, 178
History of Western Philosophy, A (Russell), 132
Hitchens, Christopher, 122–23
Hızal, Dündar, 172–73
Hızlan, Doğan, 33
Hoffmann, E. T. A., 26
Holbrook, Victoria, 16
Holland, 67, 110, 136
Holub, Miroslav, 29
hüzün (melancholy), xiii, 46, 72, 80–81, 129
hybridity, xiv, xviii

İleri, Selim, 10
India, xvi–xvii, 43–44, 58, 60–61, 76, 92–95, 97, 110, 123, 171–72
Indonesia, 122
Innocence of Memories, The, xiii, xxiv
Innocence of Objects, The, xiii, xxiv, 134
intertextuality, xii, xiv–xvi, xxiii
interview: as alternative literary history, xvii–xx; as paratext, xxi–xxii
Invisible Cities (Calvino), 75
Iran, 34, 38, 92, 145, 155
Iraq War, 47, 89
Irmak, Erkan, 151–58
Ishiguro, Kazuo, 138
Islam: book arts (*see* painting); civilization, 141, 144; and culture, 31, 155; and gender, 4, 48, 160; and literature, 21, 58, 65, 75, 98, 117, 120; mysticism (*see* Sufism); and the West, 43. *See also* secularism

Islamism, xiii, xxiv, 17, 18, 32, 42–43, 44–46, 48, 63, 67, 69–70, 86–87, 99, 121, 122–24
Istanbul: comparison to other cities, 39, 97, 105; cultural history, xi, 23, 60, 72–73, 80–81, 88, 103, 112, 119, 123, 129–30, 144, 155; European views of, 39–40, 60–61, 65, 72–73, 78, 127–28; literature and publishing, 8, 17, 55; as setting, xi, xiii, xiv, xv, xvi, xxiii, xxiv, 13, 21, 28, 39, 58, 105, 126, 142, 168; urban fabric, xii, 15, 81, 162–63
Istanbul: Memories and the City (*İstanbul: Hatıralar ve Şehir*), xi, xiii, xxi, xxiv, 39, 40, 46, 57, 60–61, 65, 72, 78–79, 80–81, 82, 92, 129, 152, 157
Italy: art (*see* painting); film, 143; literature, 40, 171

James, Henry, 21, 42, 170–71
Jameson, Fredric, 132–33
Japan, xiv, 61, 158
Journal of the Plague Year, The (Defoe), 169
journalism, xi, xxiii, 5, 49–51, 53, 67, 72, 84, 98–100, 106, 124–25, 130, 142, 174, 177
Joyce, James, xviii, 4, 15, 20, 21, 28, 31, 39, 84, 94, 100, 105, 123, 176

Kafka, Franz, 7, 49, 84, 99, 109
Kars (Turkish city), xiii, xxiv, 45, 49–51, 62–63, 84, 162
Kelile and Dimna, 155
Kemal, Yaşar, 17
Kitabu'r-Ruh, 155
Kıvrak, Pelin, xi–xxii, 174–78
Koçu, Reşat Ekrem, xxi
Kurds: minority rights, xx, 51, 62, 68, 83, 106, 138; political movements, xiii, xxiv, 18, 49, 61
Kuyaş, Ahmet, 11

La Vita Nuova (Dante), 14
Lampedusa, Giuseppe Tomasi di, 143
Leigh, Mike, 143
Leopard, The (Lampedusa), 143
London, 39, 75, 92, 94, 124, 171
Louvre Museum, 103
Love in the Time of Cholera (García Márquez), 169
Lu Xun, 133
Lukács, György, xviii, 3, 9, 12

Madame Bovary (Flaubert), 91, 108
Mallarmé, Stéphane, 84–85
Malraux, André, 105
Mann, Thomas, 3, 10, 23, 46, 55, 65, 81, 84, 87, 132
Manzoni, Alessandro, 171
Marx, Karl, 163
Marxism, xviii, 9, 31–32, 56, 87, 123
Mehmed IV (sultan), 26
Memoirs of Hadrian (Yourcenar), 158
Midnight's Children (Rushdie), 96
Milliyet Publishers' Novel Award, 8–10
Milliyet Sanat, 6, 10
Mishra, Pankaj, 120–25
Moby-Dick (Melville), 133
modernism, xiv, xvi, xviii, xxiii, 17, 31
modernity, xi, xiii, xvii, xviii, xx, 44, 72, 77, 80–81, 110, 120, 123, 148
Montaigne, Michel de, xvii, 76–77
Moor's Last Sigh, The (Rushdie), 92–93, 94
Moreau, Gustave, 105
Mumbai, 92–93
Museum of Innocence, xiii, xv, xvii, xxi, xxiv, 102–5, 111, 117–19, 134–35, 156, 163
Museum of Innocence, The (*Masumiyet Müzesi*), xi, xiii, xv, xxi, xxiv, 102–4, 117–19, 122, 129, 134–35, 148, 155–56, 160, 163, 171
Muslim. *See* Islam

My Name Is Red (*Benim Adım Kırmızı*), xii–xiii, xv, xxiii–xxiv, 30, 33–34, 35–38, 54, 57, 62, 73, 82, 92, 117, 122, 130, 145, 151–58, 167, 172

Nabokov, Vladimir, 42, 55
Naci, Fethi, 10
Nafisi, Azar, 144–48
Naipaul, V. S., 88–89
Naïve and Sentimental Novelist, The, xxiv
Naked (Leigh), 143
Name of the Rose, The (Eco), 157
nationalism: criticism of, 46, 47, 48, 50; in early Turkish Republic, 88; non-Western, 39, 43, 87; recent surge, 59, 83
naturalism, 25, 158
Neruda, Pablo, 88
Nerval, Gérard de, xvii, 39, 65, 78–79
New Life, The (*Yeni Hayat*), xii, xv, xxiii, 14, 17, 19, 29–30, 55, 153
New York. *See* Pamuk, Orhan: New York years
New York Times, xiii, 41, 165
New York Times Book Review, xiii
New York Times Magazine, xix, 17
New Yorker, xii–xiii, 100–101
Nights of Plague (*Veba Geceleri*), xiii–xiv, xvi, xxi, xxv, 157, 162, 164–73, 176
Nişantaşı (Istanbul neighborhood), xi, xxiii, 14, 23, 28, 160, 168
Nobel Prize in Literature, xi–xiii, xvii–xix, xxi, xxiv, 45, 71–73, 80, 87, 91, 92, 112, 117
Notes from Underground (Dostoevsky), 7
novel: autobiographical, 7, 23, 98; birth of, 84–85, 108–9; detective, xii, xv, 58, 108, 157; East-West, xi, xiv, 43–44, 161–62; encyclopedic, xvii, 15, 28, 85, 155; European, 20, 21, 84; global,

xi, xvi–xvii, xviii, 107; historical, xii, xviii, 3, 35, 67, 113, 127–29, 153, 155, 157–58, 162; modern, 11, 17; and museums, xiii, xv, xxiv, 103, 117–18, 134, 155; nineteenth-century, 7, 9, 11, 55, 100, 107, 130, 169; and plague, 169–70; political, xiii, xiv, xx, 41–42, 48–49, 56, 61–62, 66, 85–86, 89, 175; purpose of, 99–100, 108–9, 123–24, 130; in Turkey, xx, 4, 5, 10, 26, 50, 52, 53–54, 90–91, 106, 120–21, 136. *See also* postcolonialism; postmodernism

Occidentalism, 43, 75, 88, 113, 115
Oedipus Rex (Sophocles), xv, 141, 144, 145
Oran, Fatma, 31–32, 34–35
Orange, xxv
Orientalism (Said), 168
Orientalism, 60
Other Colors (*Öteki Renkler*), xii, xxiv, 22, 92
Ottoman Empire: architecture, xv, 166; collapse of, 60, 81; contemporary memory of, 60, 80, 120–21, 128; history, xi, xx, 20, 68, 92, 115, 122; language, 14, 20, 120; as literary setting, xiv, xvi, xviii, xxiii, xxv, 4, 17–18, 20, 79, 117, 167, 170, 172–73, 176; poetry, 53–54; relationship to Europe, xi, xvi, 113, 121; visual arts, xii, 35, 37–39, 154, 158. *See also* painting
Özcan, Celal, 26–27
Özgüven, Fatih, 9–12
Öztürk, Şeyda, 168–72

painting: European Renaissance, 36, 84, 104–5, 158; Islamic miniatures, xv, 33–38, 82, 154–58; surrealist, 105
Pakistan, 92, 122
Pamuk, Orhan: approach to interviews, xvii, xx, xxii, 52–53, 73, 97, 100, 131, 174–78; archival research, 9–10, 15, 27, 104–5, 126–27, 129–30, 167, 171–72; book sales, xiv, 11, 14, 17, 43, 52–53, 64, 138, 175; as collector, 103–4, 117–19; court case against, 21, 42–43, 46, 69, 81; doppelgänger motif, xi–xii, 16, 18–19, 26; family life, 18, 22–24, 36–37, 58–59, 88, 91, 113–14, 116, 120, 140–41, 144–45, 152, 160; and Istanbul, xi, xiv, xxi, xxiii, 14, 18, 19, 20, 45, 53, 66, 91, 92, 93–94, 109, 127, 129, 142, 149, 166–67, 177; literary style, 24–25, 28; love, 65, 89, 102–3, 117–18, 159; New York years, xii, 11, 18–19, 57–58, 75, 80, 93, 105, 136–37, 164; as painter, xi, xiv, xxiii, 37, 57, 107, 109, 152, 153–54, 168, 177; political views, xx, 15, 17, 21, 34–35, 41–44, 46–51, 55–56, 59, 66–67, 70, 82–83, 89–90, 110–11, 121–22, 130–31, 133, 141–42, 175; reception in United States, 17, 52, 122, 133, 138; and religion, 20, 67, 81–82; threats in Turkey, 52–53, 61, 63, 68, 80, 91; on the writer's mission, 76–79, 86–87, 98–99; writing process, 6, 19, 22, 24–25, 53–54, 56–57, 64, 68, 140, 142, 151, 156–57, 165–66
Pamuk, Shevket, 19, 36–37, 58–59, 88, 141, 157
pandemic, xiii, 164–66, 169–70
paratext. *See* interview
Paris, xxv, 21, 39, 49, 75, 88, 94, 105
Paris Review, xiv, xvii, xix, 52, 177
Parla, Jale, xix, 20
Persian language, 20, 21, 120–21; literature, 61, 75–76, 141, 144–45
Persian visual arts. *See* painting
photography, xiv, xxiv, xxv, 149–50
Picasso, Pablo, 95
Plague, The (Camus), 169–70, 172
Plath, Sylvia, 147

Plato, 141
Plimpton, George, 178
Politzer, Georges, 31–32
Possessed, The (Dostoevsky), 86
postcolonialism, xi, xiv, xvi, 89
postmodernism, xi–xii, xiv, xvi, xx, xxiii, 14, 17, 37, 57, 129, 133, 142, 156–57
Princes' Islands, 140, 166
Prix de la découverte européenne, xi
Proust, Marcel, 17, 46, 52, 55, 65, 87, 89, 97, 103, 105, 109, 132
Pynchon, Thomas, 123

Qur'an, 148, 155

Rahim, Sameer, 117–19
realism, xi, xvi, xviii, xxiii, 3–4, 15, 48, 52, 98–100, 107–8, 119, 120, 126, 133, 140, 146, 157–58, 166
Red-Haired Woman, The (*Kırmızı Saçlı Kadın*), xiii, xxiv, 140–42, 144–47, 159, 161, 162
Rehm, Diane, 112–16
Rimbaud, Arthur, 4
Robbins, Bruce, 131–39
Rose, Charlie, 107–9, 110–11
Roth, Philip, 169
Rumi, Jelaleddin, 13, 28, 75
Rushdie, Salman, xvi, 14, 92–101
Russell, Bertrand, 132
Russia, 18, 62, 89, 115, 132, 171

Sacks, Oliver, 29–30
Said, Edward, 60, 163, 168
Salman, Yurdanur, 20
Sartre, Jean-Paul, 68, 131
Satanic Verses, The (Rushdie), 92
Secret Face, The (*Gizli Yüz*), xii, 31
secularism: and class, 110, 115, 120, 126, 129, 138, 142, 160; conflict with religion, 45, 48, 121–22; critique of, xii, xiii, xxiv; foundation of Turkish Republic, 14, 18, 20; and politics in contemporary Turkey, 41, 63, 67, 68, 70, 88; versus *laïcité*, 139; and writers, xvii, xxiv, 75, 88, 98
Selim III (sultan), 154
Sentimental Education, A (Flaubert), 108
Shah Ismail, 154
Shah Tahmasp, 38, 154
Shahnameh (Ferdowsi), xv, 141, 144, 147, 154
Shakespeare, William, 26, 141
Sheikh Galip, 28
Silent House (*Sessiz Ev*), xi, xxiii, 8, 11, 18, 23–25, 27, 56, 112–16, 117, 119, 131, 133, 159–60, 162, 168
Simpson, Mona, 20
Smith, Adam, 71–74
Smith, Zadie, 124
Snow (*Kar*), xiii, xv, xxi, xxiv, 41–44, 45–51, 53–54, 61–64, 66, 67, 68, 73, 82, 85–86, 92, 98–99, 122–23, 162, 175, 177
Sophocles, 141, 144–45, 148
Sound and the Fury, The (Faulkner), 55
South Africa, 89–90
Star, Alexander, 41–44
Steidl, Gerhard, 149–50
Steinbeck, John, 52
Stendhal, 3, 50, 55, 85, 107, 123–24, 134–35
Stone, Judy, 3–16
Strangeness in My Mind, A (*Kafamda Bir Tuhaflık*), xiii, xxi, xxiv, xxv, 113, 126–30, 142, 146–47, 149, 159, 160–61, 162–63, 177
Sufism: and classical literature, 13, 21, 75; as literary inspiration, xii, xv, xxiii, 14, 15, 33, 75; in Turkey today, 128
surrealism, 105, 123
Switzerland, xx, 31, 46, 51

Tamer, Ülkü, 9–10
Tanizaki, Junichirō, 120

Tanpınar, Ahmet Hamdi, xiv, 31, 133
terkip (synthesis), xiv
Teuwsen, Peer, 45–51
Time Regulation Institute, The
  (Tanpınar), 133
Times Literary Supplement, 73
Tolstoy, Leo, 3, 6, 55, 65, 87, 99, 106, 132, 171, 177
Topkapı Palace, 33, 154, 157
translation: and the contemporary novel, 137; into English, xii, xxiii, 45, 112, 117; into French, xi; interaction with translators, 16, 20, 49, 74, 137–38, 173; process, 55; responses in Turkey, 65, 94, 138; untranslated work, xxiii, 55; into world languages, xiv, 17, 40, 47, 65, 70, 81, 141, 161
trial. *See* Pamuk, Orhan: court case against
Triesman, Deborah, 91–101
Tristram Shandy (Sterne), 84
Trotsky, Leon, 132
T24 (website), 165
Turgenev, Ivan, 115, 117
Turkey: and Europe, xi, xvi, 19, 20, 42, 45–47, 49, 59–60, 65, 67, 70, 72, 80, 82, 83, 94–95, 110, 113, 115, 162; Gezi Park protests, 124–25, 131; identity crisis, 13, 20, 26, 43, 49, 70, 75, 93; migration, 123, 126–27, 177; military coups, xii, xiii, xx, 8, 15, 17, 18, 21, 56, 63, 112–13, 138, 141–42, 151; minority rights, xiii, xx, 18, 49, 51, 61–62, 63–64, 68, 70, 81, 83, 92, 106, 138, 177; westernization, 14, 20, 41, 48, 59–61, 63, 88–89, 113, 115, 129, 142, 145, 160, 163
Turkish language, 14, 16, 20, 24, 52, 73, 81, 93, 120–21, 134; literature, xi, xii, xiv, xviii, xx, 3–5, 10, 31, 42, 65, 89, 97, 105–6, 120, 129, 133, 136

Ulysses (Joyce), 100, 105
United States: foreign policy, 43, 89; literature of, 97–99, 124, 133, 169
Updike, John, 45, 95
Üster, Celal, 25–26

Valsecchi, Bagatti, 104
Vatansever, Hülya, 32
Veli, Orhan, 5
Village Voice, 73
Visconti, Luchino, 143
Voltaire, 50
Voyage en Orient (Nerval), 39, 78

Walkowitz, Rebecca, 137
War and Peace (Tolstoy), 26
Welch, Stuart Cary, 154
Welfare Party, xiii
White Castle, The (*Beyaz Kale*), xi, xiv, xxiii, 11–12, 13, 15, 18–19, 25, 26, 27, 58–59, 75–76, 151, 161, 162, 168
women: in fiction, 36, 146–47, 159–61, 172–73; headscarf issue, 4, 48, 118; as readers, 90, 91; rights in Turkey, 14, 24, 114–15, 118, 147, 159–60
Woolf, Virginia, xviii, 4, 31, 46, 52, 55, 177

Yavuz, Hilmi, 10, 11, 46
Yılmaz, İhsan, 164–68
Yourcenar, Marguerite, 158

Zola, Émile, 107, 129–31

About the Editors

Erdağ Göknar is associate professor of Turkish studies at Duke University. He is translator of Pamuk's *My Name Is Red* and author of *Orhan Pamuk, Secularism and Blasphemy: The Politics of the Turkish Novel*.

Pelin Kıvrak is a literary scholar and fiction writer. She worked in the creation of Pamuk's Museum of Innocence in Istanbul and is editor of Pamuk's illustrated autobiographical book, *Uzak Dağlar ve Hatıralar* ("Memories of Distant Mountains").

Printed in the United States
by Baker & Taylor Publisher Services